D1483226

SOCIETY FOR NEW TESTAMENT STUDIES

MONOGRAPH SERIES

General Editor: R. McL. Wilson, F.B.A.

Associate Editor: M. E. Thrall

39

THE SON OF MAN

IN THE TEACHING OF JESUS

THE SON OF MAN IN THE TEACHING OF JESUS

A. J. B. HIGGINS
Professor Emeritus of Theology
Saint David's University College
Lampeter, Wales

CAMBRIDGE UNIVERSITY PRESS
CAMBRIDGE
LONDON NEW YORK NEW ROCHELLE
MELBOURNE SYDNEY

KRAUSS LIBRARY
LUTHERAN SCHOOL OF THEOLOGY
AT CHICAGO

Published by the Press Syndicate of the University of Cambridge
The Pitt Building, Trumpington Street, Cambridge CB2 1RP
32 East 57th Street, New York, NY 10022, USA
296 Beaconsfield Parade, Middle Park, Melbourne 3206, Australia

© Cambridge University Press 1980

First published 1980

Typeset by H Charlesworth & Co Ltd, Huddersfield
Printed in Great Britain by Redwood Burn Ltd
Trowbridge and Esher

British Library Cataloguing in Publication Data

Higgins, Angus John Brockhurst
The Son of Man in the teaching of Jesus. –
(Society for New Testament studies. Monograph
series; 39).
1. Son of Man – Biblical teaching
2. Bible. New Testament. Gospels
I. Title II. Series
232 BT232 79-42824

ISBN 0 521 22363 6

BT
232
.H53

CONTENTS

	Preface	page vii
	Abbreviations	ix
	Introduction	1
	PART ONE	
I	**The Son of man and ancient Judaism**	3
	F. H. Borsch	3
	C. Colpe	7
	The Similitudes of Enoch	12
	The philological problem	20
	G. Vermes and the synoptic sayings	23
	Excursus: The Son of man and the Melchizedek fragment	28
II	**The Son of man in the synoptic gospels in recent study**	29
	Excursus: The hypothesis of Barnabas Lindars	49
	PART TWO	
III	**The synoptic texts. I**	55
	1. Luke 17.22, 24, 26, 30	56
	2. Luke 18.8b	72
	3. Luke 21.36	74
	4. Matt. 10.23	75
	5. Mark 14.62	77
	6. Mark 13.26	79
	7. Matt. 25.31	79
	Conclusion	79
IV	**The synoptic texts. II**	80
	1. Luke 12.8-9; Matt. 10.32-3; Mark 8.38	80
	2. Luke 12.10; Matt. 12.32; Mark 3.28-9	84
	3. Luke 11.29-30; Matt. 12.39-40; Mark 8.12	90
	(i) R. A. Edwards, *The Sign of Jonah*	92

(ii) The eschatological correlative and the teaching of Jesus 100
(iii) The eschatological correlative and the sentence of holy law 107
4. Luke 6.22; Matt. 5.11 113
5. Matt. 16.13; Mark 8.27. 113
6. Mark 8.31; Matt. 16.20f. 114
7. Matt. 16.28; Mark 9.1 114
8. Mark 10.45; Luke 22.27 114
9. Matt. 19.28; Luke 22.28-30 115
Conclusion 116
Excursus 1: Luke 12.10 and parallels 116
Excursus 2: The sign of Jonah, and the sign of the Son of man 118
Excursus 3: Remarks on J. Jeremias, 'Die älteste Schicht' 119
Excursus 4: The Son of man and pre-existence 121
V The kernel sayings 123
Summary 123
Concluding remarks 125

Notes 127
Select bibliography 159
Index of authors 169
Index of references 172

PREFACE

It has taken very much longer than anticipated for this book to see the light of day. Other academic commitments and the responsibilities of a university chair have contributed to the delay. However, one result has been that I have been able to take account of some of the more recent literature which, to the impoverishment of my own work, would otherwise not have figured here. My opinion remains that none of the more recently proposed alternative solutions of the Son of man problem in the synoptic gospels, however new or different they may claim or may appear to be, carry such a weight of conviction as to overthrow irreparably the hypothesis they are intended to supplant.

The absence of discussion of the Johannine form of the Son of man, to which a chapter was devoted in my book of 1964, *Jesus and the Son of Man*, should occasion no surprise.

It so happened that the present study, in its final form, was completed early in the sesquicentenary year of what is now known as Saint David's University College. Since Theology has always figured prominently among the subjects of study in the College, it seems not inappropriate to dedicate this monograph to my colleagues in the Department of Theology during my tenure of the Chair from 1970 to 1976, and this I do with esteem and gratitude.

Lampeter,
August 1977

A. J. B. HIGGINS

ABBREVIATIONS

BJRL	*Bulletin of the John Rylands Library*, Manchester
BZNW	Beihefte zur *Zeitschrift für die Neutestamentliche Wissenschaft*, Berlin
CGSM	F. H. Borsch, *The Christian and Gnostic Son of Man*, 1970
EQ	*Evangelical Quarterly*, Exeter
ET	English translation
EvT	*Evangelische Theologie*, Munich
ExpT	*Expository Times*, Edinburgh
FRLANT	Forschungen zur Religion und Literatur des Alten und Neuen Testaments, Göttingen
HDB	Hastings' *Dictionary of the Bible*, second edition, revised by F. C. Grant and H. H. Rowley, Edinburgh 1963
JBL	*Journal of Biblical Literature*, Philadelphia
JR	*Journal of Religion*, Chicago
JSM	A. J. B. Higgins, *Jesus and the Son of Man*, 1964
JTS	*Journal of Theological Studies*, Oxford
LXX	The Septuagint
NEB	New English Bible
NTS	*New Testament Studies*, London
RGG[3]	*Die Religion in Geschichte und Gegenwart*, third edition, ed. K. Galling *et al.*, Tübingen 1957-62
RSV	Revised Standard Version
SB	H. L. Strack and P. Billerbeck, *Kommentar zum Neuen Testament aus Talmud und Midrasch*, Munich 1922-61
SBT	Studies in Biblical Theology, London
SJT	*Scottish Journal of Theology*, Edinburgh
SMMH	F. H. Borsch, *The Son of Man in Myth and History*, 1967
SNTSMS	Society for New Testament Studies Monograph Series, London
TDNT	*Theological Dictionary of the New Testament*, ET of *Theologisches Wörterbuch zum Neuen Testament* (see

	TWNT, below) by G. W. Bromiley, Grand Rapids, Michigan 1964-76
TU	Texte und Untersuchungen zur Geschichte der altchristlichen Literatur, Berlin
TWNT	*Theologisches Wörterbuch zum Neuen Testament*, ed. G. Kittel and G. Friedrich, Stuttgart 1933-74
ZNW	*Zeitschrift für die Neutestamentliche Wissenschaft*, Berlin
ZTK	*Zeitschrift für Theologie und Kirche*, Tübingen

Dead Sea Scrolls

CD	Cairo Damascus Document
1QM	War Scroll
1QS	Manual of Discipline
1QSa	Appendix to 1QS: Rule of the Congregation
4QCatena A	Catena of Old Testament passages, copy A
4QPatr	Patriarchal Blessings
11QMelch	Melchizedek fragments

INTRODUCTION

The appearance not only of another book about the Son of man, but of one by an author already responsible for an earlier work on the subject, may perhaps require some explanation. In the last chapter of my earlier book, *Jesus and the Son of Man* (1964), the thesis was outlined that Jesus confidently expected vindication of his mission after his death by being given, in the presence of God, a status of exaltation that involved the judgmental functions traditionally associated with the apocalyptic Son of man.[1] The present work seeks to develop this thesis, and to that extent it is a logical sequel to *JSM*. It was suggested as a worthwhile undertaking by study of subsequent contributions to the unending debate, some of which have been used in support of the thesis presented here, while others, setting out theories which appear to me to be unconvincing, have served only to strengthen my adherence to it. The contribution of the present study, therefore, is not the presentation of a fresh or novel theory, but the defence, promotion, and development, against the background of recent significant work, and by detailed investigation of the relevant texts, of the theme stated above.

The first two chapters, constituting Part One, are intended mainly as necessary prolegomena to the study of texts in Part Two. Although not an actual part of the argument, these chapters are far from being a mere catalogue of the principal views and theories put forward since 1964. At a number of points they necessarily raise and discuss some of the issues of prime importance for the underlying theme. Thus the views of Vermes on the synoptic sayings are introduced in chapter I, and are followed in the last paragraph by an indication of the different approach to them adopted in Part Two. Again, chapter II concludes with references to Jeremias' classification of the Son of man sayings in two categories: those with, and those without, parallel versions or 'rivals' lacking the term. These references serve as a transition to the constructive work that follows, for Jeremias' classification has been taken as a convenient framework for the examination of texts in Part Two.

The position adopted in regard to the three main categories of Son of man sayings remains substantially the same as in *JSM*. It seems probable, however, that the 'present' sayings in Mark 2.10; Luke 7.34, par. Matt. 11.19; and Luke 9.58, par. Matt. 8.20 are most satisfactorily understood as examples of the christologizing, into the Son of man title, of *bar nasha* used by Jesus in an indefinite sense in reference to himself as 'a son of man', 'a man', 'someone'. The passion predictions (Mark 8.31; 9.31; 10.33f.; also Mark 9.12f.; Luke 17.25; 24.7) are all creations of the post-resurrection community. Nevertheless, it is possible that they have a common *ultimate* origin in a use by Jesus of *bar nasha* in much the same way as in the 'present' sayings, and even that Mark 9.31a, 'God [logical subject] will deliver up the [or a] man to men', may be 'the ancient nucleus' underlying them.[2]

It is among the 'future' sayings alone that possibly authentic sayings about the Son of man in a messianic sense are to be sought. Coordination of these with the other two categories of sayings has often been felt to be a problem. For the early church no problem existed. All the sayings were received as from Jesus, and the three types were all placed on the same level of authenticity. Jesus was believed to have adopted as a self-designation the messianic title Son of man in referring equally to his earthly activity, his approaching death and resurrection, and his destiny as God's agent in the judgment. But attempts to uphold this traditional biblical unity, or to trace a consistent pattern linking together the three kinds of Son of man sayings, carry conviction only where certain presuppositions are held. A basic dichotomy between the present and the passion sayings on the one hand, and the future sayings on the other, underlies the unity which has been imposed upon them - a unity which does not have to be traced back to Jesus himself.

PART ONE

I

THE SON OF MAN AND ANCIENT JUDAISM

A majority of recent writers continue to support the view that there existed in pre-Christian apocalyptic Judaism a concept of the eschatological Son of man, a transcendent and pre-existent being whose primary function in the End-time would be that of a judge, delivering the righteous and punishing the wicked. Besides H. E. Tödt,[1] E. Jüngel,[2] and F. Hahn[3] may be mentioned the following. D. E. Nineham accepts the hypothesis without discussion.[4] R. H. Fuller thinks the most likely source of the Son of man concept used by Jesus and the early church to be a pre-Christian apocalyptic tradition of the Son of man 'as the pre-existent divine agent of judgment and salvation'.[5] C. K. Barrett supports the apocalyptic Son of man passages in the gospels, because 'they have a readily ascertainable setting in the Judaism with which, we may suppose, Jesus was familiar',[6] and part of the evidence is provided in the Similitudes of Enoch.[7] It is part of P. Vielhauer's[8] different thesis (that it was not Jesus but the early church that spoke of him as the coming Son of man, and that Jesus did not use the term at all) that this concept and title were derived from apocalyptic Judaism. He is followed by H. Conzelmann.[9] According to H. M. Teeple,[10] who also denies to Jesus any Son of man sayings, the Son of man Christology began in Hellenistic Jewish Christianity, perhaps in Syria, and was derived from Jewish apocalyptic.

Two major contributions, by F. H. Borsch and C. Colpe, will now be discussed.

F. H. Borsch[11]

At a time when doubts are being cast by some scholars[12] on the existence of a Son of man concept in Judaism, Borsch devotes a large part of his book to an attempt to show that not only in Judaism, but in the oriental world at large, the Son of man and related concepts were widespread and familiar. This is an approach, therefore, which draws upon the findings of the history of religions school. As the title of his book indicates, Borsch's task is two-fold, to trace a recognizable mythological Son of man (or Man) pattern in the antecedents of Christianity, and to show how this pattern was actualized and, indeed, consciously fulfilled by the historical Jesus. At this stage we are almost entirely concerned with the former of these considerations.

After an introductory chapter reviewing the main attempts at a solution of the Son of man problem in the gospels, and finding them all unsatisfactory because too narrowly based, Borsch ventures the opinion that a far wider background of thought, transcending Judaism and involving beliefs current in the centuries surrounding the rise of Christianity, requires investigation. While he is not original in suggesting a link between the Son of man in the gospels and the Man-King mythology of the Near East, his investigation appears to be the most thorough on these lines. The beliefs in question, oriental and gnostic, in a variety of forms, concern the Man hero as Adam, Anthropos, Urmensch, Heavenly Man, etc. Among the sources examined are Hippolytus, Irenaeus, Poimandres, and the Nag Hammadi, Manichaean, and Mandaean texts. Borsch writes:

> We have good cause for suspecting that there was a mythical conception of relative antiquity concerning a primal hero, conceived of as a Man who was once on earth, whose story contains some reference to defeat or death. Yet somehow he was also regarded as one who was or who was very closely allied with a glorious, cosmic Man figure of the heavens. While such legendary beliefs are never found in exactly the same guise and often appear only in fragmentary forms, and while we do not necessarily postulate some one original myth, there is reason to conclude that the variant descriptions are related.[13]

The next stage in the argument concerns the Royal Man (chapter III). Favouring the views of A. Bentzen and I. Engnell, who traced an intimate relationship between the concept of the first or primeval man and the king, Borsch finds the Jewish counterpart in the idea of Adam as the first royal man in paradise. One feature in particular, he urges, must be kept in mind: the suffering or humiliation of the royal personage or man-king before restoration to office.[14] In Judaism this applies to Adam, but also to the king, as witness a number of psalms (16; 18; 21; 22; 69; 89; 116; 118) involving suffering and lamentation, or joy at the ending of tribulations. Without necessarily committing himself to full acceptance of the view that in the Israelite New Year festival the king is the suffering servant of Yahweh, Borsch shares the opinion that the concepts of the king and the suffering servant, along with those of the Messiah, the First Man, and the Son of Man, are related in origin. So he is able to associate them with the idea of the man-king suffering in the water, derived from the myth of the primeval conflict with chaos and the water monster.

In the next chapter ('The Man in Sectarian Life') Borsch turns to the quest for evidence of more direct and immediate sources of influence on Jesus' thought. This he finds above all in sectarian Judaism. It is, of course, well known that there were a number of baptizing Jewish sects. Borsch maintains that there is sufficient evidence to warrant the assumption that in some of them there was a connection between baptismal rites and belief in the Man in some form or other. About Mandaism he expresses the opinion that 'it is no accident that the two features which seem to stand out in this regard are a baptismal practice which looks to be a form of a democratized kingship rite and various representations of a royal Man hero'.[15] He states as a hypothesis that in the first century A.D., and probably earlier, there were 'a number of Jewish-oriented sects which practised forms of baptism as an ordination/coronation rite', and that 'for a number of these groups, and often in connection with their baptismal rites, speculation about or belief in the Man (in one or more of his guises) had a significant role to play'. The sources of these two features (baptism and the Man), and their association with one another, 'reach back to the ancient kingship ideologies'.[16]

Borsch recognizes that the apparent absence of baptism (in the form in which he envisages it) and of speculation about the Man among the Essenes and the Qumran sect would militate against his theory, since they would be the most likely sources of influence on Jesus. This he tries to counter in two ways. We are reminded that the Essene initiates wore white robes and reverenced the sun. Perhaps, it is urged, there is more here than meets the eye. 'For instance, the Mandaeans also wore white robes, and they wore them as signs of their priesthood, believing themselves at baptism to have become the exalted royal priests of God, representatives of the Adam above. There are also many relics of sun-worship in their rituals.'[17] This kind of reasoning is not particularly convincing. Secondly, in the Qumran Hymns of Thanksgiving there is much language 'strikingly similar to that once associated with the sufferings of the royal figure':[18] rejection, mockery, drowning in the waters, deliverance from the pit and elevation to the presence of God.

Most of this, however, can be explained simply as imitation of the biblical psalms. More problematic, perhaps, are references in the Hymns and elsewhere to a 'man'. Borsch interprets this messianically, as others have done; but it is more likely that the term is generic, and refers to the sect.[19] In any case, since, as Borsch has to admit, no passages of this kind come from unambiguously baptismal contexts, a connection between baptism and the Man figure cannot be proved, and he has to fall back on theorizing. He suggests that it is not unlikely that some such language might have been used by some representative figure if and when a baptism took place. In which case the parallels with the language and themes studied previously may be indicative of a baptism in which the individual suffered before being exalted and coronated as a royal, Adam-like priest of God. In any case, it would appear that Qumran thinking may at least have been touched by these ideas.[20]

A brief consideration of John the Baptist and his baptism of Jesus also ends on a somewhat uncertain note, for the evidence 'does not prove that John the Baptist was a leader of the manner of sect which we are proposing, one that combined belief in a royal Man with baptism conceived of as an ordination or exaltation to association with or to the office of this Man'.[21]

Before proceeding to the New Testament material, Borsch raises three further problems. In the first place, even if the baptizing sectarian milieu was much concerned with the Man, the actual expression Son of man is not found there. This surely is very significant. Suppositions of the kind offered by Borsch cannot be said to gain in credibility by being shored up by further suppositions. Even if the 'special Man' was regarded as the son of the Man, in the sense that the king, as a royal personage, was the descendant and representative of Adam, to attempt to forge a link between this concept and the Son of man of Jewish eschatology, and then to unite them with Jesus' own use of the term,[22] is building castles in the air.

The next two considerations concern more closely, by anticipation, Borsch's theme, worked out later in the book, that Jesus, in calling himself the Son of man who laboured here upon earth, suffered death, and was vindicated by exaltation to glory, believed himself to be the historical fulfilment of the myth of the Man who must first suffer in order to reign. Firstly, the Jesus of the gospels speaks both of the Son of man in heaven and of himself as, or as the representative of, that Son of man on earth. But if he is already the Son of man on earth, why must he still suffer, whereas in the ritual pattern suffering was followed by exaltation and enthronement? The answer given by Borsch is that mythologically Jesus had already suffered and been vindicated as Son of man in his baptism; historically the suffering still awaits the Son of man.[23] Secondly, there is the difficulty that at most only *traces* of the idea of the Man's suffering before the attainment of glory are to be found in 'the more normative Judaism' contemporary with Jesus.[24] This is met by the hypothesis that the ideas from the old kingship ideologies, especially that of the King-Man's sufferings in the water, had revived to varying degrees in the baptizing sects. Borsch writes:

> We are therefore suggesting that the idea of the suffering of the Man was first grasped by Jesus in the context of this baptizing sectarianism. *Probably* it was a conception as much liturgical or liturgical-mythical as anything else. *Perhaps* only one or two of these groups would have actually practised the idea; *perhaps* they taught rather than enacted it [my italics], but we believe that the idea was present and that this stands as one of the links between kingship practice and versions of that ideology which we find in later religious forms. Here is the contemporary basis for the realization that the Man must suffer before salvation and glory can come, the realization which Jesus put to service in historical circumstances.[25]

Borsch has recourse to a vast amount of material in order to describe what he suggests was the probable background of Jesus' thought. It is highly questionable, however, whether it is possible, out of the bewildering variety of ideas from sources widely diverse in content, provenance, and date, to reconstruct a convincing and coherent mythological pattern. It is still more difficult to understand how an ancient mythological pattern, in the fragmented form Borsch discerns in baptizing sectarian Judaism, could have exerted such a powerful influence on Jesus that he consciously and deliberately regarded himself as acting it out. Later Borsch attempts to show how what he suggests probably happened, did in fact happen.[26] He must clearly be included among leading exponents of the view that first-century Judaism was familiar with a Son of man concept which could have influenced Jesus, although, as we have seen, he believes the apocalyptic Son of man was but one form of a much wider complex of ideas.

C. Colpe[27]

Colpe's authoritative article is of capital importance, and not least for the problem which concerns us in this section. In discussing the religious-historical problem, he reviews the main hypotheses for the ultimately non-Israelite origin of the Son of man concept. Most of these he rejects as inadequate.[28] Among them the following may be noted. The Babylonian Adapa, which can only be connected with the Son of man on the baseless assumption that the latter was originally a second Adam, has no eschatological, judicial, or redemptive functions. The gnostic Anthropos (Urmensch) has originally nothing to do with the Jewish apocalyptic Son of man. The latter acts only in the eschaton, not in the present; he acts as judge, and his saving act is not fusion with a part of himself, but acquittal; he remains in heaven, and does not descend to men and ascend again; he is announced by prophetic, apocalyptic writers, and is not represented in the persons of gnosis-bearing prophets. Colpe regards the Canaanite hypothesis as the most satisfactory, and accepts the view that Dan. 7 reflects the influence of the mythology known from the Ugaritic texts. The fourth beast in Daniel corresponds to the chaos monster, the Son of man to Baal, and the Ancient of Days to the king and creator god El who, after the defeat of the monster, installs Baal as world-ruler.[29] Although not containing exactly the same mythology as in Palestine, the Ugaritic texts seem to provide the closest parallel.

Colpe stresses the creativity of Jewish apocalyptic in the development of the Son of man figure. Apart from Dan. 7.27, where a collective interpretation is given, this was always understood in a messianic sense, and later led to the definite form as a title such as we find in the synoptic gospels.[30]

Under the heading 'The Son of Man in Jewish Apocalyptic', Colpe[31] not only deals in turn with Dan. 7, the Similitudes of Enoch (1 En. 37-71), and 2 Esdras 13, but also significantly prepares the way for his investigation of the synoptic gospels which follows in the long section on the Son of man in the New Testament.

Daniel 7. In the vision, the point of the comparison of the four beasts representing world powers which have exercised dominion, with the man-like figure to whom is delivered everlasting rule, is the wielding of power rather than representation of a group. Thus the man-like figure is not the representative of a specific people or kingdom, but a symbol of eschatological rule. Messianic ideas are present without this figure being an actual Messiah. The words 'with the clouds of heaven' introduce the whole scene in verses 13f., and this is enacted in the invisible heavenly world, of which the visible clouds are symbolic. In the explanation of the vision, the man-like figure first becomes the representative of the heavenly entourage of God. At a second stage (verse 21) these saints of the Most High are understood not as the heavenly host of angels, but as the pious and loyal Jews of the Maccabaean age. Thus the one like a son of man becomes the representative of the true Israel. In both cases he is a collective figure, without becoming directly a messiah or redeemer.

1 Enoch 37-71. Colpe subscribes to the view that in the Similitudes[32] the term 'son of man' is no more of a messianic title than in Dan. 7, that it describes rather the appearance of the heavenly being, and that its use is based on Dan. 7.13, which is reflected in the first relevant passage, 46.1: 'another being whose countenance had the appearance of a man'. The use of the Ethiopic demonstrative pronouns 'this' or 'that' with 'son of man' as renderings of the Greek definite article is in marked contrast to the non-use of the pronouns in this connection in the Ethiopic translation of the gospels, and does not imply a titular meaning. Again, the use of three different Ethiopic expressions for Son of man also suggests that in the Greek and Aramaic (or Hebrew) no title was intended.[33]

There remain chapters 70 and 71.[34] In 70.1 we read: 'And it came to pass after this that his [Enoch's] name during his lifetime was raised aloft to that Son of man and to the Lord of Spirits from amongst those who dwell on the earth.' In agreement with the consensus of opinion Colpe rejects R. H. Charles' alteration of the second person singular pronoun to the third person in 71.14. 'Thou art the Son of man born unto righteousness.'[35] This does not mean that Enoch is the incarnated Son of man, as though he had previously come down to earth, nor that there is a mystical identity of the two figures. Rather, Enoch is installed to the office and function of the eschatological Son of man, with perhaps the idea of the metamorphosis of the human Enoch into the heavenly being, the Son of man. This Colpe[36] sees as the theology of a Jewish group, which chose as its hero Enoch transported to heaven in the *Urzeit*, and whose head, founder or teacher possibly named himself after him. This Son of man eschatology did not originate among these devotees of Enoch, but was presupposed by them. They believed Enoch was the future Son of man and world judge. This is analogous to early Christian belief in Jesus' eschatological activity as the Son of man.

2 Esdras 13. The vision of the man from the sea, 'something like the figure of a son of man' (verse 3, Syriac text; Latin defective) represents too late a stage in the development of the Son of man to be used as background for the synoptic figure.

The Synoptic Gospels. Colpe prepares to utilize the synoptic material as a quarry for information about the Jewish apocalyptic Son of man, just as he has used the non-Christian materials, for he regards the Jewish sources as inadequate evidence for the background to the synoptic Son of man. There are insufficient resemblances in the Son of man of 1 Enoch to account for the New Testament concept, and the figure in 2 Esdras is too much of a fusion with the political Messiah to be serviceable. Consequently, the Jewish apocalyptic material in these sources does not show the antecedents of the New Testament Son of man in the period 50 B.C. to A.D.50. The oldest strata of the synoptic tradition are to be used as a fourth source for the Jewish concept.[37] For this purpose eight texts about the coming Son of man are examined.[38] I now summarize Colpe's chief statements about them.

Matt. 24.27, par. Luke 17.24. The mention of the parousia in Matthew is, as is generally agreed, a secondary feature, but the first half of the verse is perhaps older than the Lukan form. On this basis the original meaning would be, 'For as the lightning flashes from the east and shines as far as the west, so will it be with the Son of man in his day.' The Son of man who, like lightning, will be visible to all, is a heavenly saviour, and the saying is authentic.

Matt. 24.37, par. Luke 17.26. The suddenness of the Son of man's appearing will take men unawares like the flood in the days of Noah. The Son of man is himself the judge (not an advocate or accuser) whose judgment begins with his appearing. Apart from the term parousia, the saying is apparently attributed to Jesus.

Luke 17.30. Verses 28–30 are not a mere Lukan imitation of verses 26f. and the announcement of the sudden advent of the Son of man in verse 30 belongs in substance to Jesus' words.

Luke 21.36. Although verses 34–6 may be a secondary composition, the idea of standing before the Son of man may be attributed to Jesus, on the principle that what must be proved is not authenticity, but unauthenticity.

Luke 18.8b: 'but when the Son of man comes, will he find faith on earth?' This is inseparable from the preceding parable of the unjust judge. It refers not to a coming of the Son of man to earth, but to acceptance of Jesus' preaching by men on earth. Will the Son of man, when he appears in the heavenly court, be able to assert that men on earth have confessed him, answered his call to repentance and, like the widow the godless judge, implored God's help? Although in the form of a question, the saying has the same meaning as Luke 17.24, 26, 30 and 21.36, and in substance belongs to Jesus' preaching.

Luke 22.69, parr. Mark 14.62; Matt. 26.64. Colpe regards Luke's form as independent of Mark and as part of his special passion narrative source, and as superior to and older than Mark's version in not having the reference to Dan. 7.13. The judgment scene is an entirely heavenly one, in which the Son of man, seated at God's right hand, shares in the judgment, and so is not merely witness or prosecutor. The only secondary feature is *τοῦ θεοῦ* ('(the power) of God'). The idea of the exaltation of the Son of man is unknown to Jewish apocalyptic, and so the Lukan form of the saying, lacking allusion to Dan. 7.13 and speaking only of the dignity (*Hoheit*) enjoyed by the Son of man, is genuine.

Matt. 10.23 is best explained as a *Herrenwort* which has survived the tendency to ascribe to Jesus activity among the non-Jews. This is supported also by its preservation despite its apparent non-fulfilment. In view of the other sayings, the coming probably takes place in heaven, and is not a coming to earth.

Matt. 24.30a. The sign of the Son of man in heaven is taken to be neither a light nor the Son of man himself, but the standard or banner to which the eschatological people of God would rally.[39] Colpe thinks this is probably an older tradition than the use of Dan. 7.13 in verse 30b (and par. Mark 13.26), and from Matthew's special source, and indeed from Jesus himself.[40]

According to Colpe, the salient features of the Son of man in the presumed Jewish source preserved in the most primitive strata of the synoptic tradition represented by these texts, are the following.

(1) The Son of man is a heavenly saviour to whose standard or ensign, 'the sign of the Son of man', the people of God will rally.
(2) The Son of man will appear suddenly and unexpectedly.
(3) His coming is not a coming to earth, but his appearing in the court of judgment in heaven, where his function is primarily that of judge alongside God the supreme judge. Although less prominent, the role of the Son of man as advocate or prosecutor is, however, not necessarily totally absent (Luke 21.36).
(4) The Son of man's appearing on his 'day' is the signal for the inauguration of the judgment.
(5) The Son of man does not come to earth. Nor (in agreement with Jewish apocalyptic) is he exalted to heaven.

All these features are traceable in Jesus' own preaching. Colpe draws the following conclusions.[41] The hypothetical fourth tradition, independent of Daniel, 1 Enoch, and 2 Esdras, is an argument in favour of authenticity, and shows 'the variability of Son of Man expectation in Judaism'. This tradition may have been developed exclusively in the churches. Colpe suggests that there were probably charismatic circles which, after the collapse of hopes for a political Messiah, turned to apocalyptic expectations and awaited Jesus as Son of man, and so became Jewish Christians rather than Jews. He maintains, however, that it is most unlikely that it is their christology alone that is transmitted in the words of Jesus, for this would mean that the leaders of the communities prophesied as if they were uttering directly Jesus' own words – a contradiction of what is otherwise known of primitive Christian prophecy (against Käsemann). Further, the expectation of the coming Son of man cannot simply have arisen out of apocalyptic, because the decisive factor was the belief in Jesus' resurrection as the dawning of the new age. Earlier, Colpe has interpreted Mark 2.10; Matt. 11.19, par. Luke 7.34; and Matt. 8.20, par. Luke 9.58 as authentic utterances in which Jesus calls himself not the Son of man, but simply 'man', 'a man', *bar nasha*.[42] These utterances, however, could not have inspired the attribution to Jesus, in the post-resurrection period, of the idea of the coming Son of man. The explanation of the contents of the passages from the supposed fourth source must be 'that Jesus himself was a prophet in this apocalyptic tradition and that he proclaimed the Son of man'.[43]

Clearly Colpe, like Borsch, although for different reasons, is to be included among supporters of the view that there was a Son of man concept in Jewish apocalyptic circles; foremost in their company was Jesus with his own proclamation of the future Son of man.

The Similitudes of Enoch

(i) In Dan. 7 we have in all probability a corporate interpretation of an older concept of an individual, transcendent agent of redemption,[44] which appears in 2 Esdras 13 and in 1 En. 37-71 (the Similitudes). It is probably a mistake, however, to attach too much importance to the use of the Danielic vision in Mark 8.38, 13.26, and 14.62. When this has been done, it has often been in defence of the authenticity of one or more of these sayings as words of Jesus (especially the last) and, in the case of T. W. Manson and his followers, in support of a corporate interpretation of the synoptic Son of man regarded as derived directly from Dan. 7. Since 2 Esdras belongs to the latter part of the first century A.D., the vision in chapter 13 can at the most only be included as rather late evidence of an earlier concept. It is, therefore, not surprising that many scholars find virtually all the evidence for a pre-Christian Jewish apocalyptic Son of man in the Similitudes. In the nineteenth century, however, the Similitudes, or even the whole of 1 Enoch, were frequently regarded as of Christian origin.[45] A Christian origin for the rest of 1 Enoch (apart from the Similitudes) has now been proved to be impossible by the discovery of portions of the book among the Qumran manuscripts. A great amount of discussion would have been silenced if sections of the Similitudes had turned up there as well. At least their Christian origin remains a possibility, and is supported by a number of more recent critics who think that the Similitudes, or the Son of man pericopae within them, are Christian interpolations into a Jewish work.[46]

The analogy between the absence of the Similitudes from the extant portions of the Greek text of 1 Enoch and their absence from the Qumran Aramaic fragments of the book, is intriguing. It may be a mere coincidence. It is certainly arguable that their absence from the Qumran texts is purely accidental. On the other hand, the sect may have known the Similitudes, but found no place for the apocalyptic Son of man in its own messianology. This is quite a plausible explanation, for although the Son of man is a 'messianic' figure in the broad sense of the term, the messianic expectations of the men of Qumran were centred upon a royal prince-Messiah variously called the Messiah, the Messiah of Israel, the righteous Messiah, the holy Messiah, and the Messiah of (or from) Aaron and Israel.[47] Nevertheless, unless the sectarians found the Similitudes as a whole, and not only the Son of man passages, to be of no service to them, the natural conclusion is that the Similitudes were not included in 1 Enoch at that time, or at least in the copies accessible to them.[48]

Some scholars have made a great deal of this absence of the Similitudes from the Qumran manuscripts. C. F. D. Moule considers that the resultant uncertain date of the Similitudes seriously weakens the common idea that the Son of man who figures in them is a pre-Christian Jewish conception, and that the corporate symbolic figure in Dan. 7 is more probably the source of the New Testament usage.[49] M. Black has expressed similar doubts about the value of the Similitudes as 'the main prop of the theory' that apocalyptic Judaism cherished a belief in a pre-existent Son of man.[50] According to J. Barr, the absence of the Similitudes from Qumran probably means that they are post-Christian, and 'may represent syncretistic Judaistic Christianity'.[51]

An elaborate attempt to date the Similitudes has been made by J. C. Hindley.[52] His study is based upon the reference to the Parthians and Medes in 1 En. 56. 5–7:

> And in those days the angels shall return
> And hurl themselves to the east upon the Parthians and Medes, etc.

This has commonly been taken as an allusion to the Parthian invasion of 40–39 B.C.[53] Hindley disagrees on the ground that, according to the pro-Roman Josephus, the inhabitants of Jerusalem welcomed that invasion, whereas that in 1 En. 56 is regarded as hostile. He endeavours to find a date in the Christian era, made more likely, he maintains, by the absence of the Similitudes from the Qumran documents, and to this end surveys the history of Parthian relations with Rome in the first and early second centuries. He arrives at the conclusion that 1 En. 56 refers to A.D. 115–17, the time of a threat from the Parthians following Trajan's campaign against them. While recognizing, but without discussing, other factors such as the development of apocalyptic and the integrity of the Similitudes, he suggests that they are a Jewish work drawing not only on Daniel but, for polemical purposes, on the Christian use of the term Son of man. Enoch, not Jesus, is the true Son of man (71.14, 'Thou art the Son of man'). The Similitudes, therefore, are too late to serve as background material for the Son of man in the gospels, and should be ignored. The historical reasons advanced by Hindley are not sufficiently cogent, however, to establish a second-century date.

A still later date is suggested by J. T. Milik, who maintains that the Similitudes are of Greek Christian origin, and that the title Son of man is borrowed from the gospels, as is also the Elect One (Luke 23.35).[54] 1 En. 56.5–7 refers to events contemporaneous with the author (the victorious campaigns of the Persian Sassanid king Sapor I against the Roman Empire, culminating in the capture of the emperor Valerian in A.D. 260); and 47.1–4 and 62.11 refer to the persecutions of Christians under Decius and Valerian. One wonders whether such passages can be thus interpreted with any degree of probability. In any case the Similitudes, if they are really Christian, conceal their true nature so successfully that it is justifiable to speak of their total lack of Christian features.[55]

R. Leivestad is a convert to rejection of the view that certain apocalyptic circles in Judaism believed in a heavenly Son of Man.[56] Impressed by the apparent ignorance of any such concept on the part of the Qumran community, he now contends that it is nothing more than an invention of theology during the last hundred years. As part of his thesis (to be discussed in our next chapter) that Jesus' use of the term Son of man as a self-designation was neither titular nor messianic, he undertakes to show that in Judaism also the expression was neither intended nor understood as a messianic title. The Similitudes are dismissed as worthless evidence for the existence of the concept; it is hazardous to rely on a source available only in late Ethiopic manuscripts of the sixteenth century and after, and not quoted in the whole of Jewish and Christian literature. No other evidence whatever can be produced for the existence of an apocalyptic Son of Man title widely supposed to have influenced Jesus and the early Christian tradition. The true significance of 2 Esdras 13 (without, however, the man-like figure being called Son of man) is that it is perhaps the earliest example of Jewish messianic interpretation of Dan. 7.13. In the Danielic passage no individual messianic figure is intended, and Leivestad points to the familiar fact that in rabbinic interpretation the Messiah is called not Son of man, but 'cloud man'. In the absence, therefore, of Jewish examples, the existence of an apocalyptic Son of man concept rests solely upon a hypothetical exegetical inference unsupported also, Leivestad continues, by the New Testament sayings.[57]

To G. Vermes, the Similitudes are post-Christian, and therefore inadmissible as a source for Jewish thought in the time of Jesus. He makes the important point that 'since Enoch's *son of man* never talks, this work exhibits no structural similarity to the Gospel usage of the term, for there the phrase is always part of direct speech'.[58] A number of scholars have been unable to regard the Similitudes as Christian in origin because of the paucity or even total absence of Christian features in them. The difference of usage to which Vermes refers may in fact point in the same direction, for if the Son of man in Enoch were taken from the gospels, the last thing one would expect is that he should be silent. Jesus as portrayed in apocryphal Christian writings is anything but silent.

N. Perrin's attempt to overthrow as erroneous the widespread assumption of a Jewish apocalyptic concept of a transcendent, pre-existent, heavenly Son of man, the judge at the End-time, is focussed upon the imagery in the relevant texts.[59] What we have here is a use of Dan. 7.13 by subsequent seers - the authors of the Similitudes and 2 Esdras 13 - and in all three writings a use of Son of man imagery. The imagery of Dan. 7 is itself derived from the Canaanite mythology of the transference of power from one god to another. The Son of man figure is interpreted as representing the people of the saints of the Most High, 'almost certainly the Maccabean martyrs, and his coming to dominion, glory and greatness is their coming to their reward for the sufferings they have endured'.[60] Perrin supposes that the choice of one like a son of man is probably purely accidental, and 'any other cryptically designated figure would have served his purpose equally well'.[61] However that may be, the fact is that this particular figure was chosen; and even if the imagery was based on Canaanite mythology, the creativity of Jewish apocalyptic has been quite considerable. It is interesting to observe that Perrin, although joining Colpe in support of the Canaanite hypothesis,[62] does not share his acceptance of the view that Jewish apocalyptic did contain a Son of man concept,[63] although, as we have seen, Colpe regards Dan. 7, 1 Enoch and 2 Esdras 13 as inadequate evidence for it.

Adopting M. Black's view that 1 En. 70f. are the oldest part of the Similitudes, and comprise the third of three descriptions of Enoch's commission (14.8f.; 60; 70f.),[64] Perrin maintains that here we have the first use of imagery drawn from Dan. 7.13. In chapter 71 Enoch is depicted as becoming the Son of man by means of the interpretation of his translation to heaven in terms of Ezek. 1 and Dan. 7.[65] Similarly, but quite independently, the early Christian belief in Jesus as the Son of man was based upon the interpretation of his resurrection in terms of Ps. 110.1 and Dan. 7.13. There is no influence in either direction.[66]

Perrin makes much of the facts that, in the vision in 2 Esdras 13, which also uses Dan. 7, the Man from the sea is not actually called Son of man, and that his activity is described largely in terms of the Son of David Messiah in Psalms of Solomon 17. He claims that in this vision there is no transcendent Son of man concept at all, but 'a translation of Ps. Sol. 17 into the more fanciful style of apocalyptic fantasy'.[67] The two redeemer figures, the Davidic Messiah and the Man, are certainly fused in 2 Esdras 13 to a degree that makes the passage less useful, and besides, the date of composition is the first century A.D. Nevertheless, and with due allowance for the features brought out by Perrin, the strong impression remains that the basis is not merely imagery derived from Dan. 7, but another presentation of a transcendent Son of man figure. This is still more the case with the Similitudes of Enoch. While conceding the acuteness of Perrin's observations, we cannot be certain that the phenomena are adequately explained as nothing more than different applications of the imagery of Dan. 7, and that they cannot be more satisfactorily accounted for as variant usages, involving different emphases, of a Son of man concept.[68]

Most European and American scholars continue to uphold the pre-Christian Jewish origin of the Similitudes. F. Hahn maintains that their absence from the Qumran texts does not justify rejection of pre-Christian composition, and that, like the first-century 2 Esdras, they utilize an old apocalyptic tradition.[69] B. M. Metzger sees in the Son of man in the Similitudes a stage in the development from the symbolic use in Dan. 7.13 to the New Testament messianic meaning. There is nothing to suggest any allusion to Jesus in the Son of man passages in the Similitudes, which were probably written 'sometime before the reign of Herod'.[70] Vielhauer stresses that the importance of the absence of the Similitudes from the Qumran sectarians' writings should not be exaggerated, as if their collection of books could be expected to aim at completeness, like that of a modern central library (!), and that it is a mistake to jump to the conclusion that this absence implies their non-existence at the time. Until proof to the contrary is forthcoming, the Similitudes must continue to be viewed as Jewish, and the ideas they contain, including the Son of man concept, as reflecting the milieu of Jesus.[71]

Here it seems appropriate, since Vielhauer at this point reproduces a summary of an interesting hypothesis proposed by E. Schweizer, to turn to the latter's fuller statement of it.[72] Jesus' teaching included the forecast that as Son of man he would be the decisive witness, the counsel for the defence or for the prosecution, at the last judgment (Luke 12.8f.). Jesus adopted the term 'son of man' because it was not yet a definite title. 'It described, first of all, the earthly "man" in his humiliation and coming suffering. It depicted the messenger of God suffering for his people and calling it to repentance. It declared that this very "man" would confront his hearers in the last judgement, so that their yes or no to the earthly Jesus would then decide their vindication or condemnation.'[73] Jesus as the decisive witness was transformed into the actual judge through a 're-apocalyptization' of his own eschatology 'in a Jewish-apocalyptic group of the early church'.[74] Further, Schweizer suggests, this could be the actual origin of the apocalyptic Son of man in general, in the Similitudes of Enoch and 2 Esdras 13. This Jewish Christian group must have considered itself as part of Judaism, and was within Jewish apocalyptic circles. Thus the usual distinction between the Jewish or the Christian origin of such ideas is not necessarily correct. After the split between Jewish apocalyptic and Jewish *Christian* apocalyptic groups had taken place, the former retained the ideas of the latter, the Son of man being for them, of course, an entirely Jewish figure distinct from Jesus. Perhaps so. But if the Son of man concept in this form was of Christian origin, all traces of that origin have been eliminated with complete success from the Similitudes and 2 Esdras 13. Some Christian vestiges might have been expected to survive in these writings, even if only by accident, but in fact the Son of man there is entirely devoid of them.

R. H. Fuller is willing to concede that doubts about the pre-Christian origin of the Similitudes, aroused by their total absence from the Qumran writings, are well-founded. He points out, however, that the Son of man in them, as also in 2 Esdras, lacks 'the distinctively Christian differentia', especially the identification with Jesus both in his ministry and his passion. We agree, therefore, that if they *are* Christian, the Similitudes have successfully disguised the Son of man we encounter in the gospels. Fuller concludes that, despite legitimate uncertainty as to the pre-Christian date of the Similitudes themselves, they may still be treated 'with some degree of confidence as evidence for a tradition in Jewish apocalyptic which is pre-Christian'.[75] He lists as the relevant passages 46.4; 48.2; 62.9, 14; 63.11; 69.26f.; 70.1; 71.1 (*sic*, for 71.14).[76]

(ii) It is necessary to give some attention to the last two chapters, 70 and 71, because they may be evidence, not only that ancient apocalyptic Judaism held a belief in a transcendent Son of man as judge, but also that in some circles Enoch was thought somehow to have become that Son of man after his translation from earth to heaven; and because there is the possibility of some connection between Enoch as the Son of man and the Christian conception.

If 70f. were an integral part of the Similitudes, the difficulty already inherent in the notion that Enoch becomes the Son of man would be vastly increased, for then Enoch would be described as somehow becoming the object of his own proclamation. Mowinckel tried to resolve this difficulty by supposing that Enoch is translated to be *with* the Son of man.[77] The two chapters deal with the same topic from different points of view, and probably represent variant traditions. As Charles pointed out,[78] it is awkward that in 70 Enoch appears to describe his own exaltation to heaven in the third person:

> And it came to pass after this that his name during his lifetime was raised aloft to that Son of man and to the Lord of Spirits from amongst those who dwell on the earth. And he was raised aloft on the chariots of the spirit and his name vanished among them (70.1f.).

The author then reverts to the first person for the rest of the chapter:

> And from that day I was no longer numbered amongst them (70.3).

Chapter 71 begins all over again:

> And it came to pass after this that my spirit was translated
> And it ascended into the heavens;
> And I saw the holy sons of God (71.1).

It is in this chapter alone, and only in verse 14, that Enoch is unambiguously identified with the Son of man,[79] when he is addressed by the Lord of Spirits: 'Thou art the Son of man who art born unto righteousness.'

Mowinckel's interpretation cannot be correct as far as 71 is concerned, and we are left with the idea, however unintelligible it may be, that Enoch became the Son of man.

The identification of Enoch with the Son of man is, as Fuller remarks, untypical of apocalyptic. In fact, he is so dissatisfied with the various explanations of the last two chapters, and in particular of 71, that he puts the problem on one side as unsolved, and judges that nothing should be based on the equation of Enoch and the Son of man in approaching the Son of man in the gospels.[80]

In the study already referred to, M. Black suggested that 70f., in which Enoch is himself the Son of man, represent an older tradition than the rest of the Similitudes.[81] In his Manson Memorial Lecture he returned to this question. He makes a clear distinction between 37–69, where 'it is impossible to suppress the suspicion that, while there is nothing distinctively Christian about the Son of Man figure in the *Similitudes,* it may have been inspired by the Gospels', and the two final chapters, especially 71, in which the figure of Enoch-Son of man as witness at the judgment cannot be Christian 'even in inspiration'.[82] The differentiation of 70f. from the rest of the Similitudes is surely correct. If 70f. represent older tradition and are pre-Christian, the identification of Enoch as the Son of man would appear to indicate the existence of a Son of man concept in certain apocalyptic circles within Judaism.

We have earlier noted Colpe's agreement with the view that in the Similitudes (apart from 70f.) 'Son of man' is not an actual title, because it is preceded by the demonstrative adjectives 'this' or 'that',[83] although he does see in the 'man' a messianic figure.[84] Only in 70f. is the term a proper title. But there is a difficulty, for while in 71.14 Enoch is addressed as the Son of man by the Lord of Spirits, in verse 17 the expression is 'that Son of man' (as in 70.1 and in the earlier chapters).

> And so there shall be length of days with that Son of man,
> And the righteous shall have peace and an upright way
> In the name of the Lord of Spirits for ever and ever.

This seems strange after Enoch has been addressed directly as Son of man. Two explanations have been offered.[85] Verse 17 may be the author's own closing remark (the address to Enoch ending with the preceding verse), so that this agrees in having the expression 'that Son of man' as in 70.1, the beginning of the unit 70f. Alternatively, if the divine address includes verse 17, the author may be regarded as using a by now familiar expression, even though Enoch himself is actually the Son of man, in order to frame a suitable conclusion not only to this address, but to the Similitudes as a whole. Whichever explanation is adopted, the fact remains that 71.14 is the crucial part of 70f., and it is here especially that, as Colpe suggests,[86] there appears to be an analogy with early Christian belief in Jesus' future activity as the eschatological Son of man. Is there, perhaps, more than a mere analogy? Conceivably there has been some Christian influence on 70f.; but this is hard to detect, and more difficult to establish than in the case of 2 Enoch. On the other hand, this Enoch-Son of man tradition, as we find it in these two final sections of the Similitudes, has perhaps exerted some influence on Christian ideas.

In his discussion of the Similitudes, C. K. Barrett points out, in connection with 71.14, that 'we owe the manuscript tradition of Enoch mainly to Christians, who would have been much more likely to remove than to create an identification of the Son of man with Enoch'.[87] This consideration strengthens the case for the pre-Christian Jewish origin of the idea, and for its possible influence on early Christian thought. To Barrett it is improbable that 'the Enochic and the gospel developments of the Son of man theme are unrelated'.[88] But he rightly notes that whatever resemblance there may be breaks down at the crucial point. Enoch somehow became the Son of man after his exaltation to heaven without dying, whereas the gospel message is that it was precisely as Son of man that Jesus died. In the Christian version we are to recognize a probably 'conscious inversion of the conventional picture of the Son of man'.[89]

The cogency of the arguments against a pre-Christian origin for the Similitudes must be conceded. But their absence from the Qumran fragments of 1 Enoch may be fortuitous. They have not yet been proved to be Christian, and those who suspect that they may be have to admit that there is nothing distinctively Christian about them or the Son of man figure in them.

If the suggestion that 1 En. 70f. represent older tradition than the preceding chapters is correct, Christian influence on them is not at all likely. There is indeed a certain analogy between Enoch-Son of man and the Christian Jesus-Son of man belief. We cannot return, however, to Otto's hypothesis that Jesus himself was inspired by the Enoch-Son of man concept.[90] There is no trace of the Enoch tradition in the gospels; and despite a certain similarity, there is no evidence there of any conscious or deliberate equation or inversion of variant Son of man themes.

The philological problem

This aspect of the Son of man question is re-examined by G. Vermes in an appendix to Matthew Black's *An Aramaic Approach to the Gospels and Acts.*[91] A survey of the literature from Arnold Meyer and H. Lietzmann in 1896 onwards is followed by studies of numerous examples from the Targums, the Talmuds, Genesis Rabbah, and 1Q Genesis Apocryphon. The conclusion reached is that *bar nash*(*a*), 'a man', 'the man', is used not only as a substitute for the indefinite pronoun, 'one', 'someone', but also, in Galilean Aramaic, as a circumlocution for 'I'. Vermes claims that the evidence for this circumlocutional use is conclusive, and that the only essential difference between this usage and *hahu gabra*, 'that man', is that whilst the latter may refer to either 'I' or 'thou', *bar nasha* always refers to the first person. Secondly, he states that none of the hundreds of examples he has scrutinized 'suggests that *bar nāsh*(*ā*) was ever employed as a messianic designation'.[92] Finally, he presents the New Testament scholar with a dilemma. Either the Greek *ὁ υἱὸς τοῦ ἀνθρώπου* is derived from Aramaic, and so 'son of man' is not a title; or it is not a translation, but an original creation, and so invention by a Hellenist of an idiom alien to Greek has to be explained.[93] The second alternative would commend itself to at most an extremely small minority of critics. His two other statements, however, about the phrase 'son of man'[94] have both been challenged.[95]

Vermes presents his case again in a simplified and less technical form in the first part of his study of 'Jesus the son of man' in his book *Jesus the Jew*,[96] and reinforces it with an examination of 'son of man' in connection with Dan. 7.13, its exegesis in antiquity, and 2 Esdras 13 and 1 Enoch 37–71. He finds that, although the expression 'one like a son of man' in Dan. 7.13 came to acquire a messianic association, 'son of man' is never used as a title and never employed by anyone as a self-designation. The apparently deliberate avoidance of the titular use Vermes explains as due to a feeling that *bar nasha* was too commonplace to be suitable.

Black, in a critique of Vermes' observations, accepted his evidence for *bar nash* as a surrogate for the first-person pronoun 'I', but disagreed in finding it also suitable for messianic use: it receives 'eschatological overtones' in Jesus' application of it to himself as *eschatologische Persönlichkeit.*[97] The reply of Vermes to this consists of the statement that Black is reiterating, without any new proofs, a twenty-year-old thesis.[98]

Jeremias has maintained,[99] against Vermes, that *bar nash*(*a*) is not a mere surrogate or periphrasis for 'I'.[100] He points out that the often cited analogy of *hahu gabra*, 'that man', is incomplete, for when employed in first person contexts (it can also be a periphrasis for 'thou') it means 'I (and no other)', being strictly confined to the speaker, whereas *bar nash*(*a*) retains its generic or indefinite meaning 'I as man', or 'as a man', even where the speaker includes himself. Although *bar nash*(*a*), therefore, like 'one' in English, can include the speaker, it is not a periphrastic substitute for 'I'.

In his reply to Jeremias' objections, Vermes appeals to his discussion, earlier in his book, of 'the *double entente* inherent to circumlocutional speech'.[101] Again, he states in his earlier paper that 'the only essential difference between the two pronominal substitutes is that whilst *hahu gabra* may describe either "I" or "thou", *bar nasha* always refers to the first person'.[102] So far, however, as the topic under discussion is concerned, it seems that the basic distinction between the expressions is rather the different mode of reference by a speaker to himself, the former exclusive and direct, the latter indefinite and indirect.

We return to Vermes' second conclusion, based on the absence of examples, that *bar nash*(*a*) was not used in Aramaic as a messianic title or designation derived in some way from Dan. 7.13.[103]

In his discussion of this question Vermes points out that there is nothing mystical about the Aramaic preposition 'like' in the phrase 'one like a son of man' in Dan. 7.13; it is common, as in this chapter, in the description of dreams. The central figure of the narrative is a human being symbolizing the eschatological triumph of Israel over its oppressors, and not an individual. Rabbinic interpretation understood the passage as messianic without treating 'one like a son of man' as a title. Touching briefly on the pre-rabbinic exegesis in 2 Esdras 13, in which Daniel's 'one like a son of man' becomes the pre-existent royal Messiah, but is still not a title, Vermes examines in some detail the son of man in 1 Enoch. In contrast to 'the Anointed One' and 'the Lord of Spirits' the expression is not titular; it needs explanation either by a determining clause such as 'the son of man who has righteousness' (46.3; cf. 71.14), or by reference to the original vision, as in 46.2, where 'that son of man' alludes to 'another being whose countenance had the appearance of a man' in the preceding verse. Finally, Vermes issues a reminder that, since 'the son of man' in the gospels is not a genuine Greek phrase but an Aramaic one, it must make Aramaic sense. It would indeed, as he remarks, be a caricature of scholarship to admit these premises, and then to foist upon the Aramaic idiom a meaning discovered 'on unhistorical and unlinguistic grounds' for its Greek rendering in the New Testament.[104]

It is interesting that the Scandinavian scholar R. Leivestad[105] independently reaches the same conclusions in the following respects.

(1) There was no messianic Son of man concept or title in apocalyptic Judaism.[106]

(2) The Similitudes of Enoch are worthless as evidence to the contrary.

(3) Consequently, the expression 'son of man' has no messianic connotation whatsoever in any sayings which may reasonably be attributed to Jesus.

(4) The apocalyptic Son of man concept and title are a modern invention.[107]

On the other hand, the differences of view between these two scholars are even more striking than their agreements.

(1) Vermes insists that the Semitic original behind the translation Greek ὁ υἱὸς τοῦ ἀνθρώπου in the gospels must be Aramaic rather than Hebrew.[108] Leivestad, however, is not at all sure that we must decide in favour of Aramaic *bar nasha*, and suspects that that choice is generally influenced by a supposed connection with Dan. 7.13. Jesus could just as well have said *ben* (or *bar*) *adam.* Moreover, he remarks that 'the whole problem would be of minimal interest if the Semitic expression were nothing but a manner of speech, a simple circumlocution of the first person',[109] which is the very solution that Vermes seeks to establish; Leivestad even claims that the Greek expression cannot easily be explained on that supposition.

(2) As we have seen, Vermes insists that, since the Greek phrase in the

New Testament is a translation of Aramaic, its meaning must be that of the Aramaic exemplar. Leivestad maintains 'that the meaning of the term Son of man can only be defined from the New Testament',[110] a statement which could imply the very hazards against which Vermes issues warning.[111]

(3) Vermes supports by specific examples the case for *bar nasha* having been employed by Jesus as a circumlocution by a speaker in reference to himself. Leivestad prefers Hebrew *ben adam* as the original of the un-Greek phrase 'the son of man' in the gospels. He suggests that Jesus employed *ben adam* as a non-eschatological, non-messianic, humble self-designation to express his self-identification with the sons of men;[112] but he is unable to provide examples of anyone else using *ben adam* as a self-designation.[113] In itself this might not be a fatal objection, for Jesus could have invested the expression with a new meaning, but there remains the linguistic difficulty noted above under (1).

(4) The not unexpected consequence of Vermes' philological investigation is that he does not regard any of the future 'son of man' sayings as authentic. Leivestad, however, does accept some of them, e.g. Mark 8.38 and Luke 12.8, but at the expense of a reductionist piece of exegesis which takes 'me' and 'the Son of man' as simply instances of *parallelismus membrorum* to avoid repetition.

These comparisons and contrasts may serve as a reminder that it is not only the adherents of the Son of man type of interpretation who are divided among themselves.

It is more likely that the Greek for 'the son of man' in the gospels is translated from vernacular Aramaic rather than from Hebrew.[114] It is accepted that the Greek phrase must bear the meaning of its prototype or, perhaps one may add, that it should not be inconsistent with it.

G. Vermes and the synoptic sayings[115]

Discussion of Vermes' views on these sayings is included here because his solution of the problem rests on primarily philological considerations, and his investigation calls for undivided scrutiny as a whole.

Vermes divides these sayings into three groups: those unconnected with Dan. 7.13, those connected directly, and those connected indirectly with it. This involves classifying together sayings concerning Jesus' earthly activity and those foretelling his death and resurrection. Vermes maintains that 'there is no reasonable doubt why Jesus should not have uttered them', and that, if only half of them are authentic, they would supply ample evidence 'that the *son of man* circumlocution belonged to the stylistic idiosyncrasies of Jesus himself'.[116] However, traditio-historical criticism drastically reduces the number of sayings likely to be authentic below even half of the twenty in question. The Markan passion and resurrection predictions (Mark 8.31; 9.9; 9.12; 9.31; 10.33f.;[117] also Luke 24.7) are community formulations (*Gemeindebildungen*). Jesus' own prophecies of his death are phrased in metaphorical language and spoken in the first person (Mark 10.38, par. Matt. 20.22; Luke 12.50; 13.32f.).

I now deal briefly with sayings on which Vermes offers short comments in support of his interpretation.[118]

Mark 2.10. Vermes may be correct in maintaining that Jesus said '*the son of man* has authority on earth to forgive sins' instead of 'I have authority' out of modesty. Yet it may be that the full meaning intended is: 'that you may know that "even a man (in my case)", or "man though I am", or "a man, someone (you know who)" has authority on earth to forgive sins'.[119] But one wonders whether the real kernel of authenticity is 'son, your sins are forgiven (by God)' in verse 5, as in Luke 7.48.

Mark 2.27f. 'The sabbath was made for man, not man for the sabbath; so the son of man is lord even of the sabbath.'

Vermes believes that a circumlocutional use of *bar nasha* with reference to the speaker gives the best sense in the gospel context. This is not compelling, and the choice lies between a generic meaning of *bar nasha* in an utterance of Jesus, and a christological affirmation of the church.[120]

Matt. 16.13. 'Who do men say that the son of man is?'

One way to support the priority of this to the versions in Mark 8.27 and Luke 9.18 with 'I' is, with Vermes, to presuppose a contrast in Aramaic between 'sons of men' (*bene nash*) and '*the son of man*' (*bar nasha*); but this is not decisive.

Matt. 12.40, par. Luke 11.30. Only Matthew's version, alluding to the sojourn of the Son of man in the heart of the earth for three days and three nights, is relevant to Vermes' mention here, and is in any case secondary to that of Luke.

Luke 6.22, par. Matt. 5.11. There is much to be said for Vermes' preference for Luke's 'because of the son of man' to Matthew's 'because of me'. But authenticity is uncertain, and probably what is intended is the christological title Son of man.

Vermes also refers to two sayings of Jesus about criticisms directed against him. One of these, concerning speaking a word against the Son of man, which is forgivable, and speaking against the Holy Spirit, which is not

(Luke 12.10, par. Matt. 12.32), is problematical, and the parallel saying in Mark 3.28f. has 'sons of men' instead of the singular. The contrast between Jesus as 'son (or Son) of man' and the Holy Spirit as both the objects of men's evil speaking may be considered too startling to be authentic. It is certainly much less natural than the second example, the contrast between the criticism levelled against John the Baptist for his asceticism and against Jesus for his eating and drinking (Luke 7.34, par. Matt. 11.19). Here there is no cause for doubting authenticity. The main consideration is, perhaps, not whether *bar nasha*, as a christological title, supplanted the first-person pronoun 'I', although this is possible, but whether it is an example of a circumlocutional usage equivalent to 'I' favoured by Vermes. This is not the sole possibility; *bar nasha* may mean simply 'one' or 'someone': 'John the Baptist came neither eating nor drinking . . . ; a man, someone (you know who) came both eating and drinking . . .' In a third saying, Luke 9.58, par. Matt. 8.20, there is yet another contrast, between the refuges of foxes and birds and the homelessness of *bar nasha.* As in the preceding example, the church may have replaced 'I' with the Son of man title, and one can discern the appropriateness of such a logion to preaching on the self-sacrifice required of discipleship. More probably, in this undoubtedly authentic saying Jesus used *bar nasha* to point a contrast with the animals, not as a circumlocution for 'I', but in an indefinite sense, 'a man such as I', 'a man like myself' (so Colpe and Jeremias).

There remains Luke 19.10: 'The Son of man came to seek and to save the lost', where, according to Vermes, Jesus refers to himself as 'son of man' out of reserve. This is by no means certain; the sentence is commonly explained as a generalizing christological appendage to the story of Zacchaeus.

This examination of Vermes' 'preliminary assessment' of the sayings unconnected with Dan. 7.13 leads to the result that probably only Mark 2.10; Luke 7.34, par. Matt. 11.19; and Luke 9.58, par. Matt. 8.20 warrant serious consideration as words of Jesus. In all three contexts, *bar nasha* in the sense of 'a (certain) man', or 'someone (you know who)' would be appropriate as well as consistent with Aramaic usage. In practical terms it is of less importance whether *bar nasha* was used as a circumlocutional periphrasis for 'I' or not. If Jesus used it in an indirect way 'out of awe, reserve, or humility' on occasions when the first-person pronoun seemed less fitting, and perhaps more frequently than was customary, the effect would have been recognition by his hearers of a 'stylistic idiosyncrasy',[121] a strikingly characteristic habit of speech. It passed into the gospel tradition, where it came to be used as if it had been Jesus' regular self-designation in sayings concerning his earthly activity, his death and resurrection, as well as his future function as the eschatological Son of man.

There is little to say about the authenticity or otherwise of the sayings directly connected with Dan. 7.13, namely Mark 13.26 and 14.62 with their parallels.[122] But Vermes' remarks on Mark 13.26 include two statements important also in regard to all future Son of man sayings, whether with direct or indirect reference to Dan. 7.13.

(1) The contrast with the employment of 'son of man' as a 'self-designation' is not in itself adequate reason to deny the authenticity of the messianic content of the term in this saying, because there too it may conceivably be understood as a circumlocution for 'I'.[123]

(2) On the other hand, Vermes points out that he has earlier demonstrated[124] that Jesus had no messianic consciousness, and therefore could not have spoken this logion.

He concludes that both sayings come not from Jesus, but from the community utilizing Dan. 7.13 in the interests of the parousia doctrine.

Vermes also attributes to the community all the sayings indirectly connected with Dan. 7.13. The 'neutral speech-form' *son of man* that Jesus was in the habit of using was ' "eschatologized" by means of a midrash based on Daniel 7:13' by 'the apocalyptically-minded Galilean disciples of Jesus.'[125]

Vermes has shown that Jesus very probably used the term *bar nasha* in its meaning of 'a man', 'someone', in reference to himself and perhaps more often than was customary, although, as argued earlier, not necessarily as a mere substitute for 'I' or as a self-designation. He has also sought to demonstrate the complete absence of any messianic Son of man concept and title in extant pre-Christian Jewish sources. But even so, he has not proved its non-existence beyond all doubt; he assumes it on the basis of his investigation of the extant literature. Perhaps we should be satisfied. Yet there remains a feeling of dissatisfaction, and a suspicion that the hiatus between Jesus' use of *bar nasha* in an entirely 'unmessianic' sense and the Son of man in the gospels should be bridgeable otherwise than by a midrash on Dan. 7.13 thought up by early believers. It is felt by not a few scholars of repute that the uncertain date and origin of the Similitudes of Enoch render them unreliable as a source for the New Testament Son of man. In the present work, while legitimate doubts about them are recognized, they are used to illustrate certain features of the Son of man in the gospels, because there is nothing in them, or in their portrayal of the figure, that is specifically Christian. Even if the Similitudes were written in the Christian era, they may reflect earlier ideas perhaps current, although not widely known, in the time of Jesus.

As remarked earlier, Vermes' statements about Mark 13.26 are equally applicable to the future Son of man sayings in general. The implication is that in theory 'son of man' is possible in any of them, since it can be taken as a circumlocution for 'I', but that in fact this is impossible, because Jesus, having no messianic consciousness, could not have uttered them. Jesus rejected the popular idea of a political Messiah.[126] More relevant is his self-understanding of his mission (*Sendungsbewusstsein*) as it is expressed in his authoritative words and corresponding social conduct, which were not dependent on traditional messianic ideas. Vermes himself goes so far as to speak of Jesus' 'own consciousness of an immediate and intimate contact with the heavenly Father'.[127] This is at least part of what the post-Bultmannian scholars mean by an indirect or implicit christology. It includes the idea of the correspondence of the decisions to be made at the eschatological judgment in the presence of the Son of man with a man's attitude to Jesus' call to repentance.[128] Vermes has described Jesus as a first-century Galilean charismatic, as a prophet, and as one of the Ḥasidim (the pious). If Jesus was one of these, history has shown that he was the greatest of them.

Did Jesus, the founder of a movement soon to find itself unable to remain within the confines of Judaism, go beyond others to the extent of actually envisaging himself as involved in the judgment in a role associated in apocalyptic belief with 'the Son of man'? His 'christological' understanding of his mission *theoretically* makes it possible for him to have employed *bar nasha* in some of the future sayings with no or only indirect reference to Dan. 7.13, both instead of 'I',[129] which would have been more inappropriate than in referring to his earthly activity, and also in a christological sense. If these sayings had come down to us in an Aramaic form they would probably not have been so readily dismissed as unauthentic. The obliqueness and mysterious indirectness of the allusions to the Son of man in the relevant sayings, which even gave rise to the modern notion that they refer to some figure other than Jesus, indicates the possibility that their characterization of the Son of man is an original and creative adaptation of a concept current in some circles of which no other trace has survived, except perhaps in the disputed Similitudes of Enoch.[130]

The problem is stated succinctly by Vermes:

> The final dilemma which the historian is asked to solve is whether direct reference to Daniel 7:13 results from an attempt to render explicit the underlying significance of innuendoes genuinely uttered by Jesus, or whether indirect references are secondary developments from the formal quotations just investigated.[131]

We shall endeavour to show in Part Two that the former alternative has much to commend it as the true explanation of what happened in the developing tradition. The survey of recent significant work on the Son of man in the synoptic gospels in the next chapter is intended to provide more of the background to the studies that follow it along this particular line of investigation of the problem.

Excursus: The Son of man and the Melchizedek fragment

Indirect evidence of a Son of man concept in pre-Christian Judaism may possibly be reflected in the Melchizedek fragment from Qumran (11QMelch),[132] which interprets Ps. 82.1 as referring to Melchizedek.

> The heavenly one (*elohim*) stands in the congregation of God (*el*);
> among the heavenly ones (*elohim*) he judges.

It is clear from the context of this quotation that 'the heavenly one' is Melchizedek, and 'the heavenly ones' are other angelic beings. The manuscript says Melchizedek executes God's judgment upon Belial 'and all the spirits of his lot' (the evil angels), and is assisted in this by 'all the heavenly ones on high' (the good angels). This understanding is confirmed by the statement that over against the lot of Belial there stand 'the sons of light and the men of the lot of Melchizedek'. In this fragment Melchizedek appears as an eschatological figure, the champion and redeemer of the righteous and the judge of the wicked in the heavenly judgment. Flusser points out resemblances between this portrayal of Melchizedek and the Son of man in the Similitudes of Enoch and in the New Testament, and suggests influence from the Son of man concept on this picture of Melchizedek as the eschatological judge. If so, this might help to account for the absence from the Qumran literature of the Similitudes with their Son of man passages:[133] the Son of man was superfluous because his role was occupied by Melchizedek.[134]

II

THE SON OF MAN IN THE SYNOPTIC GOSPELS IN RECENT STUDY

This survey of Son of man-*Forschung* makes no claim to completeness, which in any case is probably unattainable, but seeks to review the main trends and developments since my earlier book *Jesus and the Son of Man* (1964).[1]

A number of scholars still find authentic words of Jesus in all three groups of sayings: those referring to his earthly activity, those foretelling his passion and resurrection, and those looking to the parousia and glory of the Son of man. Among them are Goppelt,[2] Moule,[3] Maddox,[4] Marshall,[5] Barrett,[6] and Bruce.[7]

Goppelt adds to the authentic sayings the following: Mark 2.10, 28; the Q present sayings Matt. 8.20, par.; 11.19, par.; 12.32, par.; the future saying Luke 12.8, regarded as more original than parr. Matt. 10.32 and Mark 8.38; and a passion prediction behind Mark 8.31, traceable to the oldest Palestinian tradition and possibly to Jesus in the form, 'The Son of man must suffer many things and be rejected (and after three days be raised up)'; this last part is implicit, because in the idea of the suffering righteous man rejection leads to exaltation.

Marshall does not take into account all the texts. The establishment of the fact (*sic*) that Jesus referred to himself as Son of man in his earthly ministry makes it impossible to believe that in the future sayings he could have referred to someone else, for he could not have spoken about two Sons of men! Jesus, therefore, refers to himself in Luke 12.8f.; 12.40, par. Matt. 24.44; Luke 18.8b; Mark 14.62. Marshall thinks also that the passion predictions should not be rejected out of hand (Luke 22.48; Mark 14.21; 8.31; 9.31; 10.33f.) and that Mark 10.45 is authentic. The reason why the earthly and passion and resurrection sayings are not brought into close relation with one another, is that 'Jesus avoided overt identification of himself with the Son of man and so sought to preserve a certain mystery regarding his person'.[8]

Barrett utilizes all three types of sayings in his reconstruction of Jesus' expectations of his fate and ultimate vindication. It is true that

'Son of man' is the only title at all likely to have been used by Jesus himself, and that it is this title which is used in the passion predictions. But it scarcely follows, if the passion material cannot be interpreted in terms of the Son of man, '(a) that we cannot approach Jesus' own understanding of the significance of his death, and (b) that the synoptic tradition contains no serious thinking on the subject at all'.[9] Broadly speaking, Barrett's scheme requires Son of man sayings from Jesus about his earthly ministry, his passion and death, and his early vindication by the glory of the Son of man (or, alternatively, by his own resurrection and that of his followers),[10] because Dan. 7, with the 'suffering' figure vindicated by receiving a universal kingdom, is taken to be the primary source of inspiration.

Schweizer[11] has proposed the hypothesis that Jesus' preaching contained the theme of his humiliation and rejection as Son of man, to be followed by his exaltation and vindication as Son of man. This clearly involves the acceptance of at least some of the sayings about the Son of man's earthly life as traceable to Jesus; indeed, Schweizer goes so far as to affirm that it is sayings of this category which are the most reliable. It also involves the acceptance as genuine of the saying referring to Jesus the exalted Son of man as witness at the last judgment (Luke 12.8, par. Matt. 10.32). With most other critics Schweizer regards the Markan passion and resurrection predictions as, in their present form, *Gemeindebildungen.* Nevertheless, he maintains that they are important as indirect evidence of an earlier stage of thought, originating with Jesus himself, concerning humiliation and rejection followed not by resurrection, as in their present form, but by exaltation. This thesis depends on the view that Jesus interpreted his mission as *Son of man* in terms of the humiliated and rejected, but finally exalted righteous man in Judaism.[12]

M. Black, to whom we are indebted for a series of valuable studies on various aspects of the Son of man problem,[13] has discussed Schweizer's approach and has made further suggestions on similar lines.[14] Schweizer regards as the sole possibly vital objection to his thesis, the fact that 'the Synoptists speak of the resurrection of Jesus, but very rarely, if at all, of his exaltation'.[15] Is this objection perhaps weightier than Schweizer allows? Black suggests that the first place to look for the concept of exaltation is not the gospels, but the early Christian hymn in Phil. 2.6-11, derived ultimately from the Aramaic-speaking church. Here (following Lohmeyer's famous monograph)[16] Jesus is described in language ('being born in the likeness of a man, and being found in fashion as a man') clearly reminiscent of Dan. 7.13. We agree.[17] Moreover, there is in the hymn no reference to the Son of man's resurrection, but to his exaltation (ὑπερύψωσεν). Black equates this (apart from probable allusion also to the crucifixion in John) with the Johannine usage of ὑψόω (John 3.14; 8.28; 12.32, 34). Therefore, as Schweizer also suggests, is the idea of Jesus' exaltation more primitive than that of resurrection? And does the Fourth Gospel provide evidence that the idea of the Son of man's exaltation and vindication actually goes back to Jesus himself?[18]

In the study we are discussing,[19] Black says that Acts 7.56 also belongs to the same category as the Philippians hymn and the four sayings in the Fourth Gospel because, in distinction from the kerygmatic speeches or sermons in Acts proclaiming the death and resurrection of Jesus, Stephen's closing words speak not of resurrection, but of exaltation. 'Behold, I see the heavens opened, and the Son of man standing at the right hand of God.' But, in fact, in contrast to Phil. 2.9 and the Johannine texts, Acts 7.56 refers to the Son of man in his exalted state, rather than to his exaltation in place of resurrection. In any case, this is what the context naturally demands. Stephen's declaration presupposes the resurrection; and so it does not necessarily fall out of the kerygmatic pattern. In both Acts 2.33 (ὑψωθείς) and 5.31 (ὕψωσεν) references to exaltation follow mention of the resurrection (2.32; 5.30). The probability is, then, greatly increased that both Phil. 2 and the four Johannine sayings also presuppose the resurrection as the natural consequence of death - death which is expressly mentioned in the hymn (whether or not the reference to crucifixion is a Pauline adaptation), and is probably included also in the Johannine use of ὑψόω. So viewed, the case for the greater antiquity of the idea of the exaltation and vindication of the Son of man, as compared with resurrection, does not seem particularly strong. It then becomes less likely also that the presumed more primitive doctrine goes back to Jesus.[20]

Black asks whether Jesus ever predicted his exaltation in terms of his resurrection:

> We come back to the question of the authenticity of the Marcan predictions of the rejection and resurrection of the Son of Man. Is it too fanciful to see in the Johannine version of this tradition, δεῖ ὑψωθῆναι τὸν υἱὸν τοῦ ἀνθρώπου, 'the son of man must be exalted' (iii.14), the most primitive form of the Gospel tradition and a genuine saying of Jesus? The resurrection prediction would then be secondary tradition, yet at the same time a quite legitimate inference from the 'exaltation' of the Son of Man, since his 'uplifting' to God, as in the exaltation and vindication of the righteous, led him through death to immortality.[21]

Although John 3.14 undoubtedly draws on early Palestinian tradition, the Markan passion and resurrection predictions also come from a pre-Markan and partly Palestinian stratum of tradition.[22] If in Phil. 2 (and in

John) 'we have an even earlier stratum of the tradition where the belief is solely in the triumph and vindication, the exaltation of the Son of man',[23] we also have in 1 Cor. 15.3f., on Paul's own admission, an already existing pattern of preaching relating to the death and *resurrection* of Christ. Is it conceivable that the idea of Jesus' exaltation, with no explicit reference to resurrection, was earlier than this pre-Pauline kerygma? Perhaps the answer is that resurrection and exaltation were not mutually exclusive ideas in the early preaching, so that either one or the other sometimes appears as in Phil. 2.9 and 1 Cor. 15.4, or both, as in Acts 2.32f. and 5.30f. In common with the other Johannine Son of man sayings, John 3.14 is not an authentic utterance of Jesus. Nor does it seem possible to attribute to him the rejection-exaltation-vindication theme or progression on the basis of any synoptic Son of man sayings; they allude neither to the successive stages of the theme, nor to exaltation as an itinerary from one status to another.

In a recent study G. Lindeskog[24] takes his departure from the key sayings: (1) Mark 8.38, par. Luke 9.26, (2) Luke 12.8f. (the par. in Matt. 10.32f. replaces the Son of man title with the pronoun, thus creating an entirely I-saying). These he calls I-Son of man sayings (*Ich-MS-Aussagen*), because they appear to distinguish between Jesus the speaker and the Son of man, as if they were different persons. Saying (2) differs from saying (1), which speaks only of 'being ashamed' (ἐπαισχύνεσθαι), in having the complementary ideas of 'confessing' and 'denying' (ὁμολογεῖν ἐν and (ἀπ) αρνεῖσθαι) and, while reflecting Semitic and Palestinian origin, is not earlier than the clash of Jewish Christianity with the synagogue, and uses technical Christian terminology. Were there originally two logia in the tradition, as in Luke, or one as in Mark, which led to the production of a secondary parallel saying? Lindeskog decides in favour of the latter alternative. The verb 'to be ashamed' in Mark represents the *Urwort*, out of which arose the double form in Luke 12.8f., presupposing the post-Easter situation.

Lindeskog also accepts as authentic in content the following earthly sayings: Luke 7.34, par. Matt. 11.19; Luke 19.10; Mark 2.10; 10.45a; and he cites in support the I-words in Mark 2.17, par. Luke 5.32 [Matt. 9.13], and Matt. 15.24 as being similar in content (especially 'I' or 'the Son of man came'). He makes a useful distinction between authenticity of form and authenticity of content. Mark 2.17 is authentic in both respects, whereas Luke 19.10 is authentic only in content.[25] This is not an original insight, but it is an important one.

The synoptic Son of man concept is described as a radical reinterpretation of the apocalyptic Son of man. Jesus as the Son of man on earth is the friend of sinners and not only, as is the Son of man in the Similitudes of Enoch, of the righteous; the suffering and dying Son of man has no antecedent in Jewish apocalyptic; and the Easter event is inexplicable from Jewish thought. We can even go as far as to say that the Jewish apocalyptic Son of man and the synoptic Son of man have nothing in common but the name. This is surely a gross exaggeration, and would mean that the early church separated Jesus from his conceptual background, or that Jesus himself did so, more thoroughly than can be reasonably established from the texts available to us.

Of all the theories proposed, Lindeskog rightly condemns the view that in the I-Son of man sayings Jesus meant someone other than himself, as the most objectionable on exegetical and historical grounds, for it contradicts the foundations of the tradition. With some justification he quotes Vielhauer to the effect that the distinction between Jesus and the Son of man is not between two persons, but between the 'status' of one and the same person, Jesus, which he occupies in this age, and the one he will enjoy in the coming age.[26] Vielhauer, however, is not referring to Jesus' own thought, but to the church's christology. As argued in *JSM*, we have to think, rather, of the future Son of man functions Jesus himself believed he would exercise.

Lindeskog adopts the view that in the I-Son of man sayings Jesus left unsolved and unexplained for his hearers what was perfectly clear, perhaps, to himself, namely, his identity with or distinction from the Son of man, as in the parabolic use of 'the householder', 'the bridegroom', and 'the son'. Like these, 'the Son of man' is a *Rätselwort*. It was the church which later said specifically that Jesus is the Son of man, that is, the coming Son of man, and therefore also the Son of man active upon earth, and especially the suffering Son of man. Lindeskog concludes with the observation that the Son of man secret is greater than the messianic secret. If its origin is obscure, the result is clear. The gospel is the story of Jesus as, above all, the Son of man.

This is altogether a stimulating and rewarding study. It emphasizes the inclusiveness of the Son of man christology as far surpassing any other in importance, in that it is a direct lineal descendant from Jesus' own mysterious allusions to the Son of man.

We now turn to recent supporters of the view that authentic Son of man sayings can only be sought among those referring to the future.

E. Jüngel[27] reaches the conclusion that, even of the future sayings, we possess in the synoptics only a few remnants of a once richer collection. Authentic sayings with, however, later modifications, are probably present in Matt. 24.27, par. Luke 17.24; Matt. 24.37–9, par. Luke 17.26, 30; Luke 11.30 (par. Matt. 12.40); Luke 12.8(9) (Matt. 10.32f.) and the associated sayings in Mark 8.38, parr. Matt. 16.27, Luke 9.26.

In *JSM*[28] I referred to several different attempts to support the view that Jesus applied to himself the eschatological Son of man concept in relation to his earthly ministry. One of these was that proposed by R. H. Fuller in *The Mission and Achievement of Jesus*, in which he brought together the kingdom of God as, although not yet fully come, yet active proleptically and in advance in Jesus' ministry, and Jesus himself as, although not yet the Son of man, yet destined to be, and performing proleptically the functions of, that eschatological figure.[29] This theory involved the acceptance as authentic logia, both of sayings about the coming Son of man, and of others relating to the earthly ministry and the passion of the Son of man. In his subsequent book Fuller has abandoned this position entirely, describing it as 'a rather artificial attempt to paper over the undeniable inconsistency within the Son of man sayings', and so to refute Bultmann's opinion that Jesus' view of his mission was quite unmessianic, and was rather that of the Son of man's forerunner.[30] In his earlier book Fuller had written that Jesus in his ministry is not to be identified '*tout court* with the coming Son of Man', although he is closely associated with him.[31] Jesus is the Son of man designate. Now that Fuller finds genuine Son of man sayings only in the future category, who is the Son of man in them? Not, as with Bultmann, a figure to whom Jesus is related as his forerunner, nor even the Jesus of the End-time still to come. But despite the differences, Fuller's new interpretation resembles Bultmann's in divorcing the Son of man concept in any shape or form from the actual person of Jesus himself in Jesus' own thought. Jesus' ministry is described as 'eschatological prophecy'. In the crucial saying at Luke 12.8f., 'the Son of man merely acts as a kind of rubber stamp at the End for the salvation which is already being imparted in Jesus'.[32] No longer is Jesus to be vindicated for his obedient ministry and passion, as Son of man. Rather is his mission, understood by himself as eschatological prophecy, to be vindicated by the Son of man at the End.[33] This suggestion is as unconvincing as that of Bultmann. Fuller maintains that the Son of man as the eschatological agent of redemption was a feature of pre-Christian Jewish apocalyptic. If we suppose Jesus to have been influenced by this concept, we must also allow for originality in his adaptation of it. In fact, any idea that Jesus envisaged the Son of man as an objective figure other than himself as his future vindicator, and therefore also as of higher status than himself, is surely erroneous, and is due to taking too literally the apparent distinction between himself and the Son of man in Luke 12.8 (Mark 8.38). To quote what I have written elsewhere, 'the authority inherent in Jesus' reported words and actions does not suggest that he would have appealed to any other than God himself as Father (Abba) in a special and unique sense'.[34]

In 1966 there appeared an article by R. E. C. Formesyn, entitled 'Was there a Pronominal Connection for the "bar nasha" Selfdesignation?'[35] This he claims to be 'a possible appendix to his [Tödt's] work, an appendix on a much repeated objection against his conclusions on the inauthenticity of the Son of Man selfdesignation'.[36] Like Bultmann, Tödt finds authentic logia only in the group of future sayings. In these the Son of man is not Jesus, but another figure to whom he is soteriologically, but not christologically, related, and who at the end will act as advocate and witness in the assessment of men's attitude to Jesus here and now. Formesyn accepts Tödt's main conclusions. The objection to Tödt's thesis he proposes to meet is: If Jesus did not call himself the Son of man, why is that title found only on his lips? Formesyn claims that his 'very simple' solution 'explains the whole problem completely'.[37] Beginning at this point, only about the last third of the article is actually devoted to the proposed solution, although the preceding two-thirds provide some valuable information and comment.

Formesyn maintains that 'Son of man' is confined to words attributed to Jesus because of its interchangeability in Aramaic with the first-person pronoun. In the 'earthly' and 'suffering' sayings this gave rise to 'messianisation' of the pronoun in them. But in the future sayings, some of which are authentic, the reverse happened, namely, 'potential pronominalisation of the Son of Man title', and this 'gave perhaps the first push to the process of identification of Jesus with the future Son of Man whom he predicted'.[38] To allow this interchangeability, there must have been a verbal similarity between the Aramaic for 'Son of man' and for 'I'. Sceptical of the use of *bar nash*(*a*) by itself in Palestinian Aramaic as equivalent to 'I', Formesyn thinks a composite locution, *hahu bar nasha*, 'that son of man', was most probably used in this sense, because it alone is 'unmistakenly [*sic*] equivalent to the *personal* pronoun', and an indefinite meaning is ruled out. Moreover, there is a close parallel in *hahu gabra*, 'that man', as a substitute for 'I'.[39] He is not at all deterred by the total absence of *hahu bar nasha* from Aramaic sources. But its absence is fatal to the theory.[40]

F. Hahn's book *Christologische Hoheitstitel* was first published in 1963.[41] He examines first the Son of man title, which he recognizes as the most important christological title in the gospels, since it is the one which might most reasonably be expected to provide clues to Jesus' preaching. His approach to the problem is similar to that of Tödt, about whose work he notes that 'it demonstrates the essential connection between primitive Christian preaching and the preaching of Jesus himself'.[42] The following quotation sums up his position.

> It must be established that of the three groups of Son of man words, those about the suffering and rising again of the Son of man can least of all lay claim to authenticity. The words about the earthly deeds may not in general be interpreted, as was customary among older critics, as misunderstood statements about 'man', as also the reproduction of 'I' by 'Son of man' is not provable from contemporary Aramaic. The priority of the sayings about earthly deeds cannot be supported by alleging that the concept of the suffering and exalted righteous one is implied. For it is only within the framework of apocalyptic that unequivocal presuppositions for an understanding of the Son of man idea are to be found, and for this reason the words about the coming Son of man stand necessarily at the beginning of the development. Only after the identification of the future Son of man with Jesus had been made could the Jesus who worked on earth in full power and authority be described likewise as the 'Son of man', and this description was finally extended to cover the statements about His suffering and rising again. If the priority of the words about the eschatological working of the Son of man is made clear, then further the origin of some of these words on the lips of Jesus cannot be disputed.[43]

According to Hahn the only sayings with a serious claim to authenticity are Luke 12.8f.; 17.24, par. Matt. 24.27; Luke 17.26f. (28f.), par. Matt. 24.37-9.[44]

There remains the denial to Jesus of any Son of man sayings at all. E. Käsemann's influential lecture of 1953 on 'The Problem of the Historical Jesus', first published in 1954, appeared in English in 1964.[45] Käsemann regards it as very questionable whether Jesus claimed for himself the title of Son of man, or indeed any other expression of messianic self-understanding.[46] Nor does he accept Bultmann's hypothesis that Jesus did employ the term, but in reference to a figure of the future distinct from himself. Mark 8.38, for example, which suggests that he might have done so, actually reflects the language of Palestinian Christian prophets uttering 'maxims of holy law for the guidance of the community', and laying down the future consequences of obedience or disobedience here and now.[47] As we have seen, it is highly improbable that by 'the Son of man' Jesus meant somebody else. Käsemann adds a further objection, when he asks what would be the position of such a figure 'if the Baptist has already ushered in the turn of the aeons and yet, for his part, still stands in the shadow of Jesus'. Although we find ourselves agreeing with Käsemann that Jesus neither used the title Son of man as a self-designation, nor applied it to some figure other than himself, his conclusion that it first entered the Jesus tradition from the church's own christological thought, and therefore that Jesus himself did not use it at all,[48] goes beyond the evidence.

In an article entitled 'The Origin of the Son of Man Christology', H. M. Teeple[49] attempts to demonstrate the unauthenticity of all the Son of man sayings by the application of certain criteria. He first discusses and disposes of the following criteria as invalid.

(1) A saying comes from Jesus if it has Palestinian Jewish concepts; but this element is uncertain, because it could be due to Jewish converts to Christianity.

(2) Some writers give a high place to the criterion, according to which a saying of Jesus is genuine if it is explicable neither from late Judaism nor from the situation of the early church. This standard is questionable, for Jesus was himself a product of late Judaism, and so even a saying containing apocalyptic elements could conceivably be genuine.

(3) A saying is authentic if it distinguishes between Jesus and the Son of man (Luke 12.8f.; Mark 8.38). This widely accepted criterion is incorrect, because such sayings are cases of literary parallelism: Jesus alone is meant. Moreover, they fit the situation of Christians brought before courts demanding denial of Jesus.

(4) The criterion that some sayings express Jesus' prophetic self-consciousness is of doubtful validity, because it is difficult to make a distinction from 'words of prophetic Jesus-consciousness of the early church'.[50]

We may accept Teeple's verdict on criteria 1, 2 and 4 with some confidence. Criterion 3, however, cannot easily be disposed of. A final decision depends on the interpretation of certain texts which require detailed re-examination.

Teeple lays down as valid criteria the following.

(1) A saying is not authentic if it reflects the early church's situation, and not that of Jesus. He recognizes, however, the need for caution in the application of this standard.

(2) A saying is probably unauthentic if it reflects Hellenistic attitudes, customs, and situations, rather than those of Palestinian Judaism - although Hellenistic thought did, Teeple says, affect Palestinian Judaism, where it appears the context is less likely to be Jesus' real teaching than the kerygma as known in the Hellenistic Jewish and Gentile worlds.

(3) A saying is not likely to be authentic if it identifies the Son of man with a human Messiah, for in the Jewish background the Son of man was not equated with, for example, the Son of David. This was only possible at a later stage, when the two streams of tradition were combined in post-Palestinian Christianity.

(4) Sayings in which Jesus appears to identify himself with the Son of man cannot be genuine, because in Jewish apocalyptic the Son of man was

considered to be pre-existent, a notion which is present in the Fourth Gospel, but absent from the synoptics.

(5) 'If a saying makes salvation depend upon loyalty to Jesus' person, it can hardly be a genuine logion of Jesus', for his basic message was, rather, repentance in response to his proclamation of the kingdom of God (Mark 1.15).[51]

Of these, the last is to be received with considerable reserve, and possibly even discarded, in view of the evidence that in fact Jesus did associate faithful discipleship and loyalty to himself with the proper response to his mission and message.

No more than the briefest summary of Teeple's application of his valid criteria can be given here. In any case, he makes no attempt to examine the Son of man texts one by one (for which he refers the reader to Vielhauer), and is content to apply the valid criteria to the three groups of sayings.

The future sayings are 'eliminated from authenticity by criterion no. 4',[52] or by criterion 1 (Luke 12.40; 17.24; 17.26-30),[53] these latter referring to the (delayed) parousia. The passion and resurrection sayings are excluded by the same two criteria. Teeple says Jesus could not have uttered them without believing that he, as Son of man, would die, whereas the Son of man is a pre-existent and eternal being. They were created by the church for the express purpose of explaining how Jesus is still the Son of man despite his death. In the present sayings, the term Son of man is shown to be a *title* referring to Jesus, as in the other two categories, and so criterion 4 is again invoked to disprove authenticity. There is, then, not a single Son of man saying in the synoptics (any more than in the Fourth Gospel), which goes back to Jesus.

Teeple maintains that the very frequency of the term Son of man ascribed to Jesus (81 times), which is often invoked as evidence of its dominical use, is actually an argument against it; such frequency is 'unnatural'.[54] It points not to Jesus' use of the term, but to its being a literary device to foster acceptance of the Son of man christology among Christians who were doubtful about it. He points out that this title occurs much more frequently in the gospels than Christ, Son of David, and Servant, and compares the Johannine emphasis on the Son and the Son of God as titles of Jesus. Frequency is no guarantee of authenticity.

What Teeple offers is a broad sweep of general and important considerations, to which due attention must be given; but this is hardly an adequate substitute for detailed examination of all the relevant texts. There remain Teeple's suggestions as to the origin of the Son of man christology, if it does not stem from Jesus. He says it is not Judean. It belongs neither to official Pharisaic doctrine nor, because of the absence from the Qumran literature of the Similitudes of Enoch with their Son of man passages, to Essenism. Nor is it Galilean, as Lohmeyer maintained.[55] Acts shows that the author did not associate this christology with the original Jerusalem church, since in the speeches of Peter and others Jesus is not the Son of man, but the Son of David; he associated it, in Stephen's speech (Acts 7.56), with Hellenistic Jewish Christianity. The christology arose, Teeple concludes, among Hellenistic Jewish Christians, probably in Syria.

As we have seen in chapter I, Perrin rejects the widespread assumption of an apocalyptic Son of man concept in ancient Judaism, in favour of Son of man imagery based upon Dan. 7.13. On this basis he examines some of the New Testament material,[56] and attempts to show that, as in the Similitudes Enoch becomes Son of man through interpretation of his translation to heaven in terms of Ezek. 1 and Dan. 7, so quite independently in Christian tradition Jesus becomes Son of man through interpretation of his resurrection in terms of Ps. 110.1 and Dan. 7.13. He maintains that, since no concept of an eschatological Son of man existed anywhere in Judaism, Jesus could not have spoken of the coming Son of man, meaning either himself or another figure. All the apocalyptic sayings are products of the early church. His discussion excludes the other two types of sayings, relating to the earthly life and to the sufferings of the Son of man.[57] The 'core' passages are classified in three groups: those clearly reflecting Dan. 7.13: Mark 13.26; 14.62; judgment sayings: Luke 12.8f. par.; Mark 8.38; comparison sayings: Luke 17.24 par.; 17.26f. par.; 11.30.

What follows is a summary of Perrin's main argument about the place of Dan. 7.13 in the origination of the Son of man christology. He finds three exegetical traditions using this passage. The first is combined with Ps. 110.1, in order to interpret the resurrection-ascension-exaltation of Jesus. The second, in connection with early passion apologetic, uses Dan. 7.13 in association with Zech. 12.10ff., which is interpreted as referring to the crucifixion (cf. John 19.37). Of special importance is Rev. 1.7 which, in introducing the idea that the Son of man who has ascended to God will return, to the consternation of the crucifiers, represents the earliest parousia use of Dan. 7.13. The third exegetical tradition is the fully developed parousia one as seen in Mark 13.26. Here the tendency is to move away from the original tradition in the direction of a purely apocalyptic expectation of the 'second coming' of Jesus as Son of man.

In an earlier article Perrin[58] follows suggestions, with special reference to Fr Barnabas Lindars,[59] that there was an early Christian type of Old Testament interpretation which, because of similarities to that of the

Qumran community, can be termed a *pesher* tradition. If we adopt the explanations offered either by Lindars or by Perrin, the familiar difficulty of the order of events in Mark 14.62 – the Son of man first sits at the right hand of Power and subsequently comes with the clouds – simply disappears.

Lindars[60] regards the second part of the text ('and coming with the clouds of heaven') as a pre-Markan addition, from Dan. 7.13, to the original form of the saying. This (Mark 14.62a) expresses the idea of Jesus' exaltation as the Son of man by conflating Ps. 110.1 and Dan. 7.13, understood as equivalent in meaning. The addition, made under the increasing influence of the parousia belief, introduced a fresh meaning quite foreign to the original saying. The *pesher* has been 'historicized' and transformed into an utterance of Jesus himself. Perrin, despite all this, admits that Jesus could sometimes have used the imagery of Dan. 7.13 'to express the concept of a future vindication of his ministry and of men's proper response to it'.[61] He sees this as a possibility as regards Luke 12.8, 'Everyone who acknowledges me before men, the Son of man will acknowledge before the angels of God', where 'the reference is only a general one' to the vindication imagery of Dan. 7.13.[62] He suggests that the oldest form of the second part of this logion was 'will be acknowledged before the angels of God', the passive being the Aramaic circumlocution for the action of God, as in verse 9, and that this form, with no mention of the Son of man, could go back to Jesus.[63] This suggestion that the Son of man is not an original element in the saying is an unproven hypothesis. Besides, to admit that Jesus could have used the imagery of Dan. 7.13 opens the door to the recognition of the possibility that his use of this imagery could also have included the actual expression Son of man in Luke 12.9.

The idea of a Christian *pesher*-type of interpretation of Old Testament passages is certainly correct, and Mark 14.62 is an outstanding example. But granted the influence of exegetical tradition based on Dan. 7.13, it does not follow that this is the actual *origin* of the Son of man christology. Its role may rather have been the secondary one of explicating the term Son of man as used only by Jesus.[64] If the Son of man sayings are all creations of early Christian exegesis, why are they invariably placed on the lips of Jesus? Perrin's theory does not answer this question.[65]

Some attention has been given earlier to some of Leivestad's views.[66] At the expense of some repetition, a more extended discussion seems appropriate here, for Leivestad, like Perrin, but on very different grounds, rejects the widespread belief in the existence of an apocalyptic Son of man concept in ancient Judaism. It is interesting to note that Colpe, who likewise finds the extant Jewish sources (Dan. 7, the Similitudes of Enoch, and 2 Esdras 13) devoid of any evidence of such a concept and title, nevertheless maintains that it did exist - in a fourth Jewish source of which traces are discernible in the earliest strata of the gospel traditions themselves. Leivestad, on the other hand, endeavours to show that the synoptic Son of man sayings themselves disprove the existence of a concept which, in his opinion, rests solely upon a hypothetical exegetical inference, and that a titular meaning of the expression Son of man does not fit them. 'Son of man' is Jesus' self-designation, not, however, as a title, but as a name, 'the Man'.[67] In distinction from Christos, a title becoming a proper name in Paul, Son of man, from being a name used by Jesus in reference to himself, acquired a certain christological meaning and titular content in later formulations as a consequence of the identification of Jesus with the Messiah. Even here, however, according to Leivestad, the emphasis is still on the name Jesus rather than on the title.

Leivestad adduces two facts in support of his argument that Son of man in the synoptic gospels is not a title.[68] The expression does not occur in confessional formulae; it does not appear either as an attribute or as a predicate - there are no forms like 'Jesus the Son of man'[69] or 'I, the Son of man', nor is it ever said that 'Jesus is the Son of man', like 'Thou art the Son of man' in 1 En. 71.14; much less does Jesus ever declare, 'I am the Son of man.'[70] But the absence of these usages is surely due rather to the early church's recognition that Jesus alone used the expression 'Son of man', but not in these ways, and to the preservation of this fact in the developing tradition.[71] His employment of it is too subtle and enigmatic to be satisfactorily explained as simply a self-imposed name. Further, since there is no certainly authentic instance of Jesus using any other name or title for himself either as attribute or as predicate, there is nothing surprising in the absence of the Son of man being used in those ways.

Leivestad issues a warning against too confident reliance on redactional analysis, as if, for instance, it could always be assumed that differences between Matthew and Luke on the one hand, and Mark on the other, when they appear to be following Mark, are due to alterations of Mark. Many such differences, it is urged, are just as likely to reflect the influence on the later evangelists of living oral tradition and church use. A form in the oldest source does not necessarily come from the oldest strand of tradition. As an example Leivestad cites Matt. 16.13, 'Who do men say that the Son of man is?' The parallel in Mark 8.27 has, 'Who do men say that I am?' (cf. Luke 9.18). The common view is that Matthew has modified Mark. But Leivestad advises us to allow for the alternative explanation, that Matthew follows a variant tradition, which has as much claim as the

Markan form to be the original. Of course, Leivestad does not claim that this decides which form is to be followed; but neither, he claims, can the matter be settled by traditio-historical methods. While the priority of Mark means a tradition represented there must be relatively old, the possibility is not excluded that a tradition in Matthew or Luke may be just as old or even older.[72] Son of man in Matthew, as in the other synoptics, he claims, is always an entirely unmessianic self-designation of Jesus. But it is difficult to follow Leivestad in seeing Matt. 16.13 as an example of this, and in equating the Son of man there with the personal pronoun in Mark 8.27.

The sayings about the Son of man's earthly work and his passion (and resurrection) present hardly any difficulties to Leivestad, despite their apparent incompatibility with the presumed apocalyptic Son of man. More problematical are the sayings about the Son of man in heavenly power and judgment. Both the *Gemeindebildungen* (e.g. Matt. 13.41; Luke 21.36) and probably authentic sayings appear to distinguish between Jesus and the Son of man as another figure, so that this feature becomes a doubtful criterion of authenticity. Leivestad[73] refers to Tödt's opinion that the church's preservation of the distinction between the 'I' of Jesus and the coming Son of man 'is intelligible only on the assumption that it was handed down in stereotyped Son of Man sayings of Jesus whose authority protected it from being modified'.[74] Leivestad's objection, that this would be surprising when Jesus' words have undergone so many other alterations, does not take account of the uniqueness of this special case involving what was known to the early church to have been a remarkable feature of Jesus' speech. Furthermore, he reasons that the complementary tenet of the traditio-historical method, that the presence of the term Son of man also in the other two classes of logia is entirely the work of the community, is quite inconsistent with the former one. We should have to posit two types of sayings: those in which Jesus speaks of the Son of man as distinct from himself, and others in which he says 'the Son of man' instead of 'I'. This would have created the impression which the church, identifying the Son of man with Jesus, would have been concerned to avoid, namely, that Jesus himself used the expression in two different senses. But what evidence is there that this impression ever actually arose in the early church?

Even in Matthew, where the Son of man's role as eschatological judge is more prominent, Leivestad regards it as unnecessary to look to Jewish apocalyptic speculations as the background. Although he concedes the possibility of understanding Son of man as a messianic title in a number of Matthaean sayings (13.41; 16.27; 24.30f.; 25.31; also 10.23; 19.28; 24.27, 37, 39, 44), he insists that it is unnecessary; it is sufficient that Jesus is meant. We are directed to the significance of the absence of warnings against false 'Sons of men' (*Menschensöhne*)!

Leivestad concludes that the witness of the synoptics reinforces his contention that Judaism was ignorant of any apocalyptic Son of man title and concept. In many cases, he claims, Son of man can *only* be understood as Jesus' self-designation, and no saying is intelligible *only* on the hypothesis of a pre-Christian titular use. The only real redeemer figure for Jews at the time of Jesus was the Messiah, and so the earliest church knew only one christological *Hoheitstitel*, Christus, and its synonyms Lord and Son of God. It is only secondarily and occasionally that Son of man has a certain titular meaning in it.[75]

Finally, we come to the most interesting questions of all. How and why did Jesus speak of the Son of man?

Leivestad speaks of 'the general impression that Jesus, in his statements about his person, his call, his way and his goal, preferred to use a circumlocution instead of the personal pronoun'.[76] He refers to the remarkable fact that there is not a single example of 'the Son of man says'; it is always 'I say'.[77] Surely this is of momentous significance. If, as Leivestad and other critics like E. Schweizer maintain, authentic Son of man utterances are to be sought first among sayings about Jesus' earthly work, it is surprising that none of his authoritative words are introduced by 'the Son of man says'. If 'the Son of man' was a name chosen by Jesus as his customary self-designation, why its total absence from this vitally important area? But if Tödt and others are correct, all becomes clear. Jesus did not use the expression in referring to his earthly ministry,[78] and therefore did not use it to preface his pronouncements.

Why Jesus chose to call himself the Son of man (or the Man) Leivestad finds inexplicable. Having consistently refuted any borrowing from apocalyptic mythology, and reiterating his conviction of the non-existence of any apocalyptic Son of man figure in Judaism,[79] he turns to conjecture. First he asks whether the frequent address to the prophet Ezekiel as *ben adam* was the inspirational source of Jesus' usage, but does no more than leave this open as a bare possibility.[80] In my view the hypothesis has nothing in its favour at all.[81] His own tentative suggestion is that the significance of the term Son of man resides in the expression itself. Jesus saw himself as the special representative of mankind. His messianic self-consciousness was not as the political 'Messiah *ben David*', but as the 'Messiah *ben adam*', and his mission was directed not to the salvation of Israel alone, but of all men. The days of the Son of man are thus comparable with the days of Noah (Luke 17.26). The name of Son of man was intelligible only to those who forsook all to follow him.[82]

Having discussed in the preceding chapter Borsch's theory of the background to the Son of man concept, we now turn more particularly to his interpretation of the synoptic material. In contrast to Perrin[83] and Leivestad, both of whom deny the existence of an apocalyptic Son of man concept in Judaism, Borsch employs this very concept (although, as we have seen, against a wider background than apocalyptic) as the foundation of his interpretation of the synoptic sayings. He has much of value to say about other solutions of the problem, and it would be tempting to invoke his support on a number of issues. His investigation includes comments on a number of the sayings, preceded by preliminary observations and followed by more extended 'related observations' on some relevant topics.[84] The following quotation states the general approach.

> The great majority of the synoptic Son of Man logia have a reasonable claim on authenticity. They indicate that Jesus may very well have spoken of the Son of Man as one who could have a function on earth, as destined for suffering and as a figure who would appear in heavenly glory.[85]

Borsch maintains that the term Son of man was not inserted by the evangelists into contexts which originally did not have it. The tendency was to remove it, so that in cases of double attestation of the same or an equivalent saying, it is the version with Son of man which is more original.[86]

Behind the apparent ambiguity of Jesus' relationship with the Son of man Borsch believes there is discernible an earlier stage of tradition, 'when Jesus was not *simply* identified with the Son of Man'.[87] 'Nowhere is Jesus reported to have made the unambiguous claim that he was in and of himself the one and only Son of Man.'[88] The clue to this mysterious statement is to be found in the discussion of 'As it is written'.[89] Here Borsch confesses difficulty in believing that the strain of '*mustness*' (δεῖ) and 'as it is written' is a wholly Christian creation. He suggests that the idea of scriptural necessity in the Son of man passion predictions is traceable to a pre-Christian element of tradition before its association with Jesus as the Son of man, and maintains that this is a better explanation than the usual one, namely, that the idea is part and parcel of the early church's understanding of scripture as fulfilled for the first time, once and for all, and uniquely, in Jesus. Earlier he has asked on what grounds the church introduced these ideas into the sayings. Did it know why Jesus must suffer as the Son of man or where it is written that he must do so? 'If so, why is there no explanation of these features? If not, are not these elements better understood as having been caused by factors in the primitive traditions?'[90] For an answer to these questions Borsch is appealing to the myth of the man-king suffering before enthronement, and not to the reflection of Christian thought about the passion of Jesus and its meaning in the light of historical event and religious experience. Further, he writes, 'It is frankly our opinion that these references [to '*mustness*' and 'as it is written'] are to be taken quite literally and that Jesus was being guided here by a work or works which spoke of the Son of Man's destiny in these terms.'[91] Jesus, in alluding to himself as the Son of man who labours among men, suffers death at their hands, and is rewarded with heavenly glory, believed that he was actualizing historically in his person and work the widespread myth of the man-king who must suffer in order to reign. In this, according to Borsch, he was influenced especially by sectarian Judaism which had preserved, although in a fragmentary form, the features of the ancient myth. Narrowing it down still further, *baptizing* sectarianism is suggested as the source of Jesus' teaching on the Son of man's suffering. 'Here is the contemporary basis for the realization that the Man must suffer before salvation and glory can come, the realization which Jesus put to service in historical circumstances.'[92] Myth becomes history. Borsch thinks, then, that the authenticity of the vast majority of the synoptic Son of man sayings of all three traditional groups is guaranteed by the coexistence of the same three spheres of thought as in the pre-Christian myth. Their reappearance in the synoptic logia, and the mutual relationship of the three groups of logia for which Borsch argues, stem from Jesus himself.

This thesis is unconvincing. It is very questionable whether a coherent mythological pattern, such as Borsch believes he can elicit from the bewildering mass of material spanning centuries, and in the form in which he reconstructs it, ever existed. It is, of course, true that the synoptic Son of man sayings bear a certain relationship to one another. But this relationship does not have to be attributed to Jesus, nor to be traced back to a hypothetical mythological pattern in order to be explained. Taken together, the sayings express the church's belief in Jesus as the Son of man who laboured upon earth, who was rejected and killed by men, but was raised from the dead by God, and who will play a decisive role at the last judgment in God's presence. Above all, we do not get from the gospels the impression that Jesus was consciously acting out, in his life and ministry, and in his expressed expectations of the future, the pattern of any myth whatsoever. Any notion of this nature is both unsupported by the gospel records, and contrary to our knowledge of Jesus' teaching as a whole. This is not to deny that he may have envisaged his ministry and its outcome as the fulfilment of the hopes of Israel. But that is not the same thing.

Morna D. Hooker, in *The Son of Man in Mark*, is another scholar who turns from form-critical and traditio-historical analysis in search of another approach. Unlike Borsch, she does not range over the whole religious-historical field in the quest for a coherent pattern, with the resultant possibility of the acceptance as authentic of a majority of the Son of man sayings, but finds it primarily in Dan. 7, where the theme, she claims, is the rejection of the righteous remnant in Israel, their sufferings, and final vindication. She discovers the same theme in Mark, where the pattern forms a logical and coherent whole. She suggests that it may be pre-Markan, and probably corresponds to Jesus' own understanding of the term Son of man as his self-designation. But she is unable to point to anything more than traces of the pattern in the other gospels. This does not inspire confidence in the correctness of her thesis.[93]

More recently R. Maddox,[94] accepting the existence of the Son of man-judge concept in apocalyptic Judaism, is prepared to receive as utterances of Jesus some sayings in all three of the familiar categories. He, too, is sceptical of the ability of form-criticism to distinguish authentic from unauthentic sayings. Instead, he concentrates on the evangelists' own representation of Jesus' words, and looks at the gospel material as a whole, in order to discern whether there emerges a significant pattern in the use of the Son of man title. Putting on one side the tripartite classification of sayings, he finds the theme of judgment not only in the future sayings, but also in those concerning Jesus' earthly activity (comparing Mark 14.62 and 2.10), and in the passion and resurrection sayings, all of which are associated with judgment directly or indirectly, in the latter case through the mention of resurrection which implies exaltation and judgment. All the synoptic Son of man sayings, then, portray Jesus as endowed with judicial authority. (The sole exception is Matt. 8.20.)[95] Maddox little doubts that this representation is essentially Jesus' own teaching. This reconstruction is scarcely convincing. The theme of judgment is over-emphasized, and to achieve his results the author has to indulge in some exegesis which is, to use his own term,[96] distinctly *recherché*.

The exponents of form-critical and traditio-historical methods are not alone in differing among themselves; they arrive at different conclusions. The three contributions discussed above admittedly reach the same destination, and all accept a majority of Son of man sayings as genuine words of Jesus, but along different branches of the 'pattern' route. They cannot all be correct. The granting of authenticity to a substantial majority of the sayings, one feels, is too neatly anticipated by the reconstructions of the several underlying patterns to win conviction.

As we have seen in the last chapter, Colpe makes the novel suggestion that the oldest strata of the synoptic tradition should be regarded as themselves a fourth source for the Jewish apocalyptic Son of man, additional to Dan. 7, 1 En. 37–71, and 2 Esdras 13, which do not adequately reveal the antecedents of the New Testament concept. He finds evidence of this source in eight texts.[97] Since to a greater or lesser degree they are at the same time, in form and/or content, authentic words of Jesus, they represent him as an eschatological prophet proclaiming the coming Son of man.

Colpe discusses the crucial question whether Jesus was conscious of being the apocalyptic Son of man of whom he spoke. His answer is that if identity is meant, we cannot use a plain yes or no.[98] Rather, Jesus' imprecise allusions to his own perfecting (*Vollendung*) and his role in the *eschaton*, his preaching of the kingdom of God, and his announcing of the coming Son of man, are parallels. His eschatological role commences with his preaching of the kingdom. The kingdom of God and the Son of man are related ideas with a common origin, as is clear from Dan. 7, and did not later diverge so far as to render incredible their coexistence in a new eschatological preaching, if not in the same sayings.[99] It is therefore unnecessary to assume either that the Son of man did not feature in Jesus' teaching at all,[100] or that it was more central to his message than the kingdom of God.[101] With this we can agree. Just as, Colpe continues, there is no opposition in Jesus' message between the kingdom of God and the Son of man, so there is none between himself and the Son of man. He suggests a *functional* equation on the part of Jesus with the coming Son of man of apocalyptic expectation,[102] and from this the early community developed a static personal identification already realized in Jesus' activity on earth. The starting point of the development was the future apocalyptic sayings - those eight sayings, at least, which Colpe distinguishes as more or less authentic - which were easily applicable, without alteration, to the idea of the return of the risen Christ. The way then lay open to further developments in the oral and literary traditions, in which Jesus came to be represented as speaking of himself as the Son of man in his present ministry, and in his predictions of his death and resurrection.

Part of Colpe's hypothesis is that the crucial eight sayings underwent a three-stage usage. First, as belonging to a fourth Jewish tradition, they express certain aspects of the apocalyptic Son of man idea prior to and contemporary with Jesus. Then they were taken over and utilized by Jesus in his own proclamation of the coming Son of man. Finally, they were adopted by the early community as they stand, to refer to the risen Jesus whose parousia as judge was expected.

This three-stage sequence of usage is improbable, and that in Colpe's eight sayings a Jewish apocalyptic tradition is discoverable is a not very convincing hypothesis. Of these sayings only Luke 17.24, 26, 30 have a strong claim to authenticity and, along with some others not included with them by Colpe, they may be regarded as indirect evidence of a current Son of man belief which Jesus adapted and reinterpreted in his own proclamation, rather than as themselves elements of an already existing Son of man tradition taken over first by Jesus and subsequently by the post-resurrection church. It is highly unlikely that an objective, individual Son of man formed part of Jesus' own mental furniture, and that he thought of even a purely functional equation with the Son of man as an existent figure distinct from himself. Colpe's treatment here, although expressed in somewhat imprecise language, is correctly orientated.[103] But needless difficulties are avoided if it is supposed that Jesus employed the Son of man terminology symbolically as an accommodation of language. On this view it was in a metaphorical and functional sense that Jesus expected to 'be' the Son of man in the *eschaton*.

J. Jeremias[104] claims to have made the first systematic attempt to examine, by traditio-historical analysis, the significance of the fact that most of the fifty-one Son of man sayings[105] in the four gospels have a close counterpart or 'rival' version without Son of man. He maintains that in these cases of double attestation the Son of man alternative is secondary, and has been introduced through misunderstanding (e.g. Luke 12.10, cf. Mark 3.28), as an addition in the reframing of older logia (e.g. Matt. 16.28, cf. Mark 9.1), in imitations of older logia (e.g. Matt. 26.2, cf. Matt. 17.22), and in new formulations (e.g. Matt. 13.37). There is no instance of the replacement of Son of man by 'I' or another expression. In the doubly attested sayings, then, it is those *without* Son of man which have the stronger claim to priority.

Still more important are the few synoptic sayings, ten in number,[106] which have been handed down in the Son of man version only, and have no competitors or rivals without Son of man. They are: Mark 13.26 parr.; 14.62 parr.; Matt. 24.27, 37b (=39b), par. Luke 17.24, 26; Matt. 10.23; 25.31; Luke 17.22, 30; 18.8; 21.36.[107] According to Jeremias, these are greatly superior to the first category, because they do not arouse the suspicion engendered by the existence of a non-Son of man rival, that Son of man in them may be secondary. While not suggesting that any of them are necessarily authentic as they stand, he claims that they must be the starting point for further investigation, rather than the established method of proceeding from the customary three-fold classification of the sayings, which in reality represents the *end* of the process in the redaction of the gospels. Jeremias points out that they are all *future* sayings. This is perhaps a significant pointer to the superior importance claimed for the future sayings on various grounds by a number of scholars; and it may therefore involve a weakening of arguments in favour of the presence of authentic sayings also in one or in both of the other traditional categories, especially as used in the various forms of pattern hypothesis framed in the interests of a more conservative approach.

Excursus: The hypothesis of Barnabas Lindars

Fr Lindars' article, 'Re-enter the Apocalyptic Son of Man',[108] appeared some time after the manuscript of the present study had been completed; fortunately, it has been found possible to include the discussion of it that follows.

Lindars accepts the findings of Vermes, that 'Son of man' was not a title current in Judaism at all, that the Aramaic *bar nasha*, presumed to underlie the Greek for Son of man in the synoptic gospels, represents an idiomatic usage as a substitute for the first-person pronoun, and that this was a characteristic of Jesus' speech. As we have seen, Vermes, while claiming that a fair proportion of the sayings may be authentic, denies that any sayings containing direct or indirect reference to Dan. 7.13 are traceable to Jesus. His understanding of 'indirect reference' is such that this means *all* future Son of man sayings.[109] Lindars soft-pedals what amounts to a quite critical dissent from Vermes in this regard. So far from seeing in them, as Vermes does, the result of a process of eschatologizing of Jesus' 'neutral speech-form' *son of man* 'by means of a midrash based on Daniel 7:13',[110] Lindars relies on them as the linch-pin of his hypothesis. This I now endeavour to summarize.

(1) Jewish apocalyptic thought embraced belief in an agent of God in the coming judgment. Two examples are cited of identification of this heavenly agent with a formerly 'historical' figure. One of these is Melchizedek (Gen. 14) in the fragmentary Qumran Melchizedek scroll (11QMelch). The other and more familiar example is from the Similitudes of Enoch (1 En. 37–71), where, in 71.14, Enoch, having been translated to heaven, is addressed by God in the words, 'Thou art the Son of man who art born to righteousness.'

Lindars believes that, despite all that has been said about them as an unreliable source, 'it may still be permissible to use the Similitudes of Enoch as evidence for the identification of an historical person with the agent of God's final intervention, conceived in Messianic terms, around the beginning of the Christian Era'.[111] But this agent is not presented as 'a single, universally accepted personality entitled the Son of man'. No such title exists, nor was there 'a single, defined concept' which the early church could have taken over ready-made.

(2) The apocalyptic idea of the agent of the divine intervention is regarded as the foundation of New Testament christology. Jesus was

believed to have filled that role as the judge and the bringer of the kingdom. This belief pervades the New Testament writings in varying degrees, but it is only in the gospels that Jesus is called the Son of man. This limitation, it seems to me, renders it misleading to describe the Son of man christology as 'basic to the New Testament'.[112] Would it not be more appropriate to call it 'the divine agent christology'?

(3) The quasi-titular use of the Son of man in the sayings tradition, since it cannot be derived from other sources, must have originated with Jesus himself. It is a reference to himself, not to another figure. The evangelists use it correctly. Jesus used the term as an oblique way of indicating his destiny as God's agent, and some at least of the 'glorification' sayings are probably authentic.

Much is made of Mark 14.62 as a possibly genuine utterance of Jesus, with or without 62b, 'and coming with the clouds of heaven'. Lindars paraphrases verse 62a after 'I am' as: 'You will see *me, being the man whom* [sic] *I really am,* sitting, etc.'[113] The change from the first person, 'I am', 'implies a certain reticence, attempting to tone down the staggering claim' to be the celestial Messiah. Lindars does also refer to Luke 12.8f., a more significant text and more likely to be authentic than Mark 14.62.

The same principle is applied to the passion sayings. Some of these, it is urged, must be authentic, in order to explain the existence of the rest, and the Son of man as a self-designation must belong to the original nucleus. This nucleus should be viewed in conjunction with the nucleus of 'glorification' sayings. 'The man destined to perform the judgement is the man who first must die.'[114] In the passion predictions the use of the Son of man is more than a matter of delicacy, avoiding 'I': the phrase denotes Jesus 'as a man with a certain destiny'.

Some further sayings are discussed. Here mention need only be made of Matt. 8.20, par. Luke 9.58 and Matt. 11.19, par. Luke 7.34. In sayings such as these, Jesus speaks of himself as Son of man when 'his personal position and destiny' are concerned. He means simply 'the man who I am', and although he uses this manner of speaking out of delicacy, 'it is not inconsistent with a higher claim which he is not disposed to divulge'.[115] This becomes clear in the glorification sayings: 'he is the man who is to be God's agent in the coming judgement'. This must have been in Jesus' mind all along; but, as others have suggested, Jesus leaves open the true nature of his vocation until he is finally challenged to state it openly (Mark 14.62).

Finally, Jesus' use of Son of man as a self-designation is 'characteristic of his style' and one of his 'personality traits', and it is suggested that it is comparable to his reticence in regard to messiahship. The most revealing statement that Lindars makes occurs in the final paragraph of his article. He claims that Jesus employed Son of man as a self-designation 'in contexts where it was necessary to allude to his personal position and destiny, and the apocalyptic application turns out to be the means whereby *all the relevant sayings can be brought under one heading'* (my italics).

Lindars' hypothesis may be likened to a single-span bridge of modern construction. At one end it rests upon acceptance of Vermes' understanding of *bar nasha* on the lips of Jesus as an idiomatic Galilean Aramaic usage adopted on occasions when for reasons of 'awe, reserve, or humility'[116] it was more appropriate than the first person, for which it served as a circumlocution or periphrasis. At the other end it rests upon the suggestion that, since (as is maintained by Vermes and others) apocalyptic Judaism knew of no concept of a particular figure called the Son of man, the titular use of the expression as a self-designation in the gospels must have originated with Jesus. Are these twin foundations equal to the task of supporting the hypothesis? Or is the result bound to be a failure of the outreaching arms of the span to meet one another? Lindars' hypothesis may be expressed thus:

(1) *bar nasha*/son of man = 'I'
(2) *bar nasha*/Son of man = 'I'

That is, in Jesus' thought and teaching the two uses of *bar nasha* become virtually identical: its idiomatic usage (1) suggested to him its adoption as a self-designation, and this new and original usage (2) determined the special shades of meaning he gave to the idiomatic expression, and is the unifying factor that brings together the three classes of sayings.

(1) The question whether or not *bar nasha* is equivalent to 'I' as a periphrasis for the first person is even now not finally settled. If it is not a periphrasis, the plausibility of the argument Lindars builds upon it is to some extent weakened. It is to be conceded, however, that a characteristic use by Jesus of 'son of man' (this appears to be established) even as an indirect self-reference, without being an actual surrogate for the first person, could, but less probably, have led to a titular use by him.

(2) Lindars goes far beyond Vermes in the content he assigns to *bar nasha* in the present and passion sayings. As has been noted above, he employs expressions like 'a man with a certain destiny', Jesus' 'personal position and destiny', with 'a higher claim' not yet to be divulged, in connection with such sayings. Note especially: 'There is a delicate irony in his comment that he, being the man that he is – and with such a destiny! – should have nowhere to lay his head'.[117] This content is introduced into these sayings from the glorification sayings, so that *bar nasha*/son of man,

from being an idiomatic method of self-reference, is upgraded to a quasi-titular self-designation, Son of man. The implication is that Jesus' use of the term was *always* coloured, to a lesser or greater degree, by messianic overtones. This impression is borne out by Lindars' claim that Jesus probably had in mind his vocation and destiny as God's agent in the judgment 'all along'.[118] This is a very bold assumption; but it is bound up with the hypothesis of the mutual relationship of the three classes of Son of man sayings.

But firstly, too few possibly authentic sayings with a present or passion reference with Son of man have survived in the tradition to allow firm conclusions of this kind about them. Secondly, it is questionable whether one can legitimately work back in this way from the apparently titular use of Son of man in the future sayings, so as to impose upon the expression in the other types of sayings what amounts to a new meaning.

(3) The problem may also be approached from the other end, from the suggestion that it was Jesus himself who initiated the use of Son of man as a quasi-titular designation, in place of the first person, in order to indicate his destined function as God's agent in the judgment, because it would tone down any suggestion of arrogance in referring to his future activity.

This is a highly speculative alternative to the admittedly unproven hypothesis of the existence of Son of man as a title independently of Jesus, and utilized by him in a unique way. It implies a leap in Jesus' thought from his human life and experience on earth to a supra-mundane, celestial sphere of activity. It may, perhaps, be asked whether (on Lindars' hypothesis) Jesus would have alluded to the judgmental functions in the heavenly court to which he believed himself to be destined, *in this particular way*; that is, whether he would have employed his alleged Son of man self-designation in alluding to his glorification, in a manner parallel and closely analogous to his use of it in sayings referring to his earthly activity and to his passion and death. One may wonder also whether Jesus' hearers would have understood any of his allusions to his glorification as Son of man, if *bar nasha*, as his quasi-titular self-designation as God's agent in the judgment, had no precedent in Jewish thought, and if his use of it in non-glorification contexts was their only clue to its new and deeper meaning.

(4) Lindars cites Enoch and Melchizedek as 'historical' persons who, in apocalyptic speculation, were exalted to the role of divine agent in the future judgment, and views them as precursors of Jesus with his self-consciousness of being the one finally destined for that role – as Son of man. If (as is not clear) it is implied that Jesus might have regarded himself as a greater than either Enoch or Melchizedek, the gospels, of course,

contain no shred of evidence for it. In any case, however, the hypothesis as a whole is not helped by the complete absence of any mention of either of these figures in Jesus' recorded teaching.

I have attempted to demonstrate that Lindars' method of bringing all the Son of man sayings 'under one heading', although attractive, is beset by difficulties that render it no more successful than others. In effect, his hypothesis amounts to a sophisticated and persuasively argued version of the 'traditional' view – that all three classes of Son of man sayings stem ultimately from Jesus, and that the Son of man designation belongs to the original nucleus of authentic sayings within each group – in the light of contemporary study, research, and discovery.

The possibility, even the probability, remains, that the problem of how to reconcile the disparate nature of the future or glorification sayings with the rest, so as to form a consistent and harmonious pattern, requires no solution, because the problem is more apparent than real. The Aramaic expression *bar nasha*, 'a man', 'the man', under the influence of Dan. 7.13, 'one like a son of man', had come to mean also Son of man in Jewish apocalyptic in a messianic sense. Is it conceivable that Jesus could have used *bar nasha* in an 'apocalyptic' sense in the complete absence of any antecedent? Just such an antecedent may be assumed to lie behind his employment of it in the glorification sayings. It is not the apocalyptic usage that is original to him; what *is* original is his functional reinterpretation of Son of man to express what he meant by his destiny as the divine agent in judgment and salvation.

Vermes' conviction that all the future sayings come from the early community rather than from Jesus, and that authentic ones are only to be found among those neither directly nor indirectly connected with Dan. 7.13, has the advantage of simplicity. But he includes under the heading of 'indirect reference' to Daniel passages where the connection is so tenuous as to be virtually non-existent. To leave out of account the future Son of man sayings is to omit a vital element in the climax of Jesus' message of the coming kingdom of God, and of his call to repentance (Mark 1.15). Lindars recognizes the supreme importance of the future sayings in the teaching of Jesus, and reinstates the apocalyptic Son of man[119] – but with a difference! Let it finally be repeated: the apocalyptic Son of man who, in Lindars' article, 're-enters', is not the same as the Son of man banished from the scene by Leivestad. He is not a recognized Jewish apocalyptic figure, but Jesus alone, self-named as Son of man, in expression of his consciousness of being *the* divine agent previously exemplified in the exalted Enoch and Melchizedek.[120]

PART TWO

III

THE SYNOPTIC TEXTS. I

In the left-hand column below are listed Son of man sayings regarded as basically authentic in *JSM*,[1] and in the right-hand column sayings without rival parallels or counterparts lacking 'Son of man' and called by Jeremias *konkurrenzlos.* The numbers preceding the references indicate the order in which the texts are discussed in this chapter. It is to be noted that they all refer to the future. Those common to both lists are italicized.

JSM	Sayings without rivals
Mark	Mark
8.38 (Luke 9.26; cf. par. Luke 12.8f.)	(6) 13.26 parr.
14.62 parr.	(5) *14.62* parr.
Q	Q
Luke 11.29f., par. Matt. 12.39f.	(1) Luke *17.24* par.
Luke 12.8f., par. Matt. 10.32f.	(1) Luke *17.26* par.
Luke *17.24*, par. Matt. 24.27	(1) Luke 17.30
Luke *17.26*, par. Matt. 24.37	
Luke	Luke
17.22	(1) *17.22*
	(2) 18.8b
	(3) 21.36
	Matthew
	(4) 10.23
	(7) 25.31

1. *Luke 17.22.* And he said to the disciples, 'The days are coming when you will desire to see one of the days of the Son of man, and you will not see it.'
***Luke 17.24.* 'For as the lightning flashes and lights up the sky from one side to the other, so will the Son of man be in his day.'**
***Luke 17.26.* 'As it was in the days of Noah, so will it be in the days of the Son of man.'**
***Luke 17.30.* '. . . so will it be on the day on which the Son of man is revealed.'**

In my earlier study of these interrelated sayings I reached the following conclusions.[2] Verse 30 is redactional, and serves as a link between the story of Lot fleeing for his life from Sodom on the day of its destruction, and the admonition to the inhabitants of Jerusalem to flee before imminent disaster. 'In that day' in verse 31 is 'the day on which the Son of man is revealed' in verse 30. The fact that the parallels in Matt. 24.27 and 37 have 'the parousia of the Son of man', while Luke 17.24 and 26 have respectively 'the Son of man in his day' and 'the days of the Son of man', prompts the question whether both Lukan expressions are identical in meaning. They were found not to be so. The day of the Son of man implied in Luke 17.24 is eschatological, whereas the plural in verse 26 refers to a period culminating in the coming of the Son of man. Formed on the analogy of 'the days of Noah', the plural form is the evangelist's alteration of an original singular in the common source; the same factor accounts for the plural in verse 22. The teaching of Luke is that the day of the Son of man will be the sudden climax of a period described as 'the days of the Son of man' inexorably leading up to it. Jesus himself did not speak of 'days' of the Son of man, but only of his 'day'. Luke 17.22, 24 and 26 were rated as all basically authentic sayings, of which the first and the third have been modified by the evangelist in accordance with his eschatological ideas.

While I have retained basically the same approach as before, further consideration has led me to some changes of emphasis. The following short review of some of the recent solutions of the difficulties of these texts may serve as introductory to my present interpretation.

Jüngel too regards Luke 17.24 and 26 as probably authentic, as well as verse 30.[3] He makes the interesting observation that the church itself would not have compared the appearing of the Son of man with the flashing of lightning because Jesus had spoken of Satan fallen like lightning (Luke 10.18)! Verse 22 he regards as an entirely Lukan introduction to the eschatological speech.[4] Pointing out that ἡμέρα, a favourite Lukan word,[5] occurs ten times in Luke 17. 22-31, he suggests 'in his day'[6] in verse 24, originally an isolated saying, is the evangelist's attempt, corresponding to parousia in Matthew, to fit the logion into the surrounding sayings under the theme of 'the day of the Son of man'. The words 'so will the Son of man be' may have been a formal expression used by Jesus himself.[7] Jüngel claims support for this suggestion in verse 26, where 'in the days of the Son of man' corresponds to parousia in Matthew and, modelled on 'in the days of Noah', means that the Son of man's coming is an event of considerable duration.[8] Against this is the improbability that the day and the days of the Son of man could have had the same meaning. Jüngel is prepared, like the present writer, to exclude 'the days of the Son of man' from Jesus' own speech, but is less convincing in wishing to exclude 'the day of the Son of man' also in this way.

Colpe agrees with Jüngel in denying that Luke 17.22 is from Jesus, but differs from him in viewing it as a *Gemeindebildung* already present in Luke's source. The expression 'the days of the Son of man' (cf. verse 26) represents a pre-Lukan or a Lukan modification of the saying.[9] Earlier, Colpe[10] says about 'in the days of the Son of man' in verse 26 that Luke himself, familiar with the idea of 'the days of Jesus' in the post-Easter period, may have introduced the thought of a temporal extension of the Son of man's activity on earth into both verses, replacing the day of the sudden coming. Other alternatives he mentions are that the expression is formed on the analogy of 'the days of the Messiah' or that, on the analogy of the days of Noah until he entered the ark,[11] it means the days which the Son of man brings to an end. On any view, Jesus did not himself speak of the days of the Son of man but only, as in verses 24 and 30, of the *day* of the Son of man.[12] Colpe adopts the view that the material in Luke 17.30 was not known to Matthew, and thinks this is more plausible than that verses 28–30 are a secondary imitation of verses 26f., in which case the mention of the Son of man would have come at the beginning and not at the end (verse 30), or than that Matthew omitted the second comparison as less graphic. Like Jüngel, Colpe maintains that verse 30 goes back in substance to Jesus.

It may be noted that Fuller[13] treats 'the days of the Son of man' in verses 22 and 26 as redactional, and as 'expressing the periodization of the history of salvation'. According to Hahn,[14] the redactional introduction Luke 17.22 has the plural 'days' because the discourse is understood as concerning Jesus the Son of man working on earth, whereas in verse 26 it denotes the time immediately preceding the parousia. Luke's purpose is to assert the different aspects of the title applied to Jesus in salvation history.

Leivestad has contributed a valuable discussion on the plural form in Luke 17.22 and 26.[15] In verse 22, he holds, the days of the Son of man must be something good, like the days of the Messiah, but in verse 26 an object of fear, days not of happiness but of judgment, and the expression is analogous in form to 'the days of Noah'. The days of Noah and of Lot are not the same as the day when Noah entered the ark and when Lot fled from Sodom. In both cases 'the days' precede 'the day'. Leivestad asks how these days preceding the day of the parousia can be aptly described as 'the days of the Son of man'; the corresponding expression 'the days of the Messiah' did not denote the messianic woes. He points out the direct comparison of the parousia of the Son of man with the days of Noah in Matt. 24.37, and thinks Luke 17.26, in which 'the days of the Son of man' correspond to the parousia in Matthew, requires the same interpretation. The Lukan language is inexact and the comparison imperfect. He asks whether we should assume a shift of meaning, and whether Jesus compared his own lifetime with the days before the flood. If so, the days of the Son of man were the days when Jesus summoned men to repentance before the final judgment. We have to assume in verse 26 an erroneous equation of the *days* of the Son of man with his *day*.

Leivestad seeks support from Luke 17.22 for what he admits may seem to be a hazardous hypothesis. This he takes to be a saying originally independent of the context in which the evangelist has placed it and which it does not fit. Luke inserted it here because he saw in it the theme 'days of the Son of man' in the eschatological sense of the happy days of messianic glory. The original meaning, however, must have been quite different – that the days to come will be so bad, that in comparison the days when the Son of man was still with the disciples will seem to them a blessed time indeed, and they will long in vain for their return. Leivestad contends that the saying is meaningless if the days of the Son of man are taken as referring to the future glory, for the statement that the disciples will long in vain ('and you will not see it') to experience even one of those days is, he argues, flatly contradicted by verse 24, in which the disciples *will* live to see the Son of man's day. But in fact this verse does not say anything directly about that at all. It merely emphasizes the suddenness of the Son of man's day. According to Leivestad, then, Luke 17.22 is an authentic saying in the wrong context, and originally had nothing to do with the eschatological day. His interpretation depends on the view that Jesus used the term Son of man (or the Man) in a completely non-eschatological sense as a self-descriptive name during his earthly ministry. The evidence for this, however, is extremely slight. In contrast to the authors referred to above, Leivestad assigns the plural form 'the days of the Son of man' to Jesus' speech,[16] but for an unconvincing reason which greatly reduces the value of an acute and independent contribution to the debate.

At the opposite extreme stands Perrin[17] who, excluding all Son of man sayings from Jesus' teaching, explains Luke 17.22-30 as early Christian apocalypticizing. Verses 23f. are to him a mere repetition, in apocalyptic language, of the authentic saying about the coming kingdom of God in verses 20f. Verses 26f. and 28-30 are successive developments, using Old Testament imagery, of the idea of the day of the Son of man, which would have been a natural way for the church to express its belief in the return of Jesus as the Son of man.

I now present a revised and (I believe) improved interpretation of these texts, in which so much depends on the meaning of 'day' and 'days'.

Luke 17		Matt. 24
22, one of the days of the Son of man		
24, the Son of man in his day	Q	27, the parousia of the Son of man
26, the days of the Son of man	Q	37, the parousia of the Son of man (= 39)
30, the day when the Son of man is revealed		

Luke 17.22. This might conceivably be reckoned as a word of Jesus. For instance, it was suggested in *JSM* (pp. 88f.) that the source had 'the day of the Son of man', the meaning being that the disciples would long in vain to see their trials and persecutions brought to a sudden end by the Son of man's day of judgment. Yet come it would when least expected, and for the faithful there would be opened a door of escape, as it was with Noah and his people. This view, however, is unsatisfactory on redaction critical grounds. It is, besides, highly unlikely that Jesus would have spoken of 'seeing' the day of the Son of man, a verb which elsewhere has as its object the Son of man 'coming in clouds with great power and glory' (Mark 13.26, par. Matt. 24.30), or similar phraseology (Mark 14.62, par. Matt. 26.64; Matt. 16.28), and belongs to the language of Christian apocalyptic. These considerations also militate against Torrey's suggestion, adopted by T. W. Manson,[18] that in the Aramaic an adverb (*laḥda*) meaning 'very much' was mistaken for the numeral 'one', and that the original meaning was 'you will greatly desire to see the day of the Son of man'.

Another way would be to suppose that Jesus, in this somewhat discouraging remark, meant that the days of the Son of man, understood as the preparatory period immediately preceding the day of the Son of man, would not begin for a very long time. They lay so far in the future that the disciples would not live to see any of them. But 'the days of the Son of man' is a Lukan expression and idea.[19] The verse has several Lukan features. One of these is the expression 'the days shall come' (ἐλεύσονται ἡμέραι), cf. 5.35 (following Mark 2.20); 21.6; ἥξουσιν ἡμέραι, 19.43; ἔρχονται ἡμέραι, 23.29. However, Luke may have found these expressions in his source.[20] 'One of the days' (μίαν τῶν ἡμερῶν) is Lukan: 5.17; 8.22; 20.1. ἐπιθυμεῖν with the infinitive (15.16; 16.21; 22.15) may be a mark of Lukan style.[21]

While it is sometimes possible to presuppose an authentic saying behind an evangelist's reframing of it in his own style, this is hardly the case here. Verse 22 is best taken as the evangelist's introduction to the section by way of presentation of his own eschatology, for which purpose he borrows by anticipation 'the days of the Son of man' in verse 26.[22] There, and consequently here also, the expression means the period leading up to the *day* of the Son of man, a period culminating in the Son of man's advent. 'The days of the Son of man' in Lukan eschatology correspond rather loosely to the days of Noah and the days of Lot, in the sense that as their days reached a sudden climax in the flood and in the destruction of Sodom, so by analogy, even if somewhat imprecisely, 'the days of the Son of man' will end in his 'day', as suddenly and as unexpectedly as those calamities. The reason why the disciples will not be able to witness even a single one of these days, the coming period of the Son of man of which the climactic 'day' is the culmination,[23] is that none of this will happen in their lifetime. This agrees with Luke's interpretation of eschatology. The consummation is destined to take place, but the time is deferred to an indeterminate and far distant future.

At the same time, although Luke in this way formulated the conception of the days of the Son of man in verse 26 on the analogy of the days of Noah and the days of Lot, and gave it a distinctive theological meaning, there is ground for the belief that it replaces there an original 'day of the Son of man' in the Q source. The first piece of evidence is Luke's version of the Q saying at verse 24 compared with Matt. 24.27.

Luke 17.24	Matt. 24.27
For as the lightning flashes and lights up the sky from one side to the other, so will the Son of man be in his day.	For as the lightning comes from the east and shines as far as the west, so will be the coming (παρουσία) of the Son of man.

The word parousia in Matthew comes from the language of the church, being fairly frequent in the New Testament letters but occurring again in the gospels only in this chapter, verses 3, 37, 39. Since Matthew introduces the word at 24.3 in his modification of Mark 13.4, the presumption is that he is responsible for it here also. The expression 'the Son of man in his day' occurs nowhere else in the New Testament. Did Luke derive it from Q? Or did he modify Q and, if so, what was the original reading in Q? There are three possibilities.

(1) Luke represents the Q text exactly: 'so will the Son of man be in his day'.

(2) 'In his day' is an addition corresponding in meaning to 'the parousia of the Son of man' in Matthew. As we have seen, Jüngel maintains that the resultant Q saying could be authentic, and that 'so will the Son of man be' may have been a formal mode of speech characteristic of Jesus. This view might gain some support from the fact of the omission of 'in his day' by some important textual witnesses.[24] Yet, despite the weight of evidence for the shorter reading, the usual one is probably to be preferred, and the omission of *ἐν τῇ ἡμέρᾳ αὐτοῦ* is to be explained as due to homoioteleuton after *ἀνθρώπου*.[25]

(3) 'The Son of man in his day' implies 'the day of the Son of man'. I have previously suggested[26] not only that this stood in Q (and was replaced in Matt. 24.27 by 'the parousia of the Son of man'), but also that it may represent Jesus' words. The Old Syriac versions (Sinaitic and Curetonian) actually read 'so will be the day of the Son of man'; this early form of the saying merits further consideration.

According to Merx,[27] the Greek text presupposed by the Old Syriac, *οὕτως ἔσται ἡ ἡμέρα τοῦ υἱοῦ τοῦ ἀνθρώπου*, 'so will be the day of the Son of man', is the *Grundform*. The introduction into the Syriac-speaking church of the usual form of the text through the Peshitta version involved the importation of the idea of the parousia into a text which in the Old Syriac referred only to the day of judgment.[28] By this, Merx appears to mean that the Old Syriac form of the saying refers to the day of judgment because 'the day of the Son of man' is the subject, while in the usual form 'in his day' is equivalent to the parousia (of the Son of man) in Matt. 24.27.[29]

It is tempting to accept this Old Syriac reading, although it is otherwise unattested, as representing the Lukan *Urtext*. If, however, the usual Greek text is the original, then we have to presuppose an alteration in the *Vorlage* of the Old Syriac to 'so will be the day of the Son of man', in order either to achieve exact formal correspondence with Matt. 24.27 (in some witnesses - c s Ambrose - the process of assimilation actually results in complete textual identity with Matthew), or to restore a supposedly more accurate Lukan text. Many will feel that if a choice has to be made between Luke and Matthew in such cases, Luke is far more likely to represent Q closely than Matthew is, and that the current term 'parousia' has replaced an original 'day'. This applies even to the usual Lukan text of the saying. But it can be argued that the text which Matthew's expression 'so will be the parousia of the Son of man' corresponds to and replaces is much more probably the Old Syriac form, 'so will be the day of the Son of man', than the usual Lukan one.[30] If this is accepted, we are justified in regarding the Old Syriac form of Luke 17.24 as reproducing the text of Q. This is further supported by investigation of verses 26f. and 28–30.

Luke 17

26. As it was in the days of Noah, so will it be in the days of the Son of man;
27. they ate, they drank, they married, they were given in marriage, until the day when Noah entered the ark, and the flood came and destroyed them all.

28a. Likewise as it was in the days of Lot,
30. so will it be on the day when the Son of man is revealed;
28b. they ate, they drank, they bought, they sold, they planted, they built;
29. but on the day when Lot went out from Sodom fire and brimstone rained from heaven and destroyed them all.

Rearrangement in the right-hand column shows clearly that the story of Lot, not found in Matthew, corresponds in poetic structure very closely to that of Noah, or rather that it did so at an earlier stage in the transmission of the tradition, for there is reason to believe that this earlier structure had already been altered to its present form in the source as it came to Luke.

Did the Lot pericope, however, stand in Q despite its absence from Matthew? If so, either Matthew deliberately omitted it,[31] or it was in Q as known to Luke but not in the form of Q familiar to Matthew, and is possibly, although not necessarily, a secondary addition intended to provide a parallel to the story of Noah.[32] The decision on this point is not unimportant; upon it depends one's estimate of the relative value of the two pericopae as possible reflections of Jesus' teaching. There is no discrepancy in content marking out the story of Lot from that of Noah. This applies also to the suggested restored structure of the former given above. The most probable view is that the second pericope was in Q, but was omitted by Matthew in the interests of brevity.[33] Verses 28–30 were probably in their present order in the source as it came to Luke, and the whole section, verses 23–37, with the possible exception of verse 32, is from Q.[34] We have to assume that a pre-Lukan redactor had already rearranged the Lot section he found in the source. His work is to be recognized in the transference of verse 30 from its original position after the name of Lot in verse 28a (the two together corresponding to verse 26) to the end of the story. The object of this was two-fold: to create a climactic conclusion to *both* stories, and to be able to use the word 'day' as a *Stichwort* linking on 'in that day' (ἐν ἐκείνῃ τῇ ἡμέρᾳ) at the beginning of verse 31, a reference to the fall of Jerusalem in a form resembling Mark 13.15f. What of verse 32, 'Remember Lot's wife' (cf. Gen. 19.26)? T. W. Manson thought that this also belongs to the pre-Lukan source which had already, even in the oral period, joined together verses 28-30 and 31f., and that the name of Lot provided the mnemonic connection which brought them together.[35] But it may quite well be a Lukan insertion. In any case we owe to the early redactor the association of the originally distinct and separate idea of the parousia with the fall of Jerusalem.[36]

In support of this view, appeal may be made to Luke's pairs of parallel pericopae in his special source; each pair is constructed on an identical or very similar pattern. The clearest examples are Jesus' warnings based upon the killing of some Galilaeans by Pilate's troops and the victims of the collapse of the tower at Siloam (Luke 13. 2-5), and the twin parables of the lost sheep and the lost coin (Luke 15. 4-10). These passages show that Luke was not in the habit of changing the order radically within one member of a pair of parallel pericopae. Consequently the evangelist himself is not likely to have been responsible for the present rearrangement of the Lot pericope, for rearrangement it surely is, having regard to the poetic structure of the two stories which is strikingly close when the second one is arranged in the order: verses 28a, 30, 28b, 29. If the story of Lot originally corresponded almost exactly in order and arrangement to the companion piece about Noah, this has an important bearing on the significance of the Son of man sayings in verses 26 and 30.

Luke 17.30. κατὰ τὰ αὐτὰ occurs elsewhere in the New Testament only in Luke 6.23 (par. Matt. 5.12 οὕτως), 26. In the present passage it is probably a Lukan stylistic use in the interests of variety instead of οὕτως in the corresponding verse 26.

ἀποκαλύπτεται. Only here in the gospels is the Son of man the subject of this verb. In the church's language as exemplified in the epistles, the subjects of this verb include God's righteousness (Rom. 1.17), God's wrath (Rom. 1.18), God's glory (Rom. 8.18; 1 Pet. 5.1), salvation (1 Pet. 1.5), the man of lawlessness, the son of perdition (2 Thess. 2.3,6), the lawless one (2 Thess. 2.8). More striking than any of these is 1 Cor. 3.13, ἡ γὰρ ἡμέρα δηλώσει, ὅτι ἐν πυρὶ ἀποκαλύπτεται ('for the Day will disclose it, because it (the Day)[37] is revealed in fire'). This quite closely resembles Luke 17.30, a text which may, therefore, be said to be framed in the language of the church, although with the Son of man as uniquely the subject of the verb;[38] there are at least comparable examples in the man of lawlessness, etc. above. It is to be expected that the Son of man would have become the subject of the verb in apocalyptic contexts;[39] that it does so only here in the New Testament is all the more surprising.

It is further suggested that the present form of verse 30, perhaps partly rewritten by Luke (κατὰ τὰ αὐτά), is the result of remodelling of an older logion, resembling verse 26b in its original form, by the pre-Lukan redactor. In its original position after verse 28a it may have been οὕτως ἔσται καὶ ἐν τῇ ἡμέρᾳ τοῦ υἱοῦ τοῦ ἀνθρώπου ('so will it be on the day of the Son of man').[40]

Luke 17.26. Verses 26f. and 28-30 are analogous in structure and content, and if they have a common and contemporary origin, verse 30 provides a clue to the original form of its parallel in verse 26b. Even if the suggested original form of verse 30 is not correct, it still refers to the *day*, in the singular, in connection with the Son of man. This verse, even in its present secondary apocalyptic form, is actually more valuable in retaining the idea of the day of the Son of man than verse 26, where the evangelist has replaced the singular with the plural. The presumption is that in verse 26b the reference was similar: 'so will it be on the day of the Son of man'. Confirmation of this has already been recognized in verse 24b, especially in its Old Syriac form which probably preserves the *Urtext*, 'so will be the day of the Son of man'.

In verse 26 'the days of the Son of man' was formed by the evangelist on the analogy of 'the days of Noah',[41] and means the days leading up to and culminating in an event comparable to the sequel of Noah's day - the flood which descended on the day on which Noah took refuge in the ark. Likewise, on the very day on which Lot escaped from Sodom, fire and brimstone rained down. In some respects the story of Lot better preserves the content of Q than does its companion piece. The absence here of 'the *days* of the Son of man' shows that, unlike the Noah pericope, this part of the source material has not been affected by the evangelist's own eschatological ideas: the notion of the *day* of the Son of man is implicit in verse 30 as it is in verse 24.

Comparison of Matthew's versions of the saying about the lightning (24.27) and the Noah pericope (24.37-9) tends to confirm our conclusions. The fact that 'the parousia of the Son of man' corresponds to 'the Son of man in his day' and much more closely to 'the day of the Son of man' (Old Syriac) in Luke 17.24, but in verses 37 and 39 to 'in the days of the Son of man' in Luke 17.26, strongly suggests that Q did not have both Luke's expressions but one only, replaced in Matthew by 'parousia'. Since we have seen that 'the days of the Son of man' is a Lukan idea, this can only have been 'the Son of man in his day', or preferably 'the day of the Son of man' as in the Old Syriac text of Luke 17.24.

The points of comparison should be noted. In Luke 17.24 the day of the Son of man (Old Syriac; the parousia in Matt. 24.27) is compared directly with the lightning, the point of comparison being two-fold: the suddenness of a flash of lightning, and its illumination of the whole night(?) sky[42] - nothing can escape its glare.[43]

In Luke 17.26, 'as it was in the days of Noah, so will it be on the day of the Son of man' (conjectured original text), the comparison is not identical in type with the preceding one. There is no *direct* comparison with the days of Noah (as in par. Matt. 24.37) in the presumed pre-Lukan form of the saying. The first part of the sentence is a general reference, and the real comparison is brought out in what follows. (Matthew's expanded explanatory version, 24.37–9, destroys the Semitic structure of the strophe as seen in Luke.)[44] What we have here is the first of two examples from Israel's history of sudden overwhelming destruction of unsuspecting evil men, as illustrations of Jesus' warning of the inevitable lightning-swift coming of the day of the Son of man. The story of Lot is a second and closely parallel illustration of the same theme.

Jesus' teaching

How much of all this represents the teaching of Jesus? We shall approach this question firstly as regards the sayings in Luke 17. 24, 26, 30, and secondly as regards the Noah and Lot pericopae as units to which belong respectively the second and third sayings.

It has been suggested above that, although 'the day of the Son of man' is clearly implied in verse 24, the *Urtext* of both Luke and Q may be represented by the Old Syriac text, 'so will be the day of the Son of man'. In verse 26 an original mention of the day of the Son of man in Q has been changed to the plural by the evangelist. Verse 30 also presupposes 'the day of the Son of man'; but the original Q saying, on the analogy of the parallel in verse 26 in its suggested original form, may have been 'so will it be on the day of the Son of man'.

Although the common rabbinic phrase 'the days of the Messiah' bears a formal resemblance to Luke's 'the days of the Son of man', its differentiation between the Messiah's rule on earth (his 'days') and the future world is inappropriate to Christian eschatology, and has no bearing on the Lukan concept.

Despite its occurrence only in Luke 17, 'the *day* of the Son of man' is not, like the plural form, of Lukan origin. Nor is a singular form, 'the day of the Messiah', found in rabbinic literature.[45] The analogy, rather, would be 'the day of the Lord' which, referring in the Old Testament to Yahweh, was frequently applied to Jesus by the early church (e.g. 1 Cor. 1.8; 5.5; 2 Cor. 1.14; 1 Thess. 5.2; 2 Thess. 2.2). Yet there is perhaps also to be taken into account 'the day of the Elect One' in 1 En. 61.5. In the Similitudes of Enoch this Elect One is the same as the Son of man, and occupies a glorious throne as the eschatological judge of the wicked and champion of the righteous: the Elect One, 1 En. 45.3; 55.4; 62.1–3; the Son of man, 62.5; 69.27, 29. It is conceivable that this idea of the day of the Elect One-Son of man, current in apocalyptic circles whose beliefs may be reflected in the Similitudes, had influenced this part of the Q tradition. On the other hand, the idea may be of entirely Christian origin, and have been formed on the analogy of 'the day of the Lord (Jesus Christ)' after the post-resurrection identification of Jesus as himself the Son of man of whom he had spoken in his preaching. If this is the true explanation, then the limitation of 'the day of the Son of man' to Luke 17 is in striking contrast with the frequency of 'the day of the Lord' in the Pauline letters. Mowinckel remarks that it is in keeping with the eschatological character of the Son of man that he should have a day of the kind indicated in the Similitudes. 'It is unlikely, therefore, that the idea is borrowed from the day of Yahweh; it belongs to the Son of Man conception.'[46] This principle applies also to the corresponding Christian usage of the day of the Lord (Jesus Christ), and the day of the Son of man in Luke 17. Indeed, according to Mowinckel, Paul, in speaking of the day of the Lord Jesus Christ, is in fact borrowing from the Son of man theology.

These considerations, and also the priority of the Son of man christology in the sense that 'Son of man' was the only title which Jesus could possibly have applied to himself, support the view that the sayings in Luke 17. 24, 26, 30, although (with the possible exception of the first) subject to modifications, derive from Jesus' preaching. If the Son of man was an element in his message, it is to be expected that he would have referred to the day of judgment associated with it. The fact that the day of the Son of man features only in these synoptic logia may be due to the vicissitudes of the transmission of the tradition.

It might be thought that the occurrence of the Noah and Lot pericopae in Luke 17 and in that order, had some connection with the appeal to these figures, and in the same order, in 2 Pet. 2.4–8, as outstanding examples of righteous men delivered from the fate of their wicked generations, and that what we find in Luke may derive from church tradition at an earlier stage rather than from Jesus. Noah and Lot are stock examples of righteous men and the objects of much elaboration in Jewish and early Christian tradition.[47] But in Luke the focus is upon the suddenness and the devastating effect of the catastrophes of the flood and of the fire and brimstone which overwhelmed the men of their generations. These twin illustrations of the suddenness of the day of the Son of man (verse 24) resemble Jesus' characteristic use of direct and graphic comparisons. They stress, too, the pervasiveness of that event like a lightning-flash illuminating everything above the horizon.

There are other marks of authenticity in both these parallel illustrations. In the first place, the motif of the sudden and unexpected end is a feature of Jesus' preaching. This is the theme of the parable of the watchful servants awaiting their master's return at any moment (Luke 12. 35-8). The immediately following short parable of the burglar (Luke 12.39, par. Matt. 24.43) makes the same point: the thief would not have succeeded if the householder had been waiting for him. The next verse is secondary: 'Do you also be ready, for the Son of man comes at an hour you do not expect.' The parable itself was addressed by Jesus to his contemporaries as a warning of the approaching eschatological catastrophe, the day of the Lord (Amos 5.18). The early church, reinterpreting, applied it to the delay of the parousia, and so added this exhortation to its members (cf. Luke 12.22; Matt. 24.3) to be prepared for the Son of man's advent at any moment. We can agree with Jeremias in finding the closest parallels to the parable of the burglar in these two parables of the flood and the destruction of Sodom as illustrations of the suddenness of the day of the Son of man.[48]

Secondly, Jesus refers elsewhere to Sodom and 'that day' (Luke 10.12), where Matthew adds 'and Gomorrah', and has 'the day of judgment' for 'that day' (Matt. 10.15). There is also Matt. 11. 23b-24:

> For if the mighty works done in you had been done in Sodom, it would have remained until this day. But I tell you that it shall be more tolerable on the day of judgment for the land of Sodom than for you.

These words, not in Luke, follow the woes on Chorazin and Bethsaida and the prediction of the fate of Capernaum reported in both gospels (Luke 10. 13-15, par. Matt. 11.21-3a). According to T. W. Manson,[49] the inclusion of the reference to Sodom in Matthew is preferable to Luke's omission of it, because it preserves the strophic parallelism characteristic of Jesus' teaching. There does not appear to be any valid reason why these sayings should not be attributed to Jesus. And if he spoke about Sodom, there is no reason why he should not have spoken also of Lot in Luke 17.28f. If this is conceded, there is no obstacle in the way of acceptance of the Lot pericope, which makes the same point, serves the same purpose of illustrating the lightning-like suddenness of the day of the Son of man, and (in its original arrangement) is identical in structure with the Noah pericope.[50]

If the material we have been considering belongs to Jesus' message, what is meant by 'the day of the Son of man'?

The day of the Son of man

We have noted that the counterparts of the first two of the three references in Luke 17 occur in Matt. 24.27, 37, 39 in the form, 'so will be the parousia of the Son of man', and that the word parousia (nowhere else in the gospels except in Matt. 24.3) is frequent in the New Testament letters, and therefore belongs to the vocabulary of the early church.

In a recent article, T. F. Glasson[51] states the reasons for rejection of the idea that Jesus himself taught that he would return in glory to judge the world, and shows how his thesis has won wide acceptance since the first appearance of his influential book, *The Second Advent*, in 1945. He makes three main points.

(1) There was no pre-Christian Jewish doctrine of the Messiah's descent in glory from heaven to earth, and this includes the Son of man in the Similitudes of Enoch who, as is clear in any case, performs his judicial functions in the presence of God in the final judgment.

(2) Therefore, if Jesus taught the doctrine, he must have originated it. But investigation of the relevant synoptic texts establishes that this is not so, and that they contain the beliefs of the church and the evangelists about Jesus. However, Glasson, by his description of the whole of Luke 17.22-37 as 'a pronouncement of doom upon the city [Jerusalem]', ignores the importance of the Son of man sayings in the passage as clues to Jesus' eschatological expectations. As for Mark 14.62, he accepts the newer orthodoxy and interprets the saying as referring to Jesus' ascent or exaltation to God, whereby he is rewarded for his endurance of humiliation and suffering, and fully vindicated. In fact, however, this hypothesis, in the form in which it is usually expressed, is as unsupported by evidence as that which Glasson has done so much to discredit.

(3) The parousia is first found in the letters to the Thessalonians. The advent of the Lord in the Old Testament (e.g. 'Then the Lord your God will come, and all the holy ones with him', Zech. 14.5)[52] becomes the advent of the Lord Jesus Christ (e.g. 'For the Lord himself will descend from heaven . . .', 1 Thess. 4.16).

Whatever else it may be, the day of the Son of man in Luke 17 is not the equivalent of, and merely another name for, the parousia of popular early Christian expectation in Matt. 24. We have found good reasons for regarding the sayings in their Lukan form as basically words of Jesus, while the parousia doctrine arose in the early church.[53]

In connection with Mark 14.62, mention has been made of the new orthodoxy, according to which some of the parousia sayings refer in fact, or originally, to Jesus' ascent or exaltation to God, and that this conception is much more likely to have been part of his future expectations. Thus Jeremias suggests as 'coming' logia to be viewed in this way, Mark 8.38;[54] 13.26; Matt. 10.23b, and concludes that 'there is much to suggest that the earliest conception was that the revelation of the Son of man would come about in the form of an assumption to God'.[55]

Against this is the absence of any pre-Christian Jewish concept of the Son of man's exaltation or assumption;[56] it is as foreign to Judaism as that of the descent to earth from heaven of the Messiah or the Son of man. 1 En. 70f. is no exception, because it is Enoch who is raised aloft to the Son of man in heaven (70.1).[57]

There is, however, one aspect of the matter to which there are parallels - the Son of man's enthronement in Matt. 25.31 and 19.28.

> When the Son of man comes in his glory, and all the angels with him, then he will sit on his glorious throne (Matt. 25.31).

The throne of the Son of man appears to be derived from Jewish apocalyptic (1 En. 62.5; 69.27, 29), likewise 'the throne of (his) glory' (1 En. 45.3; 55.4; 61.8; 62.2, 3, 5; 69.27). The nearest analogy to Matt. 25.31 and 19.28 is 62.5, 'When they see that Son of man sitting on the throne of his glory'. Matt. 25.31 has other apocalyptic features: the Son of man 'comes', he comes in glory, he is accompanied by angels. This imagery describes the Son of man's approach to the celestial throne awaiting him. The association of this imagery with the Son of man is most prominent in Matthew, and the earliest stratum of tradition is not to be found in this saying.

> Truly, I say to you, in the regeneration (παλιγγενεσίᾳ), when the Son of man shall sit on his glorious throne, you who have followed me will also sit on twelve thrones, judging the twelve tribes of Israel (Matt. 19.28).

Since this saying is freer from apocalyptic features - the Son of man does not 'come'; there are no attendant angels - it might be thought to be older than the preceding one. On the other hand (quite apart from παλιγγενεσία, a later non-Semitic feature), thrones (not in Matt. 25.31) are another apocalyptic feature:[58]

> And I will bring forth in shining light those who have loved my holy name, and I will seat each on the throne of his honour (1 En. 108.12, cf. Rev. 4.4).

The conclusion on these two Matthaean sayings is that they provide no evidence of apocalyptic influence on Jesus' thought about the Son of man, and no clue as to whether his expectations included exaltation to a celestial throne. Whatever their original basis may have been, they are both unauthentic.

Luke 22.69, which is independent of Mark 14.62, does not exhibit the pattern of exaltation followed by parousia; the glory of the Son of man consists in his session at the right hand of God. Although this may possibly be a pointer to Jesus' belief, the idea is a combination of Dan. 7.13 and Ps. 110.1. Jeremias[59] cites a number of texts in support of the view that the Son of man's exaltation was an older belief than the parousia. Luke 24.26 is not particularly appropriate, for it is of the *Christ* that it is said that he is destined to suffer and so enter his glory. In the Fourth Gospel this thought is clothed in the theologized forms of the Son of man's ascension (*ἀναβαίνειν*, John 3.13; 6.62), lifting up or exaltation (*ὑψοῦσθαι*, 3.14; 8.28; 12.34), and glorification (*δοξάζεσθαι*, 12.23; 13.31f.).[60]

The idea, then, of Jesus' exaltation as Son of man is Johannine. Suggestions that some of the parousia sayings originally had to do with exaltation are not altogether compelling. But even if exaltation was the oldest belief concerning the aftermath of Jesus' death, it does not follow that it had been his own belief. It is as hard to understand how Jesus could have thought of his exaltation to God (whether as Son of man or not)[61] as it would be to explain how he could have believed in his parousia or coming to earth. Neither conception is connected with the Son of man in Judaism.

With due allowance for difference of opinion on a number of details, it is generally agreed that Jesus' outlook was eschatological, that he expected 'the last things' fairly soon, followed by the dawning of the kingdom or reign of God. If Luke 17.20–30 contains a deposit of Jesus' preaching, there was in it a parallelism between the *coming* of the kingdom and (not the coming but) the *day* of the Son of man.[62] Verse 21a is parallel to verse 23.

> Nor will they say, 'Look, here it is!' or 'There it is.'
> (*οὐδὲ ἐροῦσιν, Ἰδοὺ ὧδε ἤ, Ἐκεῖ.*)

> They will say to you, 'Look! There!' and 'Look! Here!' Do not go running off in pursuit (NEB).
> (καὶ ἐροῦσιν ὑμῖν, Ἰδοὺ ἐκεῖ, Ἰδοὺ ὧδε· μὴ ἀπέλθητε μηδὲ διώξητε.)

In different ways, these are both negative sentences. Verse 21b, 'for behold, the kingdom of God will (suddenly) be in your midst',[63] is parallel to verse 24, 'for as the lightning ... so will the Son of man be in his day' (or 'so will be the day of the Son of man'). Jesus' expectations were not fulfilled: the kingdom did not come; and early Christian hopes were fixed instead on the parousia of Jesus as the eschatological event. If the day of the Son of man in Luke is not identical with the parousia in Matthew and if, according to the synoptic records, Jesus did not speak of his ascent or exaltation to God, what is the significance of the sayings in Luke 17 for the enquiry into Jesus' expectations, on the view that they go back in substance to him?

The comparisons of the lightning, the deluge, and the destruction of Sodom are used in Jesus' proclamation to an irreligious and unresponsive generation, as symbolic descriptions of the suddenness of the eschatological catastrophe. This is the logical result of our investigation of the redactional work of Luke, whose own eschatology has partially overlaid and obscured the original eschatology of the sayings which belong in substance to Jesus' preaching.

What is the day of the Son of man implied in Luke 17.24, 26, 30? Bearing in mind our suggested reconstructions, the day of the Son of man, if not strictly the grammatical subject, is the logical subject of all three sayings. The kingdom of God and the Son of man are related ideas. We may venture further: they were related ideas in the teaching of Jesus.

The day of the Son of man is (the inauguration of) the eschatological judgment, and is parallel to the imminent coming of the kingdom of God. 'The day of the Son of man' in Luke 17 is synonymous with 'the day of judgment' or 'that day'.[64] The judgment takes place in heaven as in 1 En. 45.3: 'On that day my Elect One shall sit on the throne of glory, and shall try their works.' He is the same as the Son of man.

> And he sat on the throne of his glory,
> And the sum of judgment was given to the Son of man (1 En 69.27).

In Luke 17 the happenings on earth are concurrent with the eschatological judgment, the day of the Son of man. Unlike all others, that day will not dawn gradually. All in a flash men will realize from events around them that the Son of man's day of judgment is in progress, and that therefore the complete and final triumph of the sovereignty of God over all evil is imminent. The related sayings in Luke 17 imply two things: the exaltation *status* already belongs to the Son of man; the judgment is in progress, for the Son of man's function is judgment. The day of the Son of man will be as sudden as lightning. 'As it was in the days of Noah . . . ', 'as it was in the days of Lot . . . so will it be on the day of the Son of man.' With virtually no apocalyptic description or elaboration, the sayings refer to the futurity of the Son of man or of his day, a day that needs no identifying description beforehand, no premonitory sign; it will be self-authenticating. The coming kingdom and the (judgment) day of the Son of man are inescapable, imminent acts of God directly associated as two aspects of the same phenomenon. Jesus announced their near approach, and warned the men of his generation to accept his message and repent while there was still time.[65]

In these sayings there is no coming or parousia of the Son of man to earth, no mention of clouds, glory, or attendant angels; there is no coming of the Son of man to a throne, and no enthronement. What makes these sayings so important above all is the absence of ascension and of any *process* of exaltation of the Son of man to God, a conception which, like the parousia doctrine of the early church, is both foreign to Jewish thought and unattested for Jesus' teaching in the synoptic tradition. There is a lacuna, an unbridged gap, between Jesus' allusions to his death, and the references to the day of the Son of man in Luke 17 which are to be understood as pointing to the judicial functions associated with the Son of man he envisaged himself as exercising in his future status of exaltation. But (to repeat) there is no mention of exaltation, assumption, or translation as a mode of transition from an earthly to a celestial status. There is, therefore, no suggestion of the bridging of the gap, or of closing the lacuna, between the two states with any notion of an event or process of exaltation, which would elevate Jesus to be the Son of man. It remained for the Fourth Gospel to do that; the Johannine Jesus himself bridges the gap by speaking of his own exaltation as Son of man.[66]

2. *Luke 18.8b.* 'But when the Son of man comes, will he find faith on earth?'

This saying, together with Luke 21.36 and Matt. 10.23, is assigned by Colpe to the hypothetical fourth tradition of the Jewish apocalyptic Son of man. According to him it comes from a pre-Lukan source,[67] and does not need to be separated from what immediately precedes it. The meaning is, Will the Son of man at his coming find upon earth that faith which a man must have in order to be numbered among the elect? The saying is concerned not with a coming to earth, but with the faith men on earth should have - acceptance of Jesus' message. Will the Son of man, when he appears in the heavenly court of judgment, be able to assert that men on earth have responded to Jesus' call to decision and persistently petitioned God, as the widow did the unjust judge? Colpe maintains that in substance the saying belongs to Jesus' preaching, and that it expresses in interrogative form the same basic idea which in Luke 17.24, 26, 30 is framed as an announcement and in Luke 21.36 as a demand.

Is the correspondence of thought, however, sufficiently close to bring the saying into the category of the authentic? Colpe's interpretation is forced and unnatural. Borsch[68] independently comes close to it when he observes that the saying probably 'envisioned the Son of man appearing in heaven to judge earthly mortals'. It is very likely, of course, that whatever its origin, it came to be understood, like others, as referring to the Son of man's descent to earth. If that was its original meaning, it must be a creation of the church. Its genuineness, however, has been defended on several grounds.

Borsch[69] recalls the frequent association, as in this saying, of 'coming' with the Son of man.[70] But in fact this association is not a mark of authenticity. Borsch defends, while admitting the impossibility of proving, the authenticity of Luke 18.8b in this regard.

For Leivestad, the term Son of man is a self-designation of Jesus. Although in this saying the Son of man is the eschatological judge, Leivestad maintains that Luke's use of the term does not support the general opinion that sayings of this kind originated in apocalyptic Son of man concepts. Regarding as characteristic of the uncertainty of *Traditionskritik* the fact that the saying in Luke 18.8b and the closely related one in 21.36 are accepted as authentic by Colpe but rejected by Bultmann and Tödt, Leivestad denies the possibility, in such cases, of a firm decision based on purely traditio-historical grounds. He has recourse to the total picture of Jesus' preaching, and sees in this saying an authentic expression of a unique pessimism at variance both with Jesus' own message and with Luke's outlook. For Leivestad, the problem lies here, and not in the Son of man terminology.[71] The pessimism of the saying is a problem only if it is a word of Jesus, and Leivestad does not present a convincing case for that.

In the revised edition of *The Parables of Jesus* (1963) Jeremias abandoned his earlier opinion that Luke 18.8b was added by the evangelist as a conclusion to the parable. This is because πλήν is not a mark of Luke's usage but of that of his source, and ἄρα (only here and in Acts 8.30 in

Lukan writings) is not Lukan either, while 'the Son of man' points to a pre-Lukan tradition because Luke never employs the term independently.[72] Jeremias further reasons that 'faith' in this saying is not attributable to Pauline influence, since the definite article before it (τὴν πίστιν) is probably an Aramaism. But even if it is an Aramaism, that and the pre-Lukan features do no more than suggest, as Jeremias says, 'an early Son of Man saying' as an integral part of the parable. Yet this still remains in doubt. Borsch concedes that authenticity cannot be proved.[73] The emphasis on faith remains problematical despite the suggestion that it should be taken as trust in God (cf. Luke 7.9, par. Matt. 8.10), or steadfastness or faithfulness.[74] There is also the unique association of faith with the coming of the Son of man. Against the view that faith in Jesus is meant and reflects church usage, Borsch urges that 'there is no reason why it could not have referred to faith in the Son of Man figure and have been so used by Jesus'. But what could Jesus have meant by faith in the Son of man at his appearing in the heavenly court? Is not this interpretation inconsistent with Borsch's own approximation to that of Colpe, namely, that the question in the saying is whether the Son of man on that occasion will be able to plead on behalf of men that they have had faith in the earthly Jesus?

In the face of these difficulties, and even if the saying is of Palestinian origin, and therefore comparatively early, it should probably still be understood as an explanatory addition to the parable of the unjust judge, expressing belief in the coming to earth of Jesus the Son of man.

3. ***Luke 21.36.*** **'But watch at all times, praying that you may have strength to escape all these things that will take place, and to stand before the Son of man.'**

This is the second of three sayings included by Colpe in his hypothetical fourth tradition of the Jewish apocalyptic Son of man. Borsch, who is not slow to admit Son of man sayings, concedes the possibility that this one is a later formation, and points out the uniqueness of 'standing before' the Son of man.[75] Jüngel[76] quotes with approval Bultmann's assessment of verses 34–6 as a late Hellenistic formulation so similar to Pauline terminology 'that one could hazard a guess that Luke was here using a fragment from some lost epistle written by Paul or one of his disciples'.[77] F. W. Beare, with reason calling this a 'hazardous conjecture', thinks rather of a Lukan composition replacing the Markan ending of the synoptic apocalypse.[78] The soundest conclusion is that, although the saying preserves an element of Jesus' teaching about the Son of man as judge, it has in itself no strong claim to authenticity.

Since, however, the phrase 'to stand before' (σταθῆναι ἔμπροσθεν) may be a Hebraism,[79] the saying could at least include an old Palestinian echo of an authentic word of Jesus such as Luke 12.8.[80]

4. ***Matt. 10.23.*** **'When they persecute you in one town, flee to the next; for truly, I say to you, you will not have gone through all the towns of Israel, before the Son of man comes.'**

In his discussion of this saying, again assigned to the fourth Jewish Son of man source, Colpe asks, on the hypothesis that it is Jewish Christian in its present form, why the community did not discard it when it was not fulfilled.[81] He contends that the view that it attained the authority of a *Herrenwort* (word of the Lord) in the brief interval between its formulation and its dissemination in the tradition, is a more arbitrary hypothesis than its acceptance as a real *Herrenwort*. Even if it is discarded as unauthentic, there remains Jesus' proclamation of the coming kingdom of God, about whose non-fulfilment the community had to be convinced even after Easter. Colpe therefore considers it highly unlikely that the church could itself have produced a saying of such a similar type. He argues that it must be authentic to have survived the tendency, very pronounced in Matthew, to ascribe to Jesus missionary work among the Gentiles, and to have overcome the offence of being an unfulfilled prediction.[82] In his evaluation of the saying he follows Jeremias' thesis that Jesus both confined his own mission to Israel, and forbade his disciples to evangelize the Gentiles. But Matt. 10.23 is not necessarily to be placed on the same level as the particularist sayings in 10.5f. and 15.24, for at the most its exclusiveness is not explicit, as in these, but only suggested indirectly. Be that as it may, Colpe treats it as a word of Jesus in which the closing reference to the Son of man's coming alludes, like Luke 18.8b and 21.36, to his appearing in the heavenly judgment. This reasoning has the merit of consistency, but is speculative. Colpe does little more than theorize about the state of mind of the primitive community and its ability (or rather, inability) to have framed a logion like the one in question.

Another attempt to uphold the genuineness of Matt. 10.23 has been made by H. Schürmann.[83] Originally addressed to the disciples in a time of persecution, the words were later applied by the primitive church to its own missionary situation. The saying, Schürmann maintains, should be regarded as related to Mark 9.1 (the near coming of the kingdom) and to Mark 13.30. More important is his suggestion, plausible enough at first sight, that the Q saying in Luke 12.11f. ('and when they bring you before the synagogues and the rulers and the authorities, do not be anxious how or what you are to answer or what you are to say; for the Holy Spirit will teach you in that very hour what you ought to say'; par. Matt. 10.19f.) was originally followed by Matt. 10.23.[84] The similarity of these sayings, both in form and content, is adduced as strong evidence for this hypothesis. Both are words of comfort (*Trostworte*) promising, respectively, the help of the Holy Spirit and of the Son of man for persecuted disciples in Palestine. One might have expected that Luke himself would have placed the saying immediately after 12.11f. if it would fit so well. Schürmann's explanation is that Luke omitted it because it did not seem to him to correspond to the missionary situation as he knew it. The hypothesis is supported by the further suggestion that Mark 13.10, 'the gospel must first be preached to all the nations', is a deliberate correction of Matt. 10.23 by Mark,[85] who knew the sayings in the order: Luke 12.11f. (cf. Mark 13.9, 11), Matt. 10.23.

Ingenious though it is, Schürmann's hypothesis is unconvincing. Hahn rejects it because it isolates Matt. 10.23 from the unauthentic sayings in 10.5f. and 15.24. Itself also unauthentic, it belongs to an early stage in the church's exclusively Jewish mission and the opposition it encountered.[86] Perrin assumes a similar situation, although emphasizing rather the parousia expectation. Moreover, the saying refers to the 'coming' of the Son of man, a feature he rightly sees as a mark of logia produced in the early church. Like Schürmann, he compares Matt. 10.23 with Mark 9.1 and 13.30 with their identical solemn introductions (*αμην λέγω ὑμῖν*), but as evidence of its later formulation.[87]

Other considerations point decisively to the secondary nature of the saying. One of these is the close parallelism, both of structure and content, between verse 23b and Matt. 16.28.

> For truly, I say to you, you will not have gone through all the towns of Israel, before the Son of man comes.
> (*αμην γὰρ λέγω ὑμῖν, οὐ μὴ τελέσητε τὰς πόλεις τοῦ Ισραηλ ἕως ἔλθῃ ὁ υἱὸς τοῦ ἀνθρώπου.*)
>
> Truly, I tell you that there are some of those standing here who will not taste death until they see the Son of man coming in his kingdom.
> (*αμην λέγω ὑμῖν ὅτι εἰσίν τινες τῶν ὧδε ἑστώτων οἵτινες οὐ μὴ γεύσωνται θανάτου ἕως ἂν ἴδωσιν τὸν υἱὸν τοῦ ἀνθρώπου ἐρχόμενον ἐν τῇ βασιλείᾳ αὐτοῦ*, Matt. 16.28.)

The second passage is a transformation of the Markan prediction of the coming kingdom of God (Mark 9.1) into one of the coming of the Son of man, the same idea as in Matt. 10.23. The logion in 16.28 thus *interprets* Jesus' message of the kingdom as referring to the return of Jesus himself.

This is what we find also in 10.23. Both sayings are therefore unauthentic.

In his discussion of Matt. 10.23, D. R. A. Hare merely mentions the possibility that in its original form it was 'a genuine prediction based upon the motif of eschatological flight'.[88] Whether 23a was at one time separate from 23b, which would then have no connection with persecution, or whether 23a was created as an introduction to 23b, Hare concludes that it was known to the evangelist as a unit. Moreover, far from being an unfulfilled prediction of Jesus referring to missionary work and persecution in Palestine, the saying is for Matthew, according to Hare, a *fulfilled* prediction referring to Jewish persecution of Jewish Christian missionaries in the Diaspora. This view he supports with 23.34, where the addition of 'from city to city' after the mention of persecution in what is a Q saying (par. Luke 11.49) is simply a borrowing from 10.23.

Whether or not Hare is right in thinking of the Diaspora as the historical setting of Matt. 10.23 in the evangelist's own understanding, it does seem to have been drawn upon by him in his redactional work. This applies to both its parts. The addition in 23.34 is taken from its first part, and the redactional form of Mark 9.1 at Matt. 16.28 is inspired by its second part. We conclude that the saying is an independent unit and was treated as such by the evangelist. It reflects the same kind of situation as Luke 6.22, persecution for the sake of the Son of man (par. Matt. 5.11 has 'persecute' and 'for my sake') probably during missionary activity among Palestinian Jews.

5. *Mark 14.62.* 'And you will see the Son of man sitting at the right hand of Power, and coming with the clouds of heaven.'

Borsch defends this as 'an approximation of something Jesus said about the Son of Man at his arraignment'.[89] Having referred to Perrin's explanation of the saying as a Qumran-like *pesher* consisting of a combination of Ps. 110.1 and Dan. 7.13, he goes on to suggest that, like the Qumran examples, this one also could be of pre-Christian origin.[90] He follows up this suggestion in a subsequent article.[91] In regard to Perrin's second *pesher* combination of Dan. 7.13 with Zech. 12.10 ('*they will see* the Son of man coming with the clouds of heaven'), Borsch questions whether there is any influence from Zech. 12.10 in the formation of Mark 14.62 itself, because in Mark 13.26 and Matt. 24.30 the link between 'they will see' and the coming Son of man symbolism appears to be prior, and the more specific reference to Zech. 12.10 in Matt. 24.30 is secondary.

Borsch also makes a good deal of 1 En. 62.5.

And they shall be downcast of countenance,
And pain shall seize them,
When they see that Son of man
Sitting on the throne of his glory.

Undoubtedly there is here a remarkably close parallel to the Markan order: seeing, the Son of man, sitting. Borsch claims that it is less likely that Mark 14.62 is a mere product of Christian textual conflation, or that it and 1 En. 62.5 illustrate parallel developments among Christian and Jewish sectarians, than that both forms are influenced by older pre-Christian ideas. This, we have already learned, is an essential element in Borsch's hypothesis of Jesus' conscious fulfilment of a pre-Christian Son of Man mythology. For this he finds support in the similarity of the language of Matt. 19.28 and 25.31 about the Son of man sitting on the throne of his glory to the Enochian phraseology, and apparently believes this reflects the use of an older and better tradition than the Markan one.[92] But since this kind of phraseology is confined among the gospels to Matthew, which in other respects also is more addicted than the others to apocalyptic thought and language, it is more likely that the resemblances between 1 En. 62.5 (cf. 69.27, 29) and Matthew are the result of borrowing either from the Similitudes of Enoch or from the tradition they represent.[93] Thus the similarity between 1 En. 62.5 and Mark 14.62 is less significant than it appears.

At the opposite extreme Perrin maintains that Mark 14.62, a conflation of Old Testament texts in *pesher* form, has been historicized and transformed into a saying of Jesus.[94]

All references to the Son of man 'coming' are secondary: Mark 8.38, par. Luke 9.26; Mark 13.26, par. Luke 21.27; Luke 12.40, par. Matt. 24.44; Luke 18.8; Matt. 10.23; 16.27, 28; 24.30; 25.31. The 'coming' of the Son of man corresponds to his 'parousia',[95] a term confined to Matt. 24.3, 27, 37, 39 in the gospels and reflecting church usage. Associated with 'coming' is 'you will see' (Mark 14.62) or 'they will see' (Mark 13.26; Matt. 16.28; 24.30).

These considerations and the *pesher* interpretation of Lindars and Perrin effectively exclude authenticity for Mark 14.62. It expresses the early Christian belief in the session of Jesus the Son of man at God's right hand and his coming (or parousia) to earth.[96]

Because it is one of the eight texts in which Colpe sees remnants of a fourth Jewish Son of man tradition, we turn to the parallel in Luke 22.69: 'But from now on the Son of man shall be seated at the right hand of the power of God.' Colpe regards this as part of Luke's special passion narrative source and as independent of Mark 14.62,[97] to which it is superior and prior in lacking the secondary parousia reference to Dan. 7.13. The only secondary feature in the Lukan version is the explanatory addition of the words 'of God' to the Semitic 'the Power' in Mark 14.62.[98] The fact that Dan. 7.13 is not quoted in Luke 22.69, as it is in Mark, agrees with the absence in Jewish apocalyptic of the Son of man's exaltation. Jesus refers only to the dignity (*Hoheit*) of the Son of man. Colpe concludes that the genuineness of Luke 22.69 is established, and that it is further supported by the absence of direct admission of Messiahship by Jesus and of the visionary apocalyptic expression 'you shall see'.

While we may agree that Mark and Luke here follow independent traditions, the association in Luke of the Son of man title with the session at the right hand of God, in allusion to Ps. 110.1, is itself a combination of Dan. 7.13 with the psalm passage,[99] and is therefore not likely to be a genuine feature.

6. *Mark 13.26*

This calls for no further comment than that it is the classic expression of early Christian expectation based on the parousia interpretation of Dan. 7.13.

7. *Matt. 25.31*

See above, pp. 69–70.

Conclusion

This investigation of Son of man sayings to which there are no non-Son of man rivals or parallels shows that they are of very unequal value when they are examined for signs of authenticity. Only the closely related sayings in Luke 17.24, 26, 30 have any real claim to be regarded as genuine utterances of Jesus. But they are extremely important, and will come up for further discussion in the next chapter.[100]

IV

THE SYNOPTIC TEXTS. II

Of the sayings listed in the left-hand column at the beginning of chapter III there remain to be investigated those having non-Son of man rivals or parallels: Luke 12.8–9 par. (Mark 8.38), and Luke 11.29–30 par. In addition, Luke 12.10, along with its parallels, is re-examined next because of its position immediately after text 1 in Luke. The chapter concludes with briefer discussions of some other pairs of sayings.

1. *Luke 12.8–9.* 'Every one who acknowledges me before men, the Son of man will also acknowledge before the angels of God; (9) but he who denies me before men will be denied before the angels of God.'[1]
***Matt. 10.32–3.* 'So every one who acknowledges me before men, I also will acknowledge before my Father who is in heaven; (33) but whoever denies me before men, I also will deny before my Father who is in heaven.'**
***Mark 8.38.* 'For whoever is ashamed of me and of my words in this adulterous and sinful generation, of him will the Son of man also be ashamed, when he comes in the glory of his Father with the holy angels' (parr. Luke 9.26; Matt. 16.27).**

Support for the superiority of the Lukan to the Matthaean version is very strong and includes Bultmann, Tödt, Hahn, Fuller,[2] Leivestad,[3] Voss,[4] and Pannenberg. Bultmann,[5] Tödt,[6] Hahn,[7] and Pannenberg[8] lay special emphasis on the alleged distinction attributed to Jesus between himself and the Son of man as a separate figure as a mark of authenticity, and maintain that the post-Easter community could not have originated it.[9] This distinction is present also in Mark 8.38 and its Lukan parallel; in the two Matthaean passages it is missing: in Matt. 10.32 Son of man is replaced by 'I', while in 16.27 the Markan saying is so transformed as to extrude the first person pronoun. Pannenberg points out that the uniqueness of Luke 12.8f. is not in itself a guarantee of genuineness.[10] But we may note that the forensic terminology makes more explicit the significance of 'the day of the Son of man' in Luke 17. 24, 26, 30, and sheds light on the allusions there to the Son of man as if to another person.

In *JSM* I defended the superiority of Luke 12.8f. to the form in Matthew, and its substantial trustworthiness as a word of Jesus which, interpreting the apocalyptic Son of man concept in a functional sense, is the root of the Son of man christology.[11] Vielhauer has also thought of the distinction between Jesus and the Son of man as not between two persons, but between two states of one and the same person. But since he denies all the Son of man sayings to Jesus, he attributes the idea not to him, but to the post-Easter community.[12] Pannenberg, conceding that this cannot be entirely excluded, yet finds difficulty in the assumption that the distinction would have been put into Jesus' mouth.[13] It is less difficult to suppose that Jesus himself may have made the distinction, as much as to say, 'I in my (future) function and status as Son of man'. Pannenberg follows Bultmann and Tödt in understanding the apparent distinction in Luke 12.8 as Jesus' own differentiation between himself and another separate being. It is of the essence of the hypothesis in *JSM*, however, that it does *not* attach to Jesus' thought any notion of a Son of man as an objective, existent figure separate and distinct from himself. Pannenberg later observes,[14] 'By virtue of the resurrection, Jesus had moved into the role of the Son of Man', because to believers after the resurrection 'it must have become meaningless to expect a second figure in addition to him with the same function and the same mode of coming'. Precisely! But would it not have been equally meaningless for the disciples to have done this *before* the resurrection? If they perhaps initially shared a current apocalyptic belief in the Son of man 'as a heavenly being' (Pannenberg), are we to suppose that they went on believing in such a figure, besides Jesus, right up to the crucifixion? This would only have been possible if Jesus had spoken about the Son of man unambiguously and in such a way as to encourage such a notion. There is no evidence whatever that he did so.

Luke 12.8f. and its parallels have been explained as an utterance of Christian prophecy in forensic language, laying down a maxim of holy law for the guidance of the community.[15] But the primitive church's use of sacred law in the ordering of its life and discipline could well have been encouraged by the known use by Jesus himself of similar formulae, of which Luke 12.8f. may be an example.[16]

Possibly Luke 12.9 may not belong to the original form of the saying; it is omitted by some witnesses.[17] But the omission may be due to homoioteleuton: verses 8 and 9 both end with τῶν ἀγγέλων τοῦ θεοῦ. This explanation would hold if verse 8 stood complete in the manuscript from which was copied the exemplar with the omission of verse 9. However, the words τῶν ἀγγέλων in verse 8 are omitted by ℵ* and Marcion. Yet this is not likely to be the original reading. The occurrence of the same omission in verse 9 too in Marcion's text strongly suggests that he may have been responsible for it in both places. The case for the usual text of verse 8 is reinforced by Rev. 3.5b,[18] which appears to be a conflation of Matt. 10.32, 'before my Father in heaven', and Luke 12.8, 'before the angels of God'. The conclusion is that the textual evidence supports verse 9 as an original part of the logion.

Whereas in Luke 12.8 the Son of man is the subject of an active verb, 'will acknowledge', in verse 9 there is a passive verb, 'will be denied'. Normally this kind of Semitic passive is a circumlocution for the action of God, and may be so here. The logical subject may, however, although unusually, be the Son of man,[19] a view which I should wish to qualify. Hahn suggests that the passive, taken in conjunction with the phrase 'before the angels' used as a circumlocution for 'before God', does not limit the act of judging to God but implies that, as in verse 8 explicitly, the Son of man is also involved, and here in the condemning of those who had denied Jesus on earth.[20] The difficulty of the passive in verse 9 is thus capable of being exaggerated. We may conjecture that although Mark 8.38, certainly secondary in its present form, depicts the Son of man as unambiguously the agent in the judgment, in Luke he plays a somewhat subordinate, or, rather, a shared judgmental role as assessor alongside or in the presence of God ('the angels of God') the supreme judge, whose prerogative it is to pronounce sentence upon those who had denied Jesus in his earthly ministry. Moreover, perhaps too firm a line should not be drawn between the Son of man as witness and the Son of man as judge.[21] He may be more the witness in acknowledging those who acknowledged Jesus, but witness and judge combined when it comes to the condemnation of those who had denied him.

The suggestion that Luke 12.9 originally corresponded in form to verse 8 - 'the Son of man will deny before the angels of God'[22] - appears to be very plausible. In Matt. 10.32f. both sentences have an active verb (although the subject is 'I'), and in Mark 8.38 the subject of the active verb is the Son of man. Yet it is not wholly satisfactory, because there is no completely convincing explanation why a change should have been made to produce the present Lukan text. The familiar suggestion that Luke made the alteration in order to achieve a better transition to the structural form of verse 10 is rather inadequate, since the result would have been a mere perpetuation, albeit in more balanced clauses, of a contradiction between verses 9 and 10a: there will be denial of him who denies Jesus on earth; there will be forgiveness of him who speaks a word against the Son of man. This *is* a contradiction if Son of man in verse 10 denotes the earthly Jesus and Jesus is the speaker. But did the evangelist perhaps understand 'Son of man' in an originally independent Q logion in verse 10 as contrasting with 'me' in verse 9, and so as a futurist use of the title on Jesus' lips, referring either to himself as the future Son of man, or to the Son of man as a figure distinct from himself? Such speculations do not get us very far. Luke 12.10 is best ignored in this connection as an independent logion, of which another version without 'Son of man' is to be found in Mark 3.28f. There is, then, no need to presuppose an earlier form of verse 9 with the Son of man as subject of an active verb.

Perrin regards the hypothetical form of Luke 12.9 as less good than the present text which, however, he holds to be a secondary modelling on the pattern of the original form of verse 8, this latter perhaps going back to Jesus and reading: 'Every one who acknowledges me before men, he will be acknowledged before the angels of God.'[23] If this is correct, Luke 12.8f., in the view of many scholars the (or a) basic text for the Son of man in the teaching of Jesus, becomes worthless in that respect.

Lindeskog[24] assigns the saying to the conflict of Jewish Christianity with the synagogue, on the ground that 'confessing' (ὁμολογεῖν) and 'denying' (ἀρνεῖσθαι) belong to the technical Christian vocabulary. They do;[25] but the linguistic data do not demand this conclusion. Nor do they support Perrin's distinction between verses 8 and 9, namely, that the former, in employing the ecclesiastical word ὁμολογεῖν in an Aramaizing construction with the preposition ἐν, is superior to the latter, in which 'denying' reflects directly the early church's liturgical language. Against this is the probability that an Aramaic word *kephar* lies behind ἀρνεῖσθαι.[26]

Of these proposals, it is that which takes the usual text as it stands, in the way outlined above, which is to be preferred.[27] The ingenious suggestions of Perrin are connected with his radical theory of christological origins and development, involving a disinclination to ascribe any Son of man sayings to Jesus. Lindeskog's dating of the Q form of the logion is rendered improbable by a correct evaluation of the Semitic background of the Christian terminology. Although it has not seemed necessary to assume an earlier form of Luke 12.9 constructed on the same pattern as verse 8, we may read the passive there as denoting the judgmental function of the Son of man as well as of God.

Among the supporters of an original saying lacking reference to the Son of man are Colpe and Jeremias.[28] Colpe[29] argues for the transformation of a saying behind Matt. 10.32f. into a Son of man saying in the oral transmission. This may have been: 'Every one who acknowledges me before men, him will men (one) acknowledge before. . . ; but he who denies me before men will also be denied before. . .' This closely resembles Perrin's suggestion except that, as we have seen, he postulates an original non-Son of man logion consisting of only the first part, about acknowledging and being acknowledged. According to Colpe, the first 'passive' is to be deduced on the analogy of 'will be denied' (*ἀπαρνηθήσεται*) in Luke 12.9, and the agent of the activity denoted by both verbs is left cryptic and undefined by the use of the 'passives'. The Son of man title was later introduced and replaced the passive verb either in the first part of the saying, as in Luke 12.8, or in the second part, as in Mark 8.38; similarly, the first-person singular pronoun was introduced into both parts in Matt. 10.32f. These formulations are parallel expressions of belief in Jesus as the (Son of man) advocate and accuser in the eschatological judgment. On the basis of Matthew's practice of introducing the Son of man title into traditional sayings rather than removing it where it was already present, Colpe maintains that the earliest form did not have it, rather than that Matthew was inconsistent and removed it.[30] Colpe is here dependent on the hypothesis of Jeremias concerning the relative value of sayings with and sayings without the Son of man.

Jeremias[31] focusses upon Luke 12.8, par. Matt. 10.32 as the outstanding example of his hypothesis that in pairs of sayings it is the forms without Son of man that are to be preferred, and that there is no instance of replacement of Son of man with 'I'. Perhaps Matthew's normal practice is irrelevant here, and the Matthaean and Lukan forms may represent parallel traditions.[32] Probably more relevant is the criticism, as framed by Borsch,[33] that 'Jeremias offers only the inference that, if in other sayings with rival parallels the Son of man is secondary, so it must be here as well.' This does not necessarily follow. Matt. 10.32 may be an exception to the non-replacement of Son of man by 'I'. Each text must still be investigated individually. While we agree with Jeremias' rejection[34] of Bultmann's view[35] that Luke 12.8 is the primary text for the belief that by the Son of man Jesus meant a future saving figure distinct from himself, and that he viewed his own mission as that of the Son of man's forerunner or prophet, this does not necessarily involve its exclusion from words attributable to Jesus; nor does its acceptance mean that two figures are intended, Jesus and the Son of man.[36] The most satisfactory interpretation remains that which assigns priority to Luke 12.8f., understood as an expression of Jesus' functional adaptation of the Son of man concept to describe his future status and judgmental role.

2. *Luke 12.10.* 'And every one who speaks a word against the Son of man will be forgiven; but he who blasphemes against the Holy Spirit will not be forgiven.'

Matt. 12.32. **'And whoever says a word against the Son of man will be forgiven; but whoever speaks against the Holy Spirit will not be forgiven, either in this age or in the age to come.'**
Mark 3.28–9. **'Truly, I say to you, all sins will be forgiven the sons of men, and whatever blasphemies they utter; (29) but whoever blasphemes against the Holy Spirit never has forgiveness, but is guilty of an eternal sin' (par. Matt. 12.31. 'Therefore I tell you, every sin and blasphemy will be forgiven men, but the blasphemy against the Spirit will not be forgiven').**

These texts pose an extremely complex and difficult problem. The Markan contrast between all the sins and blasphemies which will be forgiven the sons of men and the unforgivable blasphemy against the Holy Spirit is reproduced in Matt. 12.31 in an abbreviated form, with 'men' instead of 'sons of men',[37] and in the Markan context of the charge levelled against Jesus of possession by Beelzebul. In the next verse Matthew has incorporated the Q saying (par. Luke 12.10) contrasting speaking against the Son of man with speaking against the Holy Spirit. This serves as the conclusion to Jesus' words in verses 27f. and 30 concerning the expulsion of demons by Beelzebul (par. Luke 11.19f., 23). Matthew's addition in 12.32b, 'either in this age or in the age to come', is adapted from Mark 3.29, 'never (has forgiveness), but is guilty of an eternal sin'. Otherwise Matthew and Luke agree very closely in sense, if not altogether in form and expression.

Matt. 12.32	Luke 12.10
καὶ ὃς ἐὰν εἴπῃ λόγον κατὰ	*καὶ πᾶς ὃς ἐρεῖ λόγον εἰς*
τοῦ υἱοῦ τοῦ ἀνθρώπου,	*τὸν υἱὸν τοῦ ἀνθρώπου,*
ἀφεθήσεται αὐτῷ· ὃς δ᾽ ἂν εἴπῃ	*ἀφεθήσεται αὐτῷ· τῷ δὲ*
κατὰ τοῦ πνεύματος τοῦ ἁγίου,	*εἰς τὸ ἅγιον πνεῦμα*
οὐκ ἀφεθήσεται αὐτῷ.	*βλασφημήσαντι οὐκ ἀφεθήσεται.*

Luke's more 'literary' version results in the loss of the second instance of *casus pendens*, and in the replacement of the second occurrence of the Semitic (Aramaic?) expression 'to say a word against' (*κατά, εἰς*)[38] with the later and more technical church term 'blaspheme', as in Mark 3.29. Luke 12.10 is therefore secondary in form to Matt. 12.32.

More important is the question whether the context as well as the form of Matt. 12.32 is superior to that of Luke 12.10, and perhaps follows the order of Q. As it stands, it appears to be explanatory of the preceding saying: speaking a word against the Son of man is included among, and is singled out as the most serious of, all sins and blasphemies which are forgivable. This connection, however, involving repetition of the substance of verse 31b (par. Mark 3.29) in 32b, is the conflating work of the evangelist. While it has often been argued that Luke 12.10 occupies a less satisfactory and probably secondary position as compared with Matt. 12.32, on the other hand the lack of consistency between Matt. 12.32a and 30 (par. Luke 11.23) suggests that in Q this latter saying may not have been followed by Matt. 12.32. This is certainly true of Luke (11.23; 12.10). Another point is that Matt. 12.28 has 'the Spirit of God' where Luke 11.20 has 'the finger of God'. The latter is doubtless the wording of Q; why should Luke, whose tendency is to emphasize the role of the Spirit,[39] have altered it to 'finger'? It is suggested that Matthew, in his construction of the pericope Matt. 12.22-32 by conflation of Mark and Q, replaced Q's 'the finger of God' with the more familiar 'Spirit of God' so as to produce a closer correspondence with the Spirit in verses 31f., which he had already conflated from Mark and Q respectively. Furthermore, the fact that Matthew's conflations of Mark and Q frequently result in a difference of order[40] may also support the view that the saying under discussion did not occupy in Q the context it has in Matthew.

Does this mean that Luke 12.10 gives the saying in its Q context? The crux is that the statement, that speaking against the Son of man is forgivable, appears to contradict the immediately preceding saying that he who denies Jesus will be denied before the angels of God.[41] The more 'literary' secondary form in Luke, compared with that in Matthew, might mean that its setting could also be secondary.[42]

Lagrange asks directly, What is the meaning of the saying in Luke? His answer is that it fits the context very well if it is supposed that, while those who speak evil of Jesus the Son of man may be forgiven (10a) as outsiders who have not experienced the grace of the Holy Spirit, those (being Christians) who deny him (9) cannot be forgiven because in so doing they blaspheme the Spirit himself (10b).[43] This overlooks the difficulty that Jesus, who is represented as the speaker, refers to himself in the first person in verse 9 but as the Son of man in verse 10a. Verses 8 and 9 constitute a unit; to interpret verse 10 with the help of the preceding saying is always unsatisfactory, although it may conceivably tell us what meaning Luke may have found in verse 10. In any case, it does not demonstrate the superiority of the Lukan setting of the saying to the Matthaean one.

Lövestam says that the sins and blasphemies in Mark 3.28f. include by implication blasphemy against 'God and the divine', and these are all forgivable. By contrast, blasphemy against the Holy Spirit is not forgivable, because the Spirit represents God's salvific activity through Jesus – 'God in action'. The Q counterpart to this is Matt. 12.32, contrasting speaking words against the Son of man and speaking against the Holy Spirit.[44] The placing of this saying in Luke 12.10 is the work of the evangelist. Hostile speech against the Son of man, called denying Jesus in verse 9, was not necessarily regarded as unforgivable. Lövestam explains that this is to be deduced from the fact that Peter, despite his denial of Jesus (Mark 14.72), was not rejected, but is found offering the Jews the opportunity of repentance for rejecting him (Acts 3.17ff.). Luke, it is urged, must have distinguished between this kind of denial and unforgivable final rejection of God's offer of salvation through Jesus; that was the extreme sin of blasphemy against the Holy Spirit himself (Luke 12.10b), and results in denial 'before the angels'. The main objection to this interpretation is that it understands denying Jesus in two different ways.

In a review of Lövestam's study, E. Bammel[45] attempts to show that the Lukan form of the saying, so far from being a secondary variant of Mark 3.28f. is, in fact, the older in both form and context, and even probably renders the original Q text in the Q setting. According to Bammel, the saying must be interpreted in relation to its position in the setting of persecution in Luke 12.2ff., and especially in connection with the promise to the disciples of the help of the Holy Spirit when arraigned before the authorities. Those who blaspheme against the Spirit are not backsliding believers, but the accusers and persecutors who reject the Spirit's witness against themselves. It is these alone who are beyond all hope.[46] This interpretation would perhaps be more plausible if verses 11f. preceded instead of following verse 10.

All these uncertainties render it very difficult to draw a tolerable and satisfactory meaning out of Luke 12.10 in its context. Tödt's conclusion is to be accepted, that the juxtaposition of Luke 12.8f. and 12.10 is secondary and due to the common element 'Son of man'.[47] Attempts to interpret Luke 12.10 in its context can do no more than seek to understand its meaning for Luke. This might seem to strengthen the case for Matthew's having preserved the Q context of the saying, from which it has been dislodged by Luke. Tödt stresses that the reference to the possibility of blasphemy being forgivable belongs to the Beelzebul pericope, and is also evident in Matthew's conflation of the Markan form (Matt. 12.31) with that of Q (Matt. 12.32), despite their different content.[48]

Which is earlier, the Markan or the Q version of the saying? Lövestam,[49] for example, prefers Mark, and can find no reason to question its authenticity as revealing Jesus' consciousness of speaking and acting in the power of the Spirit. More recently, R. A. Edwards[50] has defended Mark's version as the earlier, against Tödt's preference for that of Q on the ground of the distinction Q makes between opposition to Jesus on earth as Son of man and opposition to the Holy Spirit.[51] Edwards explains the Q form as an expansion of the Markan saying involving the change of 'sons of men' to the singular as a designation of Jesus. This 'has the effect of splitting the ministry of Jesus prior to the resurrection from the ministry of Jesus as the expected Son of Man'. Edwards maintains that redaction analysis exposes the Q community's redactional activity in recasting an allusion to 'sons of men' into a saying in which a distinction is drawn between denial, by the Jews, of Jesus in his ministry as a mere misunderstanding of his importance, and denial after the resurrection as a denial of the Spirit himself. A third approach is that the Aramaic *bar nasha*, correctly understood in Mark as generic - 'sons of men', 'men' - was mistaken in Q for the title Son of man.[52]

In an important study, R. Schippers[53] claims that the Markan and the Q forms of the saying both 'have their root in one and the same logion of Jesus', which in its reconstructed original Aramaic wording[54] could mean either 'all that which men blaspheme will be forgiven them' or 'whoever shall blaspheme[55] the Son of man, it will be forgiven him'. According to Schippers, therefore, the real question is not, as is usually assumed, the priority of either the Markan or the Q form, since both are secondary as compared with the Aramaic logion, but which of them more faithfully renders the meaning intended in an Aramaic *Vorlage* from which both are derived. The Markan form reflects a situation in which *bar nasha* could not be taken in the titular sense as Son of man (Jesus on earth), because this had come to denote exclusively the eschatological judge. Consequently, the distinction between the Son of man and the Holy Spirit read out of the logion by Q would have been unintelligible. Schippers claims that Q gave the correct interpretation in so far as *bar nasha* was taken as a true singular and a quasi-title of Jesus. But he rejects the authenticity of the Q version: 'Whoever speaks a word against the Son of man, it will be forgiven him; but whoever speaks against the Holy Spirit, it will not be forgiven him.' This distinction between the Son of man and the Holy Spirit could only have arisen as the result of theological reflection after Easter and as 'a periodising of the history of salvation' (*heilsgeschichtliche Periodisierung*).[56] Schippers maintains that in the original Aramaic *Vorlage* Jesus referred to himself as the *bar nasha*, as 'the man with his mission of God in the world'. Opposition to himself as a man was forgivable; but there would be no forgiveness for those who resisted 'the eschatological act of God' manifesting itself in his Spirit-directed ministry of words and works.

These considerations lead us to the following conclusions. The Q setting of the saying is unknown, for neither the Matthaean nor the Lukan context is wholly satisfactory. In both gospels the narrative settings are the result of redactional work undertaken independently. Attempts to explain the meaning of the Q saying in its contexts can only suggest what it may have meant for the evangelists. Matthew seems to have placed it immediately after his modified and abbreviated version of Mark 3.28f. in Matt. 12.31 because of their general resemblance, particularly in their second parts. Luke was led to place it to follow Luke 12.8f. by the common element 'the Son of man'.

Despite differences of wording, the Q saying has fundamentally the same meaning in Matthew and Luke: speaking against the Son of man is forgivable, but speaking against or blaspheming (Luke) the Holy Spirit is unforgivable. It is difficult to see how this could be an authentic word of Jesus. How could he have contrasted himself as Son of man with the Spirit? On the view that he did not use Son of man as a self-designation in reference to his ministry, it becomes still more difficult to imagine what he could have meant by what would then have been a contrast between the exalted and glorious Son of man in heaven and the Holy Spirit.

Following Schippers and Colpe,[57] we presuppose one primitive Aramaic logion in the pre-Markan and pre-Q tradition. The tradition later bifurcated to form the Markan and Q sayings. It seems insufficient to account for the Q saying as a mere misunderstanding of the Aramaic generic use of *bar nasha* (rightly understood by Mark). Schippers claims that the Q version is preferable; it gives 'the right interpretation' of an utterance in which Jesus referred to himself as *bar nasha*, 'son of man', in a non-eschatological sense as God's emissary to the world. He assesses the Q form of the saying as the product of post-resurrection theological reflection by the community. But, against Schippers and with Colpe, we hold that the Q form has departed from the meaning of the underlying Aramaic logion which is more faithfully preserved in Mark 3.28f. Moreover, so far from being a misunderstanding of the Aramaic (Jeremias), the Q version is the result of a deliberate christologizing of the primitive logion, involving the replacement of the collective meaning of *bar nasha* by a singular titular meaning, 'the Son of man'. Irrespective of its different contexts in Matthew and Luke, the Q version means that the sin of outsiders in speaking against Jesus the Son of man proclaimed by the church will be forgiven (if they repent and receive baptism as believers?), but that hostile speech or blasphemy against the Holy Spirit, which is turning against and apostasy from the truth as it is in Jesus the Son of man, is unforgivable.

If Schippers' view that the Q version is the right interpretation of a saying of Jesus is rejected, what of the Markan version? We have seen that

Lövestam attributes it to Jesus. But would Jesus have emphasized a distinction between the extreme seriousness of one particular sin in contrast with all others?[58] It is more probably the language of the church, perhaps equating blasphemy against the Spirit with apostasy. The upshot is that if Q's version is in fact a christological transformation of the common Aramaic *Vorlage* more accurately mirrored in Mark's Greek, we must in this instance concede the superiority of a saying without Son of man to its rival containing the title. But this is not to accept it as a saying of Jesus; it is more likely to have originated as an oracle of a Christian prophet.[59]

3. *Luke 11.29-30.* 'This generation is an evil generation; it seeks a sign, but no sign shall be given to it except the sign of Jonah. (30) For as Jonah became a sign to the men of Nineveh, so will the Son of man be to this generation.'
***Matt. 12.39-40.* 'An evil and adulterous generation seeks for a sign; but no sign shall be given to it except the sign of the prophet Jonah. (40) For as Jonah was three days and three nights in the belly of the whale, so will the Son of man be three days and three nights in the heart of the earth.'**
***Mark 8.12.* 'Why does this generation seek a sign? Truly, I say to you, no sign shall be given to this generation' (par. Matt. 16.4. 'An evil and adulterous generation seeks for a sign, but no sign shall be given to it except the sign of Jonah').**[60]

Colpe[61] describes the explanation of the sign of Jonah in Luke 11.30 as the most important of several newly constructed Son of man sayings, and he reconstructs the original form of the refusal of the request for a sign on the basis of Mark 8.12 and Matt. 12.39 par. (as far as *δοθήσεται αὐτῇ*) as having been:

> 'How this generation seeks a sign! Truly, I say to you, no sign will be given this generation. The sign of Jonah will definitely be given to it.'[62]

εἰ μὴ τὸ σημεῖον 'Ιωνᾶ is taken as the remnant of a Semitic negative asseveration which, when complete, would have included the words *δοθήσεται αὐτῇ*, 'certainly the sign of Jonah is what will be given to it'. This reconstruction is probably correct, but it does not affect the basic meaning, which is that the sign of Jonah is what this generation will receive, and no other. Colpe adds: 'In [this] enigmatic saying Jesus was threatening a divine attestation of his person which would press the unbelieving demand for validation to its logical extreme and thus show how perverted it was.' The explanation of what this attestation would be (Luke 11.30) comes from the early community, and expands Jesus' saying into a complete analogy: 'the parousia of the risen Jesus will be the granting of the sign of Messianic accreditation' to the unbelieving generation for which repentance will then be too late, because Jesus will have come as judge. In short, Colpe rejects as unauthentic the reference to the Son of man as a sign, and regards it as an early interpretative expansion of a dominical saying.

Colpe's reconstruction of the original Aramaic behind Luke 11.29, par. Matt. 12.39; Mark 8.12 is accepted by Perrin,[63] who accordingly dismisses Mark 8.12 in its present form as an incomplete derivation from the authentic Q version.[64] While conceding the possibility that the interpretation in terms of the Son of man may have been supplied by Jesus, he prefers to assign it to the early community. It may be noted that it is more accurate to speak of the *interpretations* in Matt. 12.40 and Luke 11.30. Although agreeing with Perrin's characterization of the former as a later ecclesiastical interpretation of the sign of Jonah, we see it as also the earliest attempt to explain the Q saying at Luke 11.30. Perrin's exclusion of this also from Jesus' teaching[65] depends on his argument that its implication that the Son of man will become a sign in his coming in judgment is a concept connected with the developing exegetical tradition, and on his rejection of the hypothesis, supported by Tödt and others who accept the saying, of a pre-Christian Jewish Son of man belief.

In his listing of parallel traditions of sayings with and without Son of man, Jeremias regards Luke 11.29f., par. Matt. 12.39f. as expansions of the earlier form without the title in Mark 8.12;[66] in the oldest tradition, Jesus' refusal of a sign was absolute. As reconstructed by Colpe, however, the rejection was qualified by 'except the sign of Jonah'.[67] If this alternative is preferred, involving the assessment of Mark 8.12 as an incomplete derivation from the Q form, we may have before us a further weakening of Jeremias' thesis that non-Son of man sayings are more primitive than their counterparts with the title. If Colpe's reconstruction of the earliest recoverable form of the saying is accepted, and the reasonable assumption is adopted that Jesus referred to the sign of Jonah, as in Q, we may proceed to the problem whether he himself also compared the Son of man and Jonah as signs to their generations.

Is Matt. 12.40 or Luke 11.30 the earlier? Surely the latter is to be preferred.[68] The undefined nature of the comparison of Jonah and the Son of man as signs in Luke has greater claim to priority than Matthew's precise explanation.[69] K. Stendahl has adduced a cogent argument for the priority of Luke.[70] Justin Martyr, *Trypho* 107, omits Matt. 12.40 despite the fact that he uses the preceding verse in order to establish that Jesus was to rise from the dead on the third day. Stendahl concludes that Justin could not have read verse 40 in the gospel of Matthew he knew,[71] and that it is an early post-Matthaean exegetical intrusion into the text, elucidating how Jesus was a sign. Support is claimed from the purely Septuagintal form of Matthew's quotation from Jonah 2.1: *ἦν Ἰωνᾶς ἐν τῇ κοιλίᾳ τοῦ κήτους τρεῖς ἡμέρας καὶ τρεῖς νύκτας*. To the evangelist himself, however, as the redactional addition of *τοῦ προφήτου* shows, the sign of Jonah was Jesus' preaching: '. . . the sign of Jonah the prophet . . . they repented at the preaching of Jonah'. Without verse 40 the connection between verses 39 and 41 is perfectly clear. If Stendahl's suggestion is correct, it would obviously rule out Matt. 12.40 completely as a rival to Luke 11.30.[72] But in any case Matthew's version is clearly secondary and inferior and of no particular relevance to the present enquiry, and we need only concern ourselves with Luke's version as substantially the Q form of the saying.

(i) R. A. Edwards, The Sign of Jonah

A pupil of Perrin, Edwards adopts his view that the Son of man christology originated in the *pesher* tradition of the primitive community and, using the methods of form and redaction criticism, he claims to be able to offer the first comprehensive answer to the question, What was the sign of Jonah? He claims that it is his isolation of the 'eschatological correlative' which has brought this about;[73] sayings of this form were created in order to express an already existing expectation of the coming Son of man which originated in the *pesher* tradition. The first chapter is a historical survey of 'sign of Jonah' study by the methods of source criticism, word study and Jewish background, form criticism, and redaction criticism. The deficiencies of all these are indicated, and the way is prepared for a fresh approach. The second chapter is indispensable prolegomena to the main thesis in the third chapter; it surveys the application of redaction criticism to the theology of the synoptic evangelists and discusses the Q material and the theology of the community which put it together, in order to present the sign of Jonah in its proper Q context. A crucial point is the divergence of Edwards from Tödt's redaction critical treatment of the Son of man sayings. The reason for this is his rejection of Tödt's prior assumption that the future Son of man sayings are authentic, an assumption that Edwards claims arises from failure to maintain full use of the redaction critical method.[74] With the reminder that Tödt's assumption has been challenged by Vielhauer and Perrin, Edwards proceeds to the 'eschatological correlative', a hitherto overlooked form shared by four out of the six future Son of man sayings in Q.[75] His investigation warrants careful attention, especially in view of a rather different interpretation of the conceptual relationship of the sayings in question to be proposed later on.

The eschatological correlative is a special variety of the common Koiné Greek correlative construction (as . . . so),[76] and follows the pattern:[77]

> 'Protasis: *καθὼς* (*ὥσπερ*, *ὡς*) – verb in past or present tense
> Apodosis: *οὕτως* (*κατὰ τὰ αὐτὰ*) – *ἔσται* – *ὁ υἱὸς τοῦ ἀνθρώπου*.'

The occurrences are:

1 Luke 11.30

For as Jonah became a sign to the men of Nineveh, so will the Son of man be to this generation.

καθὼς γὰρ ἐγένετο ὁ Ἰωνᾶς τοῖς Νινευείταις σημεῖον, οὕτως ἔσται καὶ ὁ υἱὸς τοῦ ἀνθρώπου τῇ γενεᾷ ταύτῃ.

2 Matt. 12.40

For as Jonah was three days and three nights in the belly of the whale, so will the Son of man be three days and three nights in the heart of the earth.

ὥσπερ γὰρ ἦν Ἰωνᾶς ἐν τῇ κοιλίᾳ τοῦ κήτους τρεῖς ἡμέρας καὶ τρεῖς νύκτας, οὕτως ἔσται ὁ υἱὸς τοῦ ἀνθρώπου ἐν τῇ καρδίᾳ τῆς γῆς τρεῖς ἡμέρας καὶ τρεῖς νύκτας.

3 Luke 17.24

For as the lightning flashes and lights up the sky from one side to the other, so will the Son of man be in his day.

ὥσπερ γὰρ ἡ ἀστραπὴ ἀστράπτουσα ἐκ τῆς ὑπὸ τὸν οὐρανὸν εἰς τὴν ὑπ᾽οὐρανὸν λάμπει, οὕτως ἔσται ὁ υἱὸς τοῦ ἀνθρώπου ἐν τῇ ἡμέρᾳ αὐτοῦ.

Matt. 24.27

For as the lightning comes from the east and shines as far as the west, so will be the coming of the Son of man.

ὥσπερ γὰρ ἡ ἀστραπὴ ἐξέρχεται ἀπὸ ἀνατολῶν καὶ φαίνεται ἕως δυσμῶν, οὕτως ἔσται ἡ παρουσία τοῦ υἱοῦ τοῦ ἀνθρώπου.

4 Luke 17.26

As it was in the days of Noah, so will it be in the days of the Son of man.

καὶ καθὼς ἐγένετο ἐν ταῖς ἡμέραις Νωε, οὕτως ἔσται καὶ ἐν ταῖς ἡμέραις τοῦ υἱοῦ τοῦ ἀνθρώπου.

Matt. 24.37

As were the days of Noah, so will be the coming of the Son of man.

ὥσπερ γὰρ αἱ ἡμέραι τοῦ Νωε, οὕτως ἔσται ἡ παρουσία τοῦ υἱοῦ τοῦ ἀνθρώπου.

5 Luke 17.28a, 30
Likewise as it was in the days of Lot . . .
so will it be on the day when the Son of man is revealed.
ὁμοίως καθὼς ἐγένετο ἐν ταῖς ἡμέραις Λωτ . . .
κατὰ τὰ αὐτὰ ἔσται ᾗ ἡμέρᾳ ὁ υἱὸς τοῦ ἀνθρώπου ἀποκαλύπτεται.

6 Matt. 24.38f.
For as in those days before the flood . . .
so will be the coming of the Son of man.
ὡς γὰρ ἦσαν ἐν ταῖς ἡμέραις ἐκείναις ταῖς πρὸ τοῦ κατακλυσμοῦ . . .
οὕτως ἔσται καὶ ἡ παρουσία τοῦ υἱοῦ τοῦ ἀνθρώπου.

In these columns the total number of eschatological correlatives is not four, as Edwards reckons them, but six. This is, firstly, because Matt. 12.40 is no mere variant version of Luke 11.30, but a different, secondary interpretation of the sign of Jonah in Q, and at the same time an interpretation of the Q saying at Luke 11.30 which it has replaced; and secondly because Matt. 24.38f. is not another version of Luke 17.28a, 30, but a substitute for it. Matthew may have known the Lot pericope, now only extant in Luke, and replaced it with this second, longer explanatory eschatological correlative about the days of Noah.

Edwards concludes his list of future Son of man sayings in Q with Luke 12.39f., par. Matt. 24.43f. and Luke 12.8, par. Matt. 10.32. Of these two pairs of sayings the latter is the more important. Edwards calls attention to it as an example of the form 'sentence of holy law' investigated by Käsemann,[78] and (in its Lukan form) as one of the two future Son of man sayings in Q which are not eschatological correlatives.[79] These two forms, the eschatological correlative and the sentence of holy law, Edwards shows to be closely related in the usage of the primitive church. To the second category Perrin assigns the rather appropriate name 'judgment sayings' or 'eschatological judgment pronouncements'.[80] Käsemann presents a case for the existence in the early community of a tradition of judgmental pronouncements rooted in Christian prophecy and with their setting in the eucharist. They consist of two parts, with the same verb in each, referring first to human activity and then to God's eschatological activity, e.g. 'Anyone who destroys God's temple will himself be destroyed by God', 1 Cor. 3.17.[81] There are clear resemblances between the two forms; they both have to do with eschatological judgment. 'The judgmental activity of the early church was expressed in this form [sentences of holy law] and promised as the future work of God.'[82] The eschatological correlatives in Q warn of the coming of the Son of man with the same judgment that overtook the contemporaries of Noah and Lot. Since the advent of the Son of man is proclaimed because of the judgment that his coming involves, Edwards suggests that the eucharist, the setting of the sentence of holy law according to Käsemann, is also the probable setting of the eschatological correlative. Both the sentence of holy law and the eschatological correlatives are aspects of the church's judgmental activity.

However, there is also a not inconsiderable difference between them. Edwards[83] maintains that the eschatological correlative is a judgment form *created by the Q community* to express its understanding of the coming Son of man, and so is *part of the Son of man tradition*. By contrast, the 'sentences' are 'rather far removed from the Son of Man tradition': only two of them, Luke 12.8 and Mark 8.38, contain the title. Edwards explains that this is because the Q community introduced the Son of man into the already established eschatological judgment pronouncement tradition, but on a comparatively slight scale.

The consequences of this approach are self-evident: neither the eschatological correlatives with Son of man in Q nor its sole 'sentence of holy law' with Son of man (Luke 12.8) can be dominical sayings.[84] Perrin insists that Luke 12.8, like other sentences of holy law, must be attributed to early Christian prophecy. 'The minor role it plays within the form itself makes it extremely difficult to accept it as the fountainhead, not only of all eschatological judgment pronouncements, but also of the total use of Son of man in the synoptic tradition.'[85] But as we shall see, it does not necessarily follow that the last word has been said on the ultimate origin of either of these two categories of sayings.

We have followed a diversion necessitated by an attempt to trace out the main features of Edwards' thesis, and we now find ourselves at his third chapter, in which he undertakes the investigation of that to which most of what precedes is prolegomena – 'The History of the Tradition of the Sign of Jonah'.

The principle upon which Edwards proceeds is that the application of redaction criticism, as a supplement to form criticism, shows that the varying forms of the sign of Jonah material are the result of conscious modification of the tradition.

The outright refusal of a sign in Mark 8.12 also lies behind the Q form. The Markan version is Semitic and early Palestinian.[86] What is common to Mark and Q points to the older form underlying both. From this point Edwards differs from Perrin and Colpe; he holds the Markan version to be the older, and the excepting clause ('except the sign of Jonah') in Q to be an insertion by the Q community.[87] We believe this to be the wrong decision and a serious weakening of the argument based upon it. Edwards asks, 'Why is there a reference to a Sign of Jonah [in Q] rather than a simple refusal [as in Mark] ?'[88] The answer we prefer is that in its earliest recoverable Semitic form the saying refused the kind of sign requested, but promised instead the certainty of the sign of Jonah.[89] The reasoning Edwards offers for his decision is less simple.[90] Two preliminary points may be noted. Firstly, he takes the Q pericope as a whole: request for a sign (Luke 11.16; Matt. 12.38), refusal, exception, and explanation of the exception, the common theme being judgment upon this generation. Secondly, his decision that the explanation of the sign both in Matt. 12.40 and in Luke 11.30 comes not from Jesus but from the early community is the only possible one once the reference to the sign of Jonah has itself already been attributed to the community.

It is widely held that the double saying about the Queen of the South and the Ninevites was originally independent, but had already become attached to the sign pericope in Q. Edwards says both parallel sayings express the Q community's judgment on non-Christian, probably Jewish contemporaries. The units were thus 'combined by the Q community on the basis of its anti-Jewish polemic with a strong emphasis on judgment'. Although Jesus refused a sign to the Pharisees, his resurrection as Son of man was interpreted by the Q community as itself a sign. Jesus did in fact give a sign: 'his assumption is a sign because it has led to the christological cognition which is the foundation of the life of the Q community'.[91] How was this to be stated? Edwards' reply is that to the Q community the Jesus who taught on earth is the coming judge, and so his teaching of the way of salvation 'that will bring [men] through the judgment' must be continued in the community's preaching. The double saying was taken to refer to the sign of Jonah, i.e. 'Jonah is extolled as the great and effective preacher' (Luke 11.32, par. Matt. 12.41) and, in his being delivered from death, as the *vindicated* preacher. Hence the Q community's addition of 'except the sign of Jonah' to the earlier form of the saying is bound up with its christological ideas, and is 'a clarification of the enigmatic conclusion to the Ninevite comparison in the double saying: "A greater thing than Jonah is here." The limited greatness of Jonah is his preaching, therefore the absolute greatness of Jesus must be stated.'[92]

Edwards, I think rightly, says that the original wording of Q's comparison of Jonah and the Son of man as signs may have closely resembled Luke 11.30.

> By combining the words 'sign' and 'Jonah', and by placing the exception clause and the explanation between the refusal of the sign and the double saying, the Q community has created a statement affirming a sign.

The complications of this correlative compared with those in Luke 17 (Matt. 24) are, says Edwards, the result of combining the correlation of Jonah's days with those of the coming Son of man and the correlation of *the sign* of Jonah with the Son of man.[93] Thus the eschatological correlative form was adapted by the community to serve a new purpose: to stress the significance of the resurrection of Jesus as the Son of man, the coming judge, both for the church and for those who fail to respond to the church's continuation of the preaching of the message of Jesus, the preacher vindicated by his resurrection. To Edwards there is no problem about the total absence of any pre-Christian reference to 'the sign of Jonah', for the simple reason that it did not exist prior to its creation by the Q community out of the 'fortuitous juxtaposition'[94] of the saying refusing a *sign* and the double saying about the Queen of the South, and the Ninevites and *Jonah*. He goes on to claim that the isolation of the eschatological correlative as the creation of the Q community, its development within Q, and its reflection of the theology of Q, support the claim already advanced, that the Son of man tradition itself also originated in the Q community.[95] We shall now enquire into the bearing of this contention, that the Q community is the source of the Son of man tradition, upon Perrin's thesis, accepted by Edwards, that this tradition is based upon the *pesher* interpretation of an early *Mar* (Lord) christology.

Perrin divides the future 'apocalyptic' Son of man sayings into three groups:[96]

(a) sayings reflecting Dan. 7.13: Mark 13.26; 14.62.
(b) judgment sayings: Luke 12.8f. (par. Matt. 10.32f.); Mark 8.38.
(c) comparison sayings: Luke 17.24 par.; 17.26f. par.; 11.30, par. Matt. 12.40.

We are only concerned here with group (a). According to Perrin, the beginning of the process is the interpretation of the resurrection of Jesus in terms of Ps. 110.1, producing the *Mar* christology (cf. *marana tha*, 1 Cor. 16.22) and the idea of the session at God's right hand. Then, on the basis of Dan. 7.13, Jesus' resurrection was further interpreted as ascension to God as Son of man. Another exegetical tradition, based on Zech. 12.10ff., was responsible for the transference of the allusion to 'seeing' from the crucifixion to the parousia idea (Rev. 1.7) also discerned in Dan. 7.13. There are thus three exegetical tradition utilizing Dan. 7.13: the ascension tradition developed from the use of Ps. 110.1 (Mark 14.62; Acts 7.56); the passion apologetic tradition using Zech. 12.10ff. (Matt. 24.30; John 19.37; Rev. 1.7); the parousia tradition (Mark 13.26). All these traditions are earlier than any New Testament texts, which reflect 'remnants and reminiscences' of them.[97]

What, then, is the connection between Perrin's thesis, accepted by Edwards, of the origination of the Son of man tradition in *pesher* interpretations of Ps. 110.1 and Dan. 7.13 on the one hand and, on the other, the concern of Edwards to show that this tradition arose within the Q community? The second of the following quotations shows that the answer is that Edwards traces the genesis of the Son of man tradition to the Q community by narrowing down the origin of the *pesher* interpretation of an earlier *Mar* christology to that community.

> The eschatological correlative . . . is part of the future Son of Man tradition . . . The eschatological correlative was created by the Q community to express its particular theological understanding of the Son of Man who is to come.[98]

> . . . the Son of Man tradition does *originate* [his italics] in the Q community and is based upon the *pesher* interpretation of a very early *Mar* christology.[99]

One may wonder whether the evidence justifies the attribution of so much creativity, including the invention of the eschatological correlative, to the Q community, and whether there may be a simpler solution. Why, for instance, if the Son of man tradition sprang from interpretation of Dan. 7.13, is there nothing in Q as specific as Mark 14.62? Edwards discusses neither this text nor Mark 13.26.

In the article 'Son of Man' previously cited, Perrin presents in summary form the thesis of *Rediscovering the Teaching of Jesus*, and clarifies his position in certain respects. The issue between himself and Tödt, Fuller and others is whether the New Testament use of the apocalyptic Son of man title begins with a 'general' proclamation of his 'coming' (e.g. Luke 12.8f.) and later, by the use of Old Testament texts, develops into sayings like Mark 14.62 and 13.26, or whether the process is the reverse of this, so that the proclamation is couched increasingly in general terms.[100] Perrin is prevented from upholding the former alternative by his presupposition of the non-existence in Judaism of a concept of a Son of man who could be the subject of any proclamation whatever. Future Son of man sayings, which seem to some other scholars to be among those with the strongest claim to authenticity, are to Perrin mere derivatives from the 'end product', in Mark 14.62, of *pesher* interpretation;[101] in them the allusions tend to drop out, and the future expectation of the Son of man is framed more and more in general terms.

Perrin accepts Edwards' isolation of the eschatological correlative (= 'comparison saying'),[102] and agrees that it was created to give content to a previously existing Son of man expectation. 'But since', Perrin reasons, 'the expectation must necessarily exist prior to a form created to give content to it, the origin of the Son of man expectation in the New Testament cannot lie in one of these sayings';[103] it lies in *pesher* interpretation, of which Mark 14.62 is the 'end product'. In reply, it may be suggested that if it is not established that the eschatological correlative was created by the early church, or by the Q community in particular, then the connection between some of the sayings of this type and the source of the Son of man belief may be very close indeed. It may be noted further that Perrin, although accepting Edwards' tracing of the origination of the eschatological correlative to the Q community, says nothing about the Son of man expectation itself having arisen there. Nor does he claim, therefore, as Edwards does, that *pesher* interpretation of an earlier Lord christology, leading to the Son of man expectation, was produced in the Q community. There is in fact insufficient evidence for any of the three hypotheses put forward by Edwards in regard to the creative activity of the Q community, in initiating the eschatological correlative form, in introducing the Son of man *pesher* interpretation of scripture and, thereby, in originating the Son of man tradition itself.

Comparison of Perrin and Edwards in the exegesis of 'except the sign of Jonah' in Luke 11.29b par. is instructive.

To Perrin this is 'certainly authentic'.[104] To Edwards, as we have seen, it is a creation of the Q community.

Edwards has something to say about the absence in pre-Christian Judaism of any mention of the sign of Jonah.[105] On his premise the explanation is simple: the expression is the creation of the Q community out of the data 'sign' twice in Luke 11.29a par. and 'Jonah' in the originally independent saying about the Ninevites. Perrin does not discuss this question. But if acceptance of the saying as dominical has more in its favour than its attribution to the Q community, the explanation will be that 'the sign of Jonah' was a *novum* – first occurring in Jesus' teaching, and so an element of it to which the application of the criterion of dissimilarity is appropriate.

Finally, the meaning. Edwards thinks that 'the sign of Jonah' meant to the Q community which created it that Jesus was himself a sign, the vindicated preacher delivered from death – a greater than Jonah, the preacher to the Ninevites. Perrin, taking the saying in the positive sense, in accordance with Aramaic idiom, as 'the sign of Jonah will be given to this generation', considers that we do not know what it means, but offers two suggestions.[106] Either the reference may be to some future event which will vindicate Jesus' ministry, on the analogy of Jonah's deliverance, or preferably, 'the sign of Jonah' and 'the preaching of Jonah' may be taken together; the second explains the first and, while independent of one another, they are both dominical. The sign of Jonah is a reference to Jesus' preaching which, in some unexplained way, will be proved to have been effective to this generation.

Edwards' book, *The Sign of Jonah*, is a significant contribution to redaction critical study of the gospels. He has shown that this method should be concerned with the creative use and development of older traditions not only by the evangelists, but also by the early communities. It should be remembered, however, that communities do not themselves create so much as adopt and gradually adapt the work of creative individuals. Edwards does not consider the possible authenticity of the 'sign of Jonah' saying. But if there are good reasons why it may be from Jesus rather than from the community, then the possibility that its explanation in Luke 11.30 is dominical is at least open to discussion, and should not be excluded from the outset, as if the redaction critical method held the key to all exegetical problems. It may be suggested that in the present instance redaction criticism is misused. Edwards' conclusion that 'except the sign of Jonah' is an interpolation by the early community is excluded by the virtual certainty, as Colpe has shown,[107] that behind the Greek text (*εἰ μὴ τὸ σημεῖον Ἰωνᾶ*) lies the Semitic idiom of negative asseveration, which does not mean what it seems to mean ('except...'), but is equivalent to an affirmation, 'certainly the sign of Jonah (is what) will be given to it' (*δοθήσεται αὐτῇ*). If we have here in all probability a dominical saying, what of Luke 11.30? The question is open whether the sign of Jonah tradition went through such a complex process of development as is traced by Edwards, and whether a simpler solution, for instance, that Luke 11.30 may represent substantially not only the Q form of the saying, but Jesus' own explanation of 'the sign of Jonah', may be not undeserving of serious consideration.

(ii) The eschatological correlative and the teaching of Jesus[108]

Edwards has established the existence of the eschatological correlative as a form almost confined to Q. This limitation, we believe, may be connected primarily with the nature of Q as a sayings source. The identification of this form as a usage of the Q community does not exclude the possibility that it may owe something to Jesus' usage; it may even have originated as a feature of his teaching. The first appearance in Q of the eschatological correlative proves neither that it was first *used* nor that it was *created* by the Q community. Edwards finds four instances of it in Q, but more accurately there are four in Q and additionally two secondary and redactional ones in Matt. 12.40 and 24.38f.[109] Luke also shows clear signs of redactional alteration of older forms of Son of man sayings - in 17.26, where 'the days of the Son of man' probably replaces an original 'day of the Son of man', and in the rearrangement of 17.28-30 and in the apocalyptic colouring of verse 30. In the investigation of the Son of man sayings in Luke 17 in chapter III it was claimed that, except for verse 22, they could go back in substance to Jesus. Perhaps this possibility is increased in the light of the eschatological correlative.

The strong claims of Luke 11.29 to authenticity have been noted. We now turn to the twin sayings following Luke 11.30 and par. Matt. 12.40. These Q sayings are presented by both evangelists in almost identical language but in a different order - Luke 11.31f.: the Queen of the South; the Ninevites; Matt. 12.41f.: the Ninevites; the Queen of the South. If it was the mention of the Ninevites[110] (as well as of Jonah) that suggested the association of these sayings, commonly thought to have been originally independent of their present Q context, with the preceding saying, one would expect the application to be to Luke 11.30, which also mentions them, rather than to Matt. 12. 40, which does not, and to follow it immediately. It is therefore possible that Matthew may preserve the Q order of the two sayings before the replacement of the Q saying about Jonah and the Son of man as signs (Luke 11.30) by what is now Matt. 12.40 broke the connection. Luke could then be presumed to have changed this order so as to round off the whole pericope Luke 11. 29-32, as it began, with the double mention of Jonah. Against this is the fact that the order of the double sayings in Q (as presumed from Matthew) would not be chronological as it is in Luke, and that it would be difficult to understand Matthew's retention of the saying about the Queen of the South as a mere pendant to that about the Ninevites. We therefore conclude that Luke retains the Q order and that Matthew's text reverses it; perhaps this change was made in order to bring the saying about the Ninevites to follow the Q saying (Luke 11.30) before its later replacement in the text by Matt. 12.40. The twin sayings themselves contain features which may point to a dominical origin.

(1) The type of comparison is closely paralleled in the Matthaean source.

Q	Matthew
Luke 11.31f., par. Matt. 12.41f.: two instances from Israelite history are cited in parallel form, and are contrasted with the present situation - 'and behold, something greater than Solomon is here';	12.3-6: two instances, one from Israelite history, the other from cultic practice as laid down in the Torah, are cited (in interrogative form) and contrasted with the present situation - 'I tell you,

'and behold, something greater than Jonah is here' (*καὶ ἰδοὺ πλεῖον Σολομῶνος ὧδε – καὶ ἰδοὺ πλεῖον Ἰωνᾶ ὧδε*).	something greater than the temple is here' (*λέγω δὲ ὑμῖν ὅτι τοῦ ἱεροῦ μεῖζόν ἐστιν ὧδε*).

πλεῖον in Q and *μεῖζον* in Matthew are translation variants of the same Aramaic *rab min.* In both passages the neuter indicates that it is not Jesus alone as an individual but as the embodiment of the power or activity of God whose agent he is, who far surpasses all that is meant by 'the temple', the wisdom of Solomon, and the preaching of Jonah.

(2) The double sayings framed in identical form are paralleled elsewhere in Jesus' teaching: Luke 12.49f.; 13.2-5; 10.13-15, par. Matt. 11.21-4. The Matthaean version of the woes on the cities of Galilee is to be preferred to Luke's shorter form because it preserves the strophic parallelism throughout. The doubling occurs both in the contrasted pairs of cities, Chorazin and Bethsaida, Tyre and Sidon, and in the apostrophe to Capernaum contrasted with Sodom, corresponding to the woes on the other two cities.

(3) The double sayings share with Luke 10.13-15 par. and 13.2-5 the theme of repentance and judgment; they resemble much of Jesus' parabolic teaching in the warnings they issue; and the choice of Gentiles like the Queen of the South, and of the men of Nineveh as an example of the proper response to the summons to repentance, recalls Jesus' unpopular references to Samaritans.

On these grounds there appears to be no particular obstacle to the acceptance of Luke 11.31f. as dominical. The meaning will be that the appearance of the Queen of the South and the Ninevites in the heavenly court of judgment will justify Jesus' ministry. Like them, this generation should have responded to the challenge offered, a challenge of much more decisive import than the wisdom of Solomon or the preaching of Jonah.

Luke 11.30, then, is both preceded and followed by sayings with sound claims to be dominical. That in itself, if not creating a presumption in favour of its authenticity, can hardly be regarded as inimical to it. The usual critical view of Luke 11.31f., that they were originally independent of their present context after verse 30, and were attached to it because of the mention of Jonah (and the Ninevites?) in verse 32, is not necessarily correct. Taken together, verses 30-2 contain a sequence of thought too closely knit to be explained satisfactorily on any other view than that they belong together.[111]

The meaning of Luke 11.30 is that it is as the eschatological judge that the Son of man will himself be a sign to this generation, and it explains the meaning of 'the sign of Jonah' immediately before.[112] The essential significance of the sign of Jonah will be repeated in the case of the Son of man and judgment. Jonah was a sign to the Ninevites in that, as a prophet, he proclaimed impending judgment and summoned them to repentance. His preaching was vindicated as successful by their response. Jesus also called for repentance in view of the coming judgment and reign of God. But his message was not obeyed by the evil generation to which it was addressed. Since Luke 11.30 is in the form of an *eschatological* correlative construction, there cannot be a completely exact and precise comparison between Jonah and the Son of man as signs. The meaning is not that Jesus, like Jonah, was a sign in his preaching or that his preaching was itself a sign.[113] Rather, Jesus is represented as claiming that his activity among the men of his time (ὧδε) is a greater phenomenon (πλεῖον) than either the wisdom of Solomon or the preaching of Jonah, because it is God's activity, the kingdom of God in action. How the Son of man will become (ἔσται) a sign to this generation need not remain a matter of mere conjecture, as it must if verses 31f. are not taken into consideration as an integral part of the whole pericope Luke 11.29-32. The two parallel sayings in verses 31f. are the key to the understanding of verse 30. Features noted below strengthen still further the case for their authenticity.

The asyndeta at the beginning of both these sayings must have existed in Q because, whichever their original order in Q (probably that of Luke), they are retained in both gospels.

Luke: . . . τῇ γενεᾷ ταύτῃ. βασίλισσα νότου . . . ἄνδρες Νινευεῖται.
Matthew: . . . τρεῖς νύκτας. ἄνδρες Νινευεῖται . . . βασίλισσα νότου.

This absence of any editorial link reflects the antiquity of the close association in Q of verses 31f. with verse 30.

The situation is very similar in Luke 17.26f.,[114] and in 28a, 30, 28b, 29 (the original Q order); both the eschatological correlatives also (as we have now learned to call them) are followed, precisely like Luke 11.30 and Matt. 12.40, by a parallel explanatory passage added without conjunction.[115]

Luke 17.26f.: 'so will it be in the days of the Son of man'; ἤσθιον, ἔπινον, κ.τ.λ.
Luke 17.30: 'so will it be on the day when the Son of man is revealed'; 28b: ἤσθιον, ἔπινον, κ.τ.λ.

Just as the parallel illustration about Lot is seen not to be secondary once the redactional work of the evangelist is recognized as responsible for the different order as compared with verses 26f., so neither is the reference to the Queen of the South as inferior in relevance to the context as it may at first appear. Jesus and his ministry are a far greater phenomenon (πλεῖον) than Solomon's wisdom, because the wisdom of God himself is active in him (cf. 1 En. 49.3; 1 Cor. 1.24, 30).

The scene of Luke 11.31f. is the court of judgment. The Queen of the South and the Ninevites will rise up in the judgment, will appear in court[116] along with this generation, and take the witness stand to testify against it. And well qualified they will be to do so. The Queen of the South set out on a long journey solely in order to hear for herself the famed wisdom of Solomon; the Ninevites obeyed Jonah's summons to repentance. Both the Queen and the Ninevites, in their different circumstances, responded to what was available to them. Jesus' contemporaries, 'this generation', on the contrary, in failing to respond to his challenge, rejected a far greater phenomenon than the wisdom of Solomon and the preaching of Jonah. From condemnation for a rejection of this order escape is impossible without repentance *now*.

As already noted, Jonah and the Son of man cannot both be called signs in exactly the same sense. The past tense (ἐγένετο) of Jonah and the future tense (ἔσται) of the Son of man indicate that while Jonah the prophet *was* a sign to his Gentile contemporaries during his own lifetime, the Son of man *will only be recognized* as a sign by Jesus' contemporaries when they find themselves confronted by him exercising judicial functions associated with the Son of man, the judge at the end-time, in the heavenly court. Moreover, Jonah in his preaching of judgment was *a* sign to the Ninevites (Luke 11.30a), and so the judgment he foretold can be called 'the sign of Jonah' (verse 29); the Son of man will also be *a* sign for Jesus' contemporaries - as the eschatological judge in the heavenly court, when it will be too late for repentance. When thus applied to the Son of man 'the sign of Jonah' assumes a much more profound significance. The judgment, 'the sign of Jonah', of which both Jonah and Jesus warned their contemporaries, is visualized as imminent. Since the Son of man is the eschatological judge, he will be not only *a* sign to Jesus' contemporaries, as Jonah was to the Ninevites in his preaching of judgment, but *the* sign, 'the sign of Jonah'. The judgment which was the burden of the preaching of Jonah, and of which Jesus also warned his generation, is to be fulfilled, actualized and, so to speak, embodied in the juridical Son of man figure; otherwise expressed, the Son of man is the personification of God's judgment. His verdicts will be the authentication and validation of the preaching of Jesus. It will be as in Luke 12.8f.

> Every one who acknowledges me before men,
> the Son of man will acknowledge before the angels of God;
> but he who denies me before men
> will be denied before the angels of God.

Summary

Jonah was *a* sign as a preacher of judgment.
The Son of man will be *a* sign as the eschatological judge.
The sign of Jonah is

(1) judgment (a) proclaimed by Jonah and Jesus, and
(b) to be actualized and fulfilled in the final judgment court;

(2) the Son of man himself as judge in that court, as the embodiment or personification of divine judgment proclaimed by Jesus to his generation.

If Luke 11.31f. is understood as a substantially reliable record of Jesus' words intended as an explanation of the saying about Jonah and the Son of man as signs, then that saying must itself also be authentic. We have seen that there is a strong case also for the authenticity of verse 29, and that it prepares for verse 30. It is perhaps less likely that both 29 and 31f. can be sayings of Jesus if they are taken as quite independent of one another; disparate allusions to the same topic, in this case Jonah, are uncharacteristic of his teaching. There are, however, marks of genuineness in both, and when linked together by the Son of man saying of Luke 11.30 the references to Jonah cease to appear disparate, and the whole pericope, verses 29-32, forms a unity. This unity is not necessarily the result of redactional work, but could be the retention, in the construction of Luke's gospel, of a unity already present in Q and even in Jesus' own preaching. It is Matthew's form of this section that bears the greater marks of redaction, in the substitution of Matt. 12.40 for the Q saying in Luke 11.30, and in the change of order of the components of the double saying that follows.

On this interpretation of the whole passage, Luke 11.30 may be dominical for the very reason which is advanced for judging it to be a community creation, namely, because it is in the form of the eschatological correlative. In support of our standpoint, further reference may be made to resemblances between Luke 11.30 in its context and the Son of man sayings of Luke 17 in their context.

Luke 17.24 states in general terms the suddenness of the Son of man in his day (or, of the day of the Son of man), comparing it with the familiar natural phenomenon of a lightning flash. The meaning, however, is designedly incomplete, and the precise significance of the comparison only comes to expression in the following illustrations from Israelite history. The emphasis common to Luke 11.30 and 17.24 is the *futurity* of the Son of man, which is clarified in the sequels to both sayings. The parallel sayings about the Queen of the South and the Ninevites refer directly to the judgment. But Luke 17.24 refers to the judgment in the allusion to the day of the Son of man, and this is repeated in the two examples of the calamitous punishment visited upon the evil generations in the days of Noah and of Lot.[117] Thus these sayings, Luke 11.30 on the one hand, and 17.24, 26, 28a, 30 on the other, along with the material respectively associated with them, together constitute *a unitary conception with two main features, the futurity of the Son of man, and judgment.* The latter is stated directly in the sequel to Luke 11.30, in the scene of the Queen of the South and the Ninevites rising up in court (ἐν τῇ κρίσει) to testify against (κατακρινεῖ, κατακρινοῦσιν) 'this generation'. In the sayings of Luke 17 the idea of judgment is unequivocally expressed in the juridical terms 'Son of man' and 'day' - 'the judgment day of the Son of man'.

This close correspondence of ideas in Luke 11.29-32 and 17.24, 26-30, amounting to a unitary conception in which features in the one passage are matched by counterparts in the other, means that the question of the authenticity of the former depends not only on the arguments already advanced, but also on one's estimate of the sayings in Luke 17. These we have seen to be symbolic descriptions of the suddenness of the eschatological catastrophe. The day of the Son of man inaugurates the judgment, and is parallel to the coming of the kingdom of God. In announcing the near approach of these two manifestations of the same phenomenon, Jesus warned his contemporaries to repent and accept his message while there was still time. Luke 11.30 in its setting focusses upon another aspect of the judgment: not the manner of its coming, but how it will go ill with this unresponsive generation on the day of trial itself in the presence of the Son of man, who is the embodiment of the divine judgment of which Jesus had warned it.[118]

In contrast to virtually all other future Son of man sayings,[119] these make no reference to the 'coming' of the Son of man and lack apocalyptic descriptions. It may also be noted that Luke 11.29-32 and 17.24, 26-30 are both pessimistic in outlook and without any qualification such as 'unless you repent' (Luke 13.3, 5). Much else of what has been said earlier about the sayings in Luke 17 applies also to Luke 11.30, for this too, in its setting, presupposes the exaltation status of the Son of man and his function as the eschatological judge.

All these considerations suggest that the eschatological correlative originated not in the early Christian community, but in Jesus' own teaching. The Q examples in Luke 11 and 17 contain within themselves the source of the early Christian Son of man belief - they are sayings of Jesus.

Matt. 12.40 and 13.40 illustrate subsequent borrowing of this form. The former replaced the Q saying at Luke 11.30. Matt. 13.40, like Luke 11.30 and 17.26, 28a + 30, is followed by an asyndetic explanation: 'the Son of man will send his angels . . .' Furthermore, Matthew's substitution of 'the parousia of the Son of man' (Matt. 24. 27, 37, 39) for his 'day' in Luke is a redactional adjustment to the church's parousia doctrine. These Matthaean examples, however, are perhaps not so much the redactional work of the evangelist as an independent individual, as illustrations of the community's employment of a form of expression characteristic of Jesus' preaching and introduced by the evangelist into his gospel.

There remains one more saying which can be discussed appropriately at this point. Luke 12.39f., par. Matt. 24.43f. is the only future Son of man saying in Q which is neither an eschatological correlative nor a sentence of holy law. It does, however, resemble the correlative in some respects, but this is due to the second sentence having been appended to the genuine parable of the burglar.[120] Best understood probably as a Christian prophet's hortatory comment upon and application of Jesus' parable, it introduces the unexpected coming of the Son of man as the reason for watchfulness. In a somewhat similar way, in the only synoptic eschatological correlative outside Q, Matt. 13.40f., the Son of man is introduced in the explanatory addition to the apodosis of the correlative, and not in the apodosis itself.[121] In effect, if not actually in form, the homiletic exhortation in Luke 12.40 par., 'so (καί) you be ready', serves as apodosis of a comparison (or correlative) of which the short parable serves as protasis.[122]

(iii) The eschatological correlative and the sentence of holy law

In section (i) attention was directed to the relationship between these in the life of the primitive community. According to Käsemann, the 'sentences', of which examples occur in the synoptic gospels and elsewhere in the New Testament, reflect the language of Palestinian Christian prophets making judgmental pronouncements in the setting of the eucharist. Perrin's names for them, 'judgment sayings' or 'eschatological judgment pronouncements',[123] especially the latter, in parallel with 'eschatological correlatives', are very appropriate; but we retain 'sentences of holy law' as the established and convenient term. Käsemann regards the 'sentences' as the most significant of the various forms of prophetic proclamation to be found in the earliest prophet-directed community.[124] The eschatological correlative, like the 'sentences', is probably to be located in the eucharist. Both forms 'are used for quite similar purposes' and both are aspects of the church's judgmental activity.[125]

In section (ii) it was maintained that the last word on the question of the ultimate source of both types of saying has not necessarily been said, and reasons were given for the possibility that the eschatological correlative employed in the primitive church did not originate there, but was derived from Jesus' usage. Since the eschatological correlative and the sentence of holy law are similar in some ways and are both used in the church's judgmental activity, there is a possibility that the origin of the latter also is to be sought in Jesus' usage. Hahn has made the point that, while sacred law may in fact have played a decisive part in prophetic activity in the community, as Käsemann claims, this does not imply that Jesus himself could not also have used the form, just as he used other traditional forms in his sayings.[126] This argument is considerably strengthened if, as has been suggested in section (ii), the eschatological correlative originated with Jesus, because the 'sentence' shares certain features with it.

(1) As we have seen, both types of saying are judgmental in character.

(2) The eschatological correlative could have been created in a Semitic milieu.[127] For the sentences of holy law this is assured if, as Käsemann claims, they reflect the judgmental language of Palestinian Christian prophets, whose background would have been the Jewish scriptures: 'holy Scripture provided the primitive Christian prophets with the stylistic form in which to clothe their sentences of holy law'.[128] Significant parallels to the 'sentences' of Christian prophets are to be found in the pronouncements of rabbis on sins forgivable and unforgivable. Since in rabbinic Judaism the Holy Spirit is the Spirit of prophecy and inspiration, it is not surprising that unforgivable sins include speaking against the Torah and denying that it is from God.[129]

(3) There is a resemblance of form. There are only two examples of sentences of holy law with the Son of man as subject, Luke 12.8 and Mark 8.38. Both of them resemble the eschatological correlative in two respects. Firstly, as in the correlative the Son of man is the conceptual and sometimes also the grammatical subject of the apodosis, so the Son of man is the subject of the second part of both these 'sentences'. Secondly, the use of *καί* to introduce this second part, immediately before the Son of man, is equivalent to *οὕτως* (*κατὰ τὰ αὐτά*, Luke 17.30) in the eschatological correlatives.[130] Luke 12.8 may be rephrased as an eschatological correlative: 'as a man confesses me, so the Son of man will confess him'. These considerations may be recognized as perhaps lending further support to the superiority of Luke 12.8, with Son of man, over against Matt. 10.32, with 'I' as subject of the second part. Perhaps, therefore, it is premature to dismiss Son of man in Luke 12.8 and Mark 8.38 as simply an exceptional use, in the general judgment tradition exemplified by the 'sentences', of

the Son of man concept otherwise associated with the other judgment tradition expressed in the eschatological correlative.

In preparation for the next stage in the argument there still remains something more to be said about Käsemann's sentences of holy law pronounced by prophets in the early church.[131] This can conveniently be done with some reference to Mark 3.28f. (parr. Luke 12.10; Matt. 12.31f.), which has recently been re-examined as a 'test case' for the Christian prophets hypothesis vital to Käsemann's theory.[132] Study of these texts earlier in this chapter has shown that Mark 3.28f. is closer than Q to the common Aramaic *Vorlage*, and that the Q version is the result of deliberate christologizing of the Aramaic *bar nasha*, used in a collective or generic sense, into the title Son of man. Both the Markan and the Q forms we can now call 'sentences of holy law', and both, because of the references to blasphemy or speech against the Holy Spirit, are church pronouncements rather than words of Jesus.

Two related issues, then, are involved here: the wider issue of the utterances of prophets in the early community, and the more restricted issue of the nature of those of their utterances described by Käsemann as 'sentences of holy law', declarations of the *ius talionis*, God's judgmental action and recompense corresponding to man's conduct. The following brief discussions of these two matters serve as a preparation for the resumption of the comparison of the two kinds of saying with which this section (iii) is concerned.

Early Christian prophets

Bultmann states that 'the Church drew no distinction between [such] utterances by Christian prophets and the sayings of Jesus in the tradition'.[133] M. E. Boring has shown that Bultmann was not the first to suggest the presence (in the synoptic gospels) of utterances of Christian prophets.[134] The idea has not won unanimous acceptance. Thus Moffatt, noting Paul's distinction between the Lord's instruction on divorce and his own ruling in cases where one of the partners had been converted to Christianity after marriage (1 Cor. 7.10-13, cf. also verses 25f.), thought this was an indication that 'although as a prophet he had divine revelations, he did not cast them into the form of what Jesus had once said, in order to invest them with authority . . . he drew a line between such authenticated sayings and his own opinions, even when the latter were "opinions" in a judicial sense'.[135] Clearly Moffatt would not have been sympathetic towards the theory, as discussed today, that the synoptic gospels contain sayings of Christian prophets. More recently F. Neugebauer has subjected Bultmann's arguments to critical examination.[136] Like Moffatt, this scholar refers to 1 Cor. 7 as evidence of the supreme authority accorded to an indisputable word of Jesus by the primitive church. He maintains that, if Spirit-inspired utterances of prophets had been assigned the same rank as Jesus' words, the church would have been led by prophets, whereas the sources reveal that the highest office was not the prophetic, but the apostolic.[137] It should be remembered, however, that Paul himself was in effect both apostle and prophet.[138]

Although the role of prophets in the formation of the tradition can be exaggerated, the synoptic gospels, when subjected to traditio-historical and redaction criticism, furnish evidence of the roles played in the development of the tradition by prophets, apostles and evangelists in the post-resurrection Spirit-directed community.[139] Jeremias attributes the increase of the occurrences of 'Father' as a name for God on the lips of Jesus in the Fourth Gospel (and also in the Gospel of Thomas) to Christian prophets 'who spoke in the name of the exalted Lord and with his words'.[140] Although this is the Fourth Gospel, yet on the reasonable assumption that much in the Johannine discourses has been derived and adapted from homiletical material, we have again to think, as in the case of the synoptics, of the part played by prophets and teachers. In comparison with the synoptic tradition, the role of Christian prophecy in the development of the Johannine sayings tradition may differ in degree more than in substance.

The previously mentioned article of Boring seeks to present evidence that Mark 3.28f. originated as an oracle of an early Christian prophet. The main points are these. The saying (and also its parallels) is an independent logion ill fitting the present context. Initial 'amen', chiastic structure, and legal form are probably characteristics of Christian prophetic speech. The saying (if not from Jesus) is, in view of its claim to authority, probably from a prophet rather than 'a scribal or didactic elaboration of Jesus' words'.[141] A logion exalting the Holy Spirit to the extent that this does is more likely to be derived from a prophetic than from a non-charismatic setting. Boring cites the injunction in the Didache 11.7 against testing a prophet speaking under the inspiration of the Spirit - 'for every sin will be forgiven, but this sin will not be forgiven' - and judges it to be the oldest extant and the correct interpretation of Mark 3.28f., in terms of Christian prophecy. Whether this estimate is correct or not, there is little room for doubt that the logion is a Christian prophetic utterance and that, on the wider plane, the evidence adduced from elsewhere in the New Testament in the earlier part of Boring's study is fully adequate for the recognition of examples such as this in the synoptic tradition.

Sentences of holy law

Käsemann's thesis has been criticized by K. Berger in a long and valuable article, in which he attempts to show that it is untenable on form critical grounds.[142] According to Berger, the so-called 'sentences of holy law' supposed to have been pronounced by Christian prophets in fact originated in the sphere of Wisdom literature. Sayings of the Wisdom type were brought into association with the person of Jesus by being formulated with introductory 'amen' (followed by 'I say to you'), and so became apocalyptic instruction as if from him. As examples are cited relative sentences with future apodosis in Mark 3.28f.; 9.41; 10.15; 10.29f.; 11.23 (Berger, p. 32). Berger believes that no conclusions can be drawn from the form of sentence as to authorship, whether of Jesus or of prophets. Sentences like Luke 12.8f. do not differ in essentials from the rest (pp. 33f.).

Although there are undeniable resemblances of form between Käsemann's 'sentences' and sayings from Wisdom literature,[143] the eschatological content of the former stands out as conspicuously distinctive in contrast with the latter. One has only to compare Mark 3.28f. with the other texts Berger lists with it to be immediately conscious of a change of atmosphere, a sharpening of stringency and severity lacking in the others.[144] Content, therefore, is more important than similarity of form in these instances. As for Luke 12.8f., its crucial significance in the teaching of Jesus has been re-emphasized earlier in this chapter.

If the use of introductory *αμην* did in fact originate with Jesus and not, as Berger has claimed,[145] in the Hellenistic Jewish church, his theory of adaptation and reformulation of Wisdom sayings as apocalyptic instruction by Jesus, through the introduction of this word, becomes much less probable than Käsemann's hypothesis. The Hellenistic period of the church was subsequent to the *floruit* of the Palestinian prophets in the early community, who would already have used it themselves.

If the resemblances noted above between the eschatological correlative and the sentence of holy law are taken into account – both are judgmental in character, both may be of Semitic origin, there is a certain formal similarity – the case for a Wisdom *Sitz im Leben* is seriously weakened. In our view Käsemann's hypothesis is fully vindicated. Going further, we suggest that not only the eschatological correlative, but also the sentence of holy law utilized in their work by early Christian prophets originated in Jesus' own preaching. Continuing the comparison of these two kinds of saying in (1), (2) and (3) above, we turn in (4) to other factors tending to reinforce those already considered.

(4) It has been noted that the dominical sayings in the form of the

eschatological correlative in Luke 11.30 and 17.24, 26, 28a + 30 constitute, with their contextual material, a unitary conception of the Son of man with two primary features, futurity and judgmental status. We have also seen that, along with a secondary partial parallel in Mark 8.38, Luke 12.8f. is the sole instance of a sentence of holy law including the Son of man as subject. This saying may now be brought into association with the eschatological correlative;[146] the result is *a consistent unitary conception of the Son of man shared by all of them.*

In Luke 17.24, 26-30 the emphasis is on the 'day' of the Son of man as judge, its suddenness, its all-embracing and devastating effects. Luke 11.30 in its setting points to the Son of man as the fulfilment of the sign of Jonah and as the embodiment of judgment.

Luke 12.8f. remains fundamental in this connection. It expresses Jesus' unique reinterpretation of the Son of man concept as a symbolic description of his anticipated judicial role after his vindication. It directs attention to the crucial issue arising in the judgment, whether a man has confessed (and so followed) Jesus, or has denied (and so forsaken) him. The future judgmental status and function of the Son of man in this saying are presupposed in the sayings in Luke 11 and 17. Luke 12.8f. foretells the consequences of men's reactions to the challenges implicit in Jesus' teaching recorded in Luke 11.29-32 and 17.24, 26-30 - confessing or denying, as the case demands, on the part of the Son of man himself.

Luke 11.29f. has served as the point of departure for the preceding extended discussion of the eschatological correlative and the sentence of holy law, and their connection with the teaching of Jesus. The sayings of both types, described as forming together a consistent unitary Son of man conception, are distinguished from all others as the *kernel sayings*, as the irreducible minimum of Jesus' authentic teaching on the subject[147] (to which ultimately all Son of man sayings in the gospels owe their existence), and as surviving remnants of a larger number which have been lost in the course of transmission of the tradition.

Of these sayings, those in Luke 17 alone among Son of man sayings without rivals or parallels lacking the term are basically authentic. This category, however, to which Jeremias attaches primary importance, is of unequal value, since the majority of its sayings appear not to be authentic. The other two kernel sayings, Luke 12.8f. and 11.29f., belong to Jeremias' other category, those having non-Son of man parallels. Jeremias maintains that in such doubly attested sayings those without Son of man have the stronger claim to priority. This is not borne out by our findings on these two texts, although there remain further pairs of sayings to be taken into account in less detail. So far as the kernel sayings are concerned – and their outstanding importance is generally acknowledged – neither of the categories as such is superior to the other; both are represented in the kernel sayings to approximately the same extent.

The first chapter of Borsch's *CGSM* is entitled 'The Priority of the Son of Man in Rival Parallel Sayings', in deliberate contrast to Jeremias' thesis,[148] and re-examines eleven examples. We now submit to a fresh analysis, in the light of Borsch's conclusions as well as those of Jeremias, further sayings additional to those already investigated in the present chapter.

4. ***Luke 6.22.*** **'Blessed are you when men hate you, and when they exclude you and revile you, and cast out your name as evil, on account of the Son of man.'**
Matt. 5.11. **'Blessed are you when men revile you and persecute you and utter all kinds of evil against you falsely on my account.'**

The priority of the Lukan version is to be supported on the following grounds. The second person in *all* the beatitudes in Luke is more likely to be original than the third person in Matthew, because in both gospels they are addressed to the disciples (Luke 6.20; Matt. 5.1f.). It is therefore probable that the more significant differences between the two forms of this particular beatitude are attributable to Matthew's modifications of a common original. 'Cast out your name as evil' is translation Greek from Aramaic. That the Son of man stood in a common source is suggested by the theme of future reward, and the beatitude may have been inspired by a saying of Jesus, like Luke 12.8f., on loyalty to himself in his ministry being rewarded by the Son of man in heaven. Matthew's 'on my account' is due to his equation of Jesus and the Son of man.[149]

5. ***Matt. 16.13.*** **'Who do men say that the Son of man is?'**
Mark 8.27 (par. Luke 9.18). **'Who do men say that I am?'**

The Markan version could quite well be an authentic question of Jesus to his disciples, and it is difficult to see how Matthew can be more original here. Borsch, however, supports Matthew on the basis of his thesis of a linkage between the Son of man, Elijah, John the Baptist, and Jesus in 'very early traditions'.[150] The question in Matt. 16.13 is taken to mean something like, 'Who do men say that the person is who at this time occupies the role of Son of man?' This is my wording, but fairly represents the interpretation of Borsch, who takes the 'I' in Mark to be an alteration due to interest in Jesus as Messiah.[151] This is interesting and ingenious, but hardly convincing enough to warrant acceptance of the priority of Son of man in Matt. 16.13 over the first person in Mark.

6. *Mark 8.31 (par. Luke 9.22).* **And he began to teach them that the Son of man must suffer many things.**
Matt. 16.20f. **Then he strictly charged the disciples to tell no one that he was the Christ. From that time Jesus began to show his disciples that he must go to Jerusalem and suffer many things.**

The absence of Son of man in Matthew at this point is explained by Jeremias as necessitated by its insertion by anticipation in 16.13 at the beginning of the pericope.[152] We have already seen reason to assign priority to the parallel Mark 8.27, with the first-person pronoun (with Jeremias, and against Borsch). There can be little room for doubt that Matthew[153] has removed the reference to the Son of man in his parallel to Mark 8.31.

7. *Matt. 16.28.* **'Truly, I say to you, there are some standing here who will not taste death before they see the Son of man coming in his kingdom.'**
Mark 9.1 (par. Luke 9.27). **'Truly, I say to you, there are some standing here who will not taste death before they see that the kingdom of God has come with power.'**

Borsch[154] argues strongly for the Matthaean version on the following grounds. Matthew may here be using, not Mark, but an independent source; Matt. 16.27 may be more original to the context than is Mark 8.38; similarly, Matt. 16.28 itself may be more original than Mark 9.1, which breaks the continuity of thought; the language of 'coming' suits the Son of man better than the kingdom of God. None of these points are decisive. There is no evidence of use of an independent non-Markan source at this point. Despite the apocalyptic colouring of its second part, Mark 8.38 is more closely akin to the Q parallel Luke 12.8f. than is Matt. 16.27, where the apocalyptic is heightened. It is widely held that Mark 9.1 does not belong to its present context; and this tends to confirm the suspicion that the consistent picture of the apocalyptic Son of man as judge in his kingdom in Matt. 16.27f. is a re-writing of Mark. Finally, Mark 9.1 speaks not of seeing the kingdom of God *coming*, but says, '. . . before they have seen the kingdom of God already come (ἐληλυθυῖαν) in power' (NEB). In any case, 'seeing the Son of man coming' is apocalyptic language.

8. *Mark 10.45 (par. Matt. 20.28).* **'For the Son of man also came not to be served but to serve, and to give his life as a ransom for many.'**
Luke 22.27. **'I am among you as one who serves.'**

The two forms of this saying are independent. It has been maintained that 'I' in Luke, despite the secondary character of the Lukan tradition in some other respects, is more original than Mark's Son of man, a decision which must stand.[155]

9. ***Matt. 19.28.*** **'Truly, I say to you, in the new world, when the Son of man shall sit on his glorious throne, you who have followed me will also sit on twelve thrones, judging the twelve tribes of Israel.'**
Luke 22. 28–30. **'You are those who have continued with me in my trials; and I assign to you, as my Father assigned to me, a kingdom, that you may eat and drink at my table in my kingdom, and sit on thrones judging the twelve tribes of Israel.'**

These passages, as Borsch says, probably derive ultimately from a common tradition, but have features suggesting that they have not been taken from a single intermediate source. Matthew has apocalyptic features absent from Luke: 'the throne of (his) glory' (1 En. 45.3; 55.4; 61.8; 62.2, 3, 5; 69.27); the throne of the Son of man (1 En. 62.5; 69.27, 29); thrones (also Luke 22.30. Rev. 4.4, like Matt. 19.28, has both 'throne' and a definite number of thrones; cf. also 1 En. 108.12, 'I will seat each on the throne of his honour'). The apocalyptic elements in Matthew's form of the saying may be due simply to his tendency to utilize apocalyptic imagery; the Son of man may be an example of his predilection for the title as a name for Jesus, rather than a primitive Semitic feature lacking or smoothed away in Luke. 'The new world' is literally 'the regeneration' (*παλιγγενεσία*), a later non-Semitic element. Borsch rightly judges the Lukan form to be the result of rephrasing, and favours Matthew's briefer version.[156] On the face of it, too, Matthew's introduction of the saying with *αμην λέγω ὑμῖν* lends it verisimilitude; but the expression is not confined to sayings with a strong claim to authenticity. A sign of later tradition in Luke is 'my kingdom' (cf. Luke 23.42, 'your kingdom'). On balance, Matt. 19.28 may be taken as a possible apocalyptic echo of a traditional Son of man saying.[157]

These results may be tabulated thus:

	(a) Priority of form with Son of man	(b) Priority of form without Son of man
1.	Luke 12.8f. (par. Matt. 10.32f.)	
2.		Mark 3.28f. (parr. Matt. 12.32; Luke 12.10)
3.	Luke 11.29f. (Matt. 12.39f.) (par. Mark 8.12)	
4.	Luke 6.22 (par. Matt. 5.11)	
5.		Mark 8.27 (par. Matt. 16.13)
6.	Mark 8.31 (par. Matt. 16.20f.)	
7.		Mark 9.1 (par. Matt. 16.28)
8.		Luke 22.27 (par. Mark 10.45)
9.	Matt. 19.28 (par. Luke 22.28–30)	

Conclusion

This analysis of sayings additional to the first three investigated at length for other purposes in the main part of this chapter confirms the findings, in those cases, on the question of priority. Full support can be given neither to the thesis of Jeremias, that, where a Son of man saying has a rival parallel without the expression, the latter is the more primitive, nor to the contrary thesis of Borsch, that the evidence tends to point to the priority of the form with the Son of man designation. There are too many other factors involved for either the presence or the absence of the Son of man to serve as a valid criterion of the priority, and therefore of the possible authenticity, of a saying.

Excursus 1: Luke 12.10 and parallels

See above pp. 84–90.
Colpe, 'Der Spruch' = 'Der Spruch von der Lästerung des Geistes', in *Der Ruf Jesu und die Antwort der Gemeinde: Exegetische Untersuchungen Joachim Jeremias zum 70. Geburtstag gewidmet von seinen Schülern*, ed. E. Lohse with C. Burchard and B. Schaller, Göttingen 1970, pp. 63–79. Colpe's transliterations are given below in a simplified form.

On somewhat similar lines to Schippers, Colpe argues that neither Mark's nor Q's version of the saying is prior to the other, but that both developed independently from one Aramaic logion. He reconstructs this as:

kol hobin wekol gidduphin
yishtebequ lebar nasha

All sins and all blasphemies (slanders)
can be forgiven man,

or – an easier transition to the Q form – as:

kol hoba
wekol giddupha di amir lebar nasha
yishtebeq (leh)

Every sin
and every blasphemy (slander) spoken by man
can be forgiven (him).

In the Aramaic *Vorlage bar nasha* meant 'man' in the generic sense. From being the object of 'forgive' it became the object of blasphemy or slander. In Luke 12.10, par. Matt. 12.32, 'Son of man' is not due to misunderstanding of the Aramaic, but is a christological statement, in terms of the Son of man, facilitated by the ambiguity of *bar nasha* ('Der Spruch', pp.

67f., 76). 'Only what is spoken against man could later become what is spoken against the Son of Man.'[158] The next step in the development would have been the distinction in Q between forgivable blasphemy (slander) against the Son of man and unforgivable blasphemy against the Holy Spirit. This development

> was most likely in a post-Pentecost community which was conscious of possessing the Spirit and which, in the light of the faith in the risen and ascended Lord made possible thereby, viewed the earthly life of the Son of Man as a preparatory age of salvation. On this view rejection of Jesus would not be so serious a breach with God as rejection of the Spirit of the exalted Lord who was to be given after the resurrection of Jesus.[159]

The climax of development is reached in the combination of Mark and Q in Matt. 12.31f., which has the effect of expressing explicitly the church's belief that before his parousia (but not afterwards) even blasphemy of or speaking against the Son of man is included in men's forgivable sins ('Der Spruch', p. 77).

A brief comparison of Colpe's conclusions with those of Schippers may now be given. They agree that Mark and Q represent independent developments from one Aramaic saying. Colpe's view is that this originally referred only to man's sins and blasphemies being forgivable, while Schippers presupposes a single ambiguous saying which could also mean that he who blasphemes the Son of man will be forgiven. According to Colpe, this second understanding of the saying only came about at a later stage when *bar nasha*, meaning 'man' as the object of God's forgiveness, was reinterpreted as the Son of man as the object of men's blasphemy or slander – a christological statement facilitated by the ambiguity of *bar nasha*. Both scholars agree in regarding the Q version of the saying, distinguishing blasphemy against the Son of man as forgivable from blasphemy against the Holy Spirit as unforgivable, as having originated in the post-Easter community. Schippers claims that the Q version is an adaptation of a word of Jesus distinguishing himself as 'son of man' in a non-eschatological sense as God's messenger, opposition to whom is forgivable, from his Spirit-directed ministry, opposition to which is unforgivable. Colpe, however, does not trace the saying to Jesus in any shape or form; with this we agree. On the other hand, Schippers' restoration of the underlying Aramaic has the merit of simplicity. Perhaps it would be permissible to accept his restoration of the ambiguous primitive logion, and to apply to it Colpe's interpretation of an unauthentic saying about slanders against man having been given a christological interpretation in Q.

Excursus 2: The sign of Jonah, and the sign of the Son of man

'The sign of Jonah' (Luke 11.29, par. Matt. 12.39) has no antecedent in Jewish literature. Luke 11.29f. has been interpreted in the text thus:[160] the Son of man in his eschatological function of judge in the celestial court will be *a* sign (as Jonah was a sign as a preacher of judgment), and at the same time 'the sign of Jonah', the embodiment of divine judgment proclaimed by Jesus to his generation. It has been claimed as all from Jesus' preaching; 'the sign of Jonah' is a new and unexampled expression and idea.

Can 'the sign of the Son of man' (Matt. 24.30a) also be traced to Jesus? Colpe adopts a positive attitude to this question, and includes the saying, 'Then will appear the sign of the Son of man in heaven', among his eight sayings which he regards as belonging to a fourth Jewish Son of man source. He considers that it probably belongs to Matthew's special material; its meaning is not explained, as would be expected were it a secondary feature, and it 'presents something hard to understand and veils what is said'; it is hardly possible for it to have come from any other source than Jesus' preaching.[161]

According to Rengstorf, 'the sign of the Son of man' may be a fixed phrase adopted by the evangelist for his own purpose, and the expression is so enigmatic that 'it can hardly be explained as the work of the community or a redactor'.[162]

If the argument in this chapter is on the right lines, 'the sign of the Son of man' can hardly also mean, alongside 'the sign of Jonah', the Son of man himself in any sense, and at the same time derive from Jesus.[163] The sign of the Son of man is distinct from, and precedes, the coming on the clouds: cf. Matt. 24.3, 'And what will be the signal for your coming?' (NEB). The sign of the parousia of Jesus and of the end of the age in verse 3 is the sign of the Son of man in verse 30, and precedes his actual parousia. So it seems that the sign of the Son of man must be something distinct from the Son of man, a premonitory sign of some kind heralding his coming. It is thought by some that its precise form cannot be determined. The most satisfactory suggestion is that of T. F. Glasson, that *σημεῖον* in Matt. 24.30a means a standard or ensign associated with the trumpet (verse 31) in the eschatological gathering together of the elect people of God (e.g. Isa. 11.12; 18.3; 27.13).[164]

Two observations may be made. Firstly, the close association of verses 3 and 30f. in Matt. 24 should be stressed. The question of the disciples, 'What is the sign (*σημεῖον*) of your coming (*παρουσία*) and of the end of the age?' receives the ultimate reply, 'And then shall appear the *σημεῖον* (sign, ensign, standard) of the Son of man in heaven . . . and they shall see the Son of man coming on the clouds of heaven.' Secondly, 'sign' on the one hand, and 'standard' or 'ensign' on the other, need not be regarded as mutually exclusive meanings of *σημεῖον* in this passage. It must certainly mean 'sign' in view of the reference back to verse 3. Moreover, the idea of a sign in heaven is not peculiar to Matthew. With *τὸ σημεῖον τοῦ υἱοῦ τοῦ ἀνθρώπου ἐν οὐρανῷ* may be compared the three signs or portents in heaven in the Apocalypse.

12.1, *καὶ σημεῖον μέγα ὤφθη ἐν τῷ οὐρανῷ* – a woman clothed with the sun.
12.3, *καὶ ὤφθη ἄλλο σημεῖον ἐν τῷ οὐρανῷ* – a great red dragon.
15.1, *καὶ εἶδον ἄλλο σημεῖον ἐν τῷ οὐρανῷ μέγα καὶ θαυμαστόν* – seven angels with the plagues.

Unlike these signs, the sign of the Son of man is not described. The reason may be that the evangelist is borrowing a known Christian apocalyptic expression and concept; no elucidation is required, because *σημεῖον* has a second meaning of ensign or standard. Possibly this arose as an apocalyptic development from the sign of Jonah in Q. It is significant that Matthew, the most given to apocalyptic language among the synoptists, refers to the sign of the Son of man as well as to the sign of Jonah.

Perhaps one may go a stage further than Glasson, and ask what device was emblazoned on the ensign, standard, or banner of the Son of man. It may be suggested that it was a representation of the greatest of all signs, the cross[165] – the sign of Jesus' triumph over death and, as the sign that heralds his coming as Son of man to execute judgment, the cause of terror to the tribes of the earth.

Excursus 3: Remarks on J. Jeremias, 'Die älteste Schicht'[166]

(1) Jeremias[167] cites Matt. 13.37, 'The sower of the good seed is the Son of man', and Matt. 13.41, 'The Son of man will send his angels', both belonging to the interpretation (verses 37–43) of the parable of the wheat and the tares, along with the Gospel of Thomas 57 as a non-Son of man parallel because it lacks the interpretation. He has shown conclusively elsewhere that the interpretation of the parable is the work of the evangelist himself.[168] The presence in Thomas of a form of the parable lacking the explanation is irrelevant to the question of the priority of non-Son of man parallels to Son of man logia. It is far more likely that the gnostic compiler knew and deliberately omitted the apocalyptic-eschatological explanation, in order to make room for a gnostic one,[169] as in the next example.[170]

Luke 12.39f. par. Matt. 24.43f.	Thomas 21b	Thomas 103
If the householder had known at what hour the thief was coming, he would not have left his house to be broken into. You also must be ready; for the Son of man is coming at an unexpected hour.	If the householder knows that the thief is coming, he will be watching before he comes (and) will not let him break into his house of his kingdom to carry away his goods. But you must keep watch against the world; gird up your loins with great power, so that no robber may find a way to come to you. For the thing which you await will be found.	Blessed is the man who knows in which part (of the night) the robbers will come, so that he will arise and collect his . . . and gird up his loins before they come in.

The substitution of the gnostic explanation for that in Q naturally involves the omission of the Son of man.[171]

It is inappropriate to cite the Gospel of Thomas among synoptic examples of rivals or parallels to Son of man sayings. In the only occurrence of the Son of man title in Thomas, at saying 86 (Luke 9.58, par. Matt. 8.20), the addition of 'and to rest' is another way of giving a gnostic slant to a canonical saying, expressing the thought of rest as the state of blessedness.[172]

(2) We can only regard as proper counterparts or parallels pairs of sayings in the same context. This is not the case, for instance, with the following texts.[173]

Form with Son of man	Form without Son of man
Mark 9.9 (par. Matt. 17.9)	Mark 14.28 (par. Matt. 26.32)
when the Son of man rises from the dead	after I am raised up

Again, one can hardly view as genuine parallels occurrences of the Son of man and 'I' at different points in the same passage.

Mark 14.21b (parr. Matt. 26. 24b; Luke 22.22)	Mark 14.18 (parr. Matt. 26.21; Luke 22.21)
the Son of man is betrayed	(one of you) will betray me

Mark 14.41 (par. Matt. 26.45)	Mark 14.42 (par. Matt. 26.46)
the Son of man is betrayed	he who betrays me

These instances illustrate the considerable degree of interchangeability of the title and the personal pronoun.

(3) To Mark 14.18 above, Jeremias adds John 13.21 (identical with Mark except for double *αμην*), and to Mark 14.42, John 19.11. To Mark 14.21a (par. Matt. 26.24a), 'the Son of man goes' (*ὑπάγει*), and its par. Luke 22.22 with *πορεύεται*, he gives as counterparts having 'I go' (*ὑπάγω* and *πορεύομαι* respectively) John 7.33 and 14.2, and other passages in each case. One may question the validity of this use of Johannine passages as if they were true parallels between gospel and gospel in corresponding contexts.

Jeremias also lists closely similar sentences with and without the Son of man in the Fourth Gospel.[174] Their relationship is, of course, complex. In some cases it is arguable that the two types of sentence do not merely illustrate interchangeability of the designation and the first-person pronoun (or Son, or Son of God), but indicate the use of a Son of man source. Priority should probably be assigned to at least some of the Johannine Son of man sayings over their non-Son of man counterparts.

Excursus 4: The Son of man and pre-existence

Hamerton-Kelly, in *Pre-existence, Wisdom, and the Son of Man,* writes:

> Jesus referred to himself, in his earthly ministry, as the Son of Man. Although the Son of Man was not a defined concept in Judaism at that time, it was, at least, a recognized image, one of whose recurrent components was the idea of pre-existence. In using this self-designation, Jesus implied his own pre-existence.[175]

The three statements contained here are all questionable.

(1) There are probably no Son of man sayings that can be attributed to Jesus except those referring to the future, and they require a functional interpretation.

(2) Earlier, Hamerton-Kelly speaks of 'a relatively stable group of ideas' associated with the term Son of man, which was not 'a well-defined figure or "concept" in Jewish apocalyptic'.[176] This corresponds broadly to the first part of the second statement in the quotation above. Hamerton-Kelly admits that Tödt himself recognizes differences in the way the Son of man is presented in Dan. 7, 1 En. 37–71, and 2 Esdras 13, but he dissents from Tödt's view that, nevertheless, behind these texts and in the background of the gospels there lies the idea of a definite Son of man figure. He prefers Perrin's hypothesis of varied application of Son of man imagery.[177] I believe,

however, that it remains permissible to speak of a recognizable Son of man 'concept' as the common centre of which the several portrayals are expressions, adaptations, and developments. Among these, Jesus' teaching about the Son of man is the most original and far-reaching.

(3) Hamerton-Kelly argues that, since New Testament texts are customarily elucidated by reference to their historical background, and since pre-existence was a constant idea in apocalyptic Son of man imagery, Jesus in using the 'self-designation' Son of man implied his own pre-existence.[178] This reasoning is unsound in so far as it fails to take account of the possibility of new and original thought in Jesus' adoption of the Son of man idea. Tödt's insistence[179] that the concept of pre-existence cannot be found in synoptic Son of man sayings is fully justified.

V

THE KERNEL SAYINGS

Summary

The antiquity of a saying attributed to Jesus may be tested in several ways; but antiquity does not guarantee authenticity. In his study of Son of man sayings and their non-Son of man rivals or parallels, Jeremias is concerned with the question of the priority of one or the other of the two types. Clearly, investigation of the relative age of traditional sayings must precede the further inquiry into authenticity. The present study has not found sufficient evidence to justify acceptance of either Jeremias' preference for the non-Son of man parallels, or Borsch's contrary arguments in favour of the Son of man versions as the more primitive type. Jeremias' other thesis is that the oldest Son of man sayings of all are likely to be those without non-Son of man rivals (*konkurrenzlos*). Our investigation, however, has produced the result that the only sayings of this category to which authenticity can be assigned with any degree of probability are the three closely associated sayings in Luke 17.24, 26f., 28–30. These, together with Luke 12.8f. and 11.29f., the only authentic sayings of the other category, constitute the 'kernel sayings'.

Full account has been taken of the 'sentence of holy law' investigated by Käsemann (Perrin's 'eschatological judgment pronouncement' or 'judgment saying'), and of the 'eschatological correlative' (Perrin's 'comparison saying') more recently isolated by R. A. Edwards. Both these types are represented among the kernel sayings: Luke 12.8f. is a sentence of holy law, and Luke 11.30; 17.24, 26, 28a + 30 are eschatological correlatives. This is not surprising, since the two types resemble one another in both form and judgmental purpose.

The kernel sayings refer only to the future activity of the Son of man. He will be a sign; he will acknowledge and deny men in the presence of God in the judgment; he (or his day) will be like a lightning flash; it will be on the day of the Son of man as it was in Noah's generation, as it was in the days of Lot.

The kernel sayings all come from Q.

The kernel sayings together form a unitary conception of the eschatological functions of the Son of man.

Luke 17.24, 26-30 emphasizes and warns of the suddenness of the (judgment) day of the Son of man.

Luke 11.29-32, taken as an original unit of dominical teaching, points to the Son of man as a sign, as the sign of Jonah, i.e. to the fulfilment of judgment in the celestial court, and to the Son of man as the embodiment of divine judgment, as himself the judge.

Luke 12.8f. presupposes the judgmental status and function of the Son of man in the other two passages, and formulates the vital principle that the verdict will depend on a man's attitude to Jesus and his message. The Son of man will be more than an ordinary witness in the great judgment; he will be judge, but not the sole judge nor the presiding judge. He will exercise his judicial functions as assessor alongside God the supreme judge, from whom he receives authorization to judge,[1] and in whose presence ('before the angels of God', Luke 12.8f.) he will testify for or against a man as advocate or accuser, as the case may be.

Although the Son of man kernel sayings are the only substantially genuine cases, echoes of Jesus' words may be discernible in some secondary formulations: Matt. 19.28; 24.30a;[2] Luke 21.36.

The status of the kernel sayings as substantially authentic words of Jesus is supported by their general agreement with his other teaching, by their mutual coherence constituting a consistent unitary Son of man conception, and by the Semitic (Aramaic) elements of their language, including poetic form and parallelism.

It is also supported by the distinctiveness of the Son of man conception. On the reasonable assumption (still not disproved) of the existence of a Son of man concept in Judaism, Jesus was unique in applying to it a completely new and original non-personal, functional interpretation, as a means of expressing, in veiled and often misunderstood language, his beliefs about the eschatological judgment, including the ideas of the Son of man as a 'sign', and of 'the sign of Jonah', itself also a new creation. Further, if authentic Son of man sayings are confined to the kernel sayings, Jesus' thought on the subject must have differed also from that of the early church. For it is the church's beliefs, not those of Jesus, that are expressed not only in the sayings regarding the *Son of man's* ministry on earth,[3] and those foretelling his passion, death and resurrection, but also in those about the Son of man as coming, whether *simpliciter*: Matt. 10.23; Luke 12.40, par. Matt. 24.44; Luke 18.8b, or as coming in glory, on or with the clouds of heaven, or with the angels: Matt. 13.41; 16.27, 28; 24.30; 25.31; Mark 8.38b; 13.26; 14.62, and in the parousia sayings in Matt. 24. 27, 37,

39.[4] The absence of all these apocalyptic features from the kernel sayings is surely significant; virtually the only item of apocalyptic imagery is the Son of man himself.[5] But this is so interpreted that for Jesus the Son of man is not a personal figure, but a symbolical description of his own expected dignity, status and function as judge.

The criterion of multiple attestation, along with variation of form, is satisfied for Luke 11.29f. by Mark 8.12, and for Luke 12.8f. by Mark 8.38. The Q sayings in Luke 17 are reported also in part in Matt. 24.26f., 37-9, the remainder only in Luke 17.28-30. In common with a good many other sayings attributable to Jesus, including those not attested by more than one source or tradition, all these have claims to authenticity on other grounds.[6] That the sayings source Q is the source to which they all belong is also in their favour, rather than the reverse.

The kernel sayings are independent of, and older than, the *pesher* interpretation of Dan. 7.13, and owe nothing to it. They come from Jesus and, apart from some redactional modifications, have retained substantially their original form.

The *pesher* texts narrow down the Son of man concept exhibited in the kernel sayings from Jesus' general proclamation. That is, Mark 13.26 and 14.62, reflecting Dan. 7.13 directly, and all texts (listed above) reflecting it indirectly in references to the Son of man as 'coming', with or without the mention of the clouds of heaven, or to his parousia, detail and particularize, with varying degrees of apocalyptic embroidery, the representation of the Son of man's future activity in the kernel sayings.

The Son of man christology originated neither in *pesher* interpretation of Ps. 110.1 and Dan. 7.13, nor in the theology of Q, but in Jesus' own preaching.

Concluding remarks

It is remarkable that Jesus is not recorded as ever prefacing with the words, 'The Son of man says', or 'I, the Son of man, say', any of his authoritative pronouncements - for example, the antithesis between the Torah and his teaching ('You have heard that it was said . . . , but I say to you . . . ', Matt. 5.21f., etc.), and the amen sayings (always in the form, 'Amen, I say to you'). The explanation suggests itself that, so far from being a self-designation, the term Son of man was confined to Jesus' clothing of his message of his anticipated judicial function in the judgment in symbolic imagery. Two of the kernel sayings are relevant here. The original form of the sign of Jonah saying probably ran: 'How this generation seeks a sign! Truly, I say to you, no sign will be given this generation. The sign of Jonah will certainly be given to it' (Mark 8.12, par. Luke 11.29, to which belongs verse 30 as also Jesus' word). Likewise, the saying about the Son of man confessing and denying is introduced with 'I say to you' (Luke 12.8). Not even in alluding mysteriously and enigmatically to the future does Jesus offer any clue to the meaning of 'the Son of man', as, for example, by declaring, 'I, the Son of man, say to you'.[7]

'Son of man' is the only christological title derived from Jesus' own usage.[8] The Son of man christology is the earliest christology in the sense that it developed out of an element of Jesus' own proclamation. It is to his use of the title and concept that all Son of man sayings in the four gospels ultimately owe their existence. Through its understanding that Jesus was himself the Son of man, the early church, by increasing the use of the term in future references and by extending it to Jesus' earthly ministry, passion and resurrection, restored to it a personal content which, in Jesus' usage, although referring to his future status, it did not possess.

Even if the surviving authentic Son of man sayings are confined to the few kernel sayings, this does not mean that the Son of man, as interpreted by Jesus, played a minor role in his thought. The future activity of the Son of man appears to have occupied a significant place in his thought of the future. Just as the kingdom of God, already active in his words and works, was an earnest of the kingdom as it would be in its total fullness, so his earthly ministry would be followed by the transcendent activity of the Son of man sharing in judgment and rule. Jesus envisaged his mission as destined, in no very distant future, to be validated and vindicated through his being given a status of exaltation in the presence of God, there to fulfil the functions of the 'Son of man'.

The Son of man is not only the judge of the wicked; he is also the bringer of salvation.[9] A judge acquits or pardons as well as pronounces guilty. The Son of man will acknowledge those who have acknowledged Jesus (Luke 12.8). The apparently uncompromising and unrelieved harshness of sayings like Luke 11.31f. and 17.26f., 28–30 does not exclude all possibility of forgiveness. Even though the Queen of the South and the Ninevites will join in testifying against 'this generation' in the judgment, there is still time for those who are ready to repent. Even though the men of Noah's day were drowned by the flood, and the men of Lot's day were destroyed by the rain of fire and sulphur, a remnant escaped. There is an unexpressed but implied 'unless you repent' (cf. Luke 13.3, 5). The burden of Jesus' message was the approach of the kingdom in all its fullness and power, and the urgent need of repentance in view of its coming (Mark 1.15). Jesus' choice of Son of man terminology, in conjunction with the striking and dramatic imagery of the kernel sayings (and probably of others that have not survived in the tradition), served to awaken a sense of urgency and to reinforce and intensify his call to repentance.

NOTES

Introduction

1 Admittedly the hypothesis of a Jewish apocalyptic Son of man title and concept has in recent years come under heavy attack. It remains permissible, however, to question whether Jesus could have originated the use of the Son of man term in an 'apocalyptic' sense, as Barnabas Lindars has recently suggested (see Excursus to chapter II), and to ask whether some of the future sayings with which the present study is concerned may themselves constitute evidence for earlier usage. Professor John Bowker's article, 'The Son of Man' (*JTS* N.S. 28, 1977, pp. 19–48), appeared too late for more than brief mention here. Unconvinced both by Lindars' argument for Jesus' originality in calling himself Son of man as God's agent, and by the claim of Vermes that *bar nasha* in Jesus' teaching is an idiomatic Aramaic circumlocution for the first-person singular pronoun, Bowker aims to show that Jesus spoke of himself in no apocalyptic sense, but – linking the two major biblical meanings of 'son of man' – as man subject to death and yet destined for vindication by God.

It should be noted that in the present study the form 'Son of man' is regularly employed except where the variations 'Son of Man' and 'son of man' are required in discussion of the work of scholars who use the one or the other.

2 See J. Jeremias, *New Testament Theology* I, London 1971, pp. 281f. The saying, however, is not necessarily a *mashal* or riddle, as Jeremias claims, on the ground that *bar nasha* could also be understood as the title Son of man.

Chapter I

1 H. E. Tödt, *The Son of Man in the Synoptic Tradition*, London 1965, chapter 1, 'The Transcendent Sovereignty of the Son of Man in Jewish Apocalyptic Literature'.

2 E. Jüngel, 'Jesus und der Menschensohn', *Paulus und Jesus* (Hermeneutische Untersuchungen zur Theologie 2), Tübingen [4]1972, pp. 215–62.

3 F. Hahn, *The Titles of Jesus in Christology*, London 1969, chapter 1.

4 D. E. Nineham, *The Gospel of Saint Mark*, Harmondsworth 1963, pp. 46f.

5 R. H. Fuller, *The Foundations of New Testament Christology*, London 1965, pp. 34–43 (p. 42).

6 C. K. Barrett, *Jesus and the Gospel Tradition*, London 1967, p. 32.

7 *Ibid.*, p. 94, following E. Sjöberg, *Der Menschensohn im äthiopischen Henochbuch*, Lund 1946.

8 P. Vielhauer, 'Gottesreich und Menschensohn in der Verkündigung Jesu' in *Festschrift für Günther Dehn*, ed. W. Schneemelcher, Neukirchen 1957, pp. 51–79, and 'Jesus und der Menschensohn: zur Diskussion mit Heinz Eduard Tödt und Eduard Schweizer', *ZTK* 60, 1963, pp. 133–77; both reprinted in Vielhauer, *Aufsätze zum Neuen Testament*, Munich 1965, pp. 55–91 and 92–140.

9 H. Conzelmann, 'Gegenwart und Zukunft in der synoptischen Tradition', *ZTK* 54, 1957, pp. 277ff.; 'Jesus Christus', *RGG* III[3], cols. 630f., ET *Jesus*, ed. J. Reumann, Philadelphia 1973, pp. 43–6; *An Outline of the Theology of the New Testament*, London 1969, pp. 131–7.

10 H. M. Teeple, 'Origin of the Son of Man Christology', *JBL* 84, 1965, pp. 213–50, especially pp. 244, 250.

11 F. H. Borsch, *The Son of Man in Myth and History*, London 1967 (cited as *SMMH*).

12 Leivestad, Perrin, Vermes.

13 *SMMH*, p. 87.

14 *Ibid.*, pp. 121f.

15 *Ibid.*, p. 210.

16 *Ibid.*, pp. 218f.

17 *Ibid.*, p. 220.

18 *Ibid.*, p. 221.

19 A. R. C. Leaney, *The Rule of Qumran and its Meaning*, London 1966, p. 157, on 1QH 3.7–10 and 1QS 4.20–3.

20 Borsch, *SMMH*, p. 223.

21 *Ibid.*, p. 225.

22 *Ibid.*, p. 226.

23 *Ibid.*, pp. 226–9.

24 *Ibid.*, p. 229.

25 *Ibid.*, p. 230.

26 *Ibid.*, p. 219.

27 C. Colpe, '*ὁ υἱὸς τοῦ ἀνθρώπου*', *TDNT* VIII, 1972, pp. 400–77.

28 *Ibid.*, pp. 408–15.

29 *Ibid.*, pp. 415–19; cf. J. A. Emerton, 'The Origin of the Son of Man Imagery', *JTS* N.S. 9, 1958, pp. 225–42.

30 Colpe, '*ὁ υἱὸς τοῦ ἀνθρώπου*', p. 420.

31 *Ibid.*, pp. 420–30.

32 Leaving chapters 70f. aside at this stage.

33 The first occurrence is in 46.2: 'And I asked the angel who went with me and showed me all the hidden things, concerning that Son of man.' Whether the variant expressions for 'Son of man' are simply due to careless translation of a single Greek phrase or represent three different expressions in Aramaic (or Hebrew) underlying the Greek remains uncertain, but the former alternative is perhaps more likely.

34 Colpe, '*ὁ υἱὸς τοῦ ἀνθρώπου*', pp. 426f., regards these chapters as an addition or appendix.

35 R. H. Charles, *The Book of Enoch or 1 Enoch Translated from the Editor's Ethiopic Text*, Oxford 1912, *ad loc.*

36 Following in the main C. P. van Andel, *De Structuur van de Henoch-Traditie en het Nieuwe Testament*, Utrecht 1955.

37 Colpe, 'ὁ υἱὸς τοῦ ἀνθρώπου', p. 429: 'one must conclude that the oldest stratum of the Synoptic tradition suggests a Jewish Son of Man tradition which provisionally constitutes a fourth source alongside those already mentioned'.

38 *Ibid.*, pp. 433–7. The eight sayings 'yield a self-contained apocalyptic picture and seem to stand up to critical analysis' (p. 433).

39 Following Glasson, 'The Ensign of the Son of Man (Matt. XXIV. 30)', *JTS* N.S. 15, 1964, pp. 299f.

40 Colpe, 'ὁ υἱὸς τοῦ ἀνθρώπου', p. 437: 'It is hardly possible that there could be any other source for it than Jesus' own preaching.'

41 *Ibid.*, pp. 438f.

42 *Ibid.*, pp. 430–3.

43 *Ibid.*, p. 438. Colpe's German text reads: 'Jesus muss als Prophet selbst in dieser apocalyptischen Tradition gelebt und den Menschensohn angekündigt haben', *TWNT* VIII, p. 441, lines 27–8. The translation in *TDNT*, 'and that He proclaimed Himself to be the Son of Man', is incorrect; three paragraphs later (p. 439, last paragraph) Colpe makes quite clear his opinion that Jesus did not do this.

44 See A. J. B. Higgins, *Jesus and the Son of Man*, London 1964 (cited as *JSM*), p. 15; Fuller, *Foundations*, pp. 36f.

45 A. Hilgenfeld and G. Volkmar held the former view, J. C. K. von Hofmann, H. Weisse, and F. Philippi the latter; for further literature see *JSM*, p. 198 n. 2.

46 *Ibid.*

47 1QSa (= 1Q28a) 2.12, 20; 2.14; 4QPatr 3; Cave 1, fragment 30, line 2; CD 12.23f.; 14.19; 19.10f.; 20.1; see my article, 'The Priestly Messiah', *NTS* 13, 1966–7, pp. 211–39 (pp. 215–19). On the absence of 'transcendental' messianism from the Qumran literature, see F. M. Cross, *The Ancient Library of Qumran and Modern Biblical Studies*, p. 150 n. 7; he attributes the absence of the Similitudes from this literature to their 'post-Essene' composition.

48 M. Burrows, *More Light on the Dead Sea Scrolls,* New York 1958, p. 72.

49 C. F. D. Moule, *The Phenomenon of the New Testament*, London 1967, p. 34 n. 21.

50 M. Black, 'The Son of Man Problem in Recent Research and Debate', *BJRL* 45, 1962–3, pp. 305–18 (p. 312).

51 J. Barr, 'Messiah', HDB, p. 651.

52 J. C. Hindley, 'Towards a Date for the Similitudes', *NTS* 14, 1967–8, pp. 551–65. Borsch's remarks in *The Christian and Gnostic Son of Man*, London 1970 (cited as *CGSM*), p. 19 n. 67, on Hindley's suggestions are very much to the point: most of the materials in the Similitudes are difficult to date in relation to known historical events; evidence of Christian influence upon them is slight or non-existent; cf. Jeremias, *Theology* I, p. 269 n. 5.

53 Colpe, 'ὁ υἱὸς τοῦ ἀνθρώπου', p. 423 n. 180, supports a date before the destruction of Jerusalem in A.D. 70 which, he urges, would surely have been mentioned had it already taken place, and after 40–38 B.C. Despite the non-appearance of the Similitudes among the Qumran texts, he inclines to a dating nearer the earlier than the later period.

54 J. T. Milik, 'Problèmes de la littérature Hénochique à la lumière des fragments araméens de Qumrân', *Harvard Theological Review* 64, 1971, pp. 333–78 (pp. 373–8); cf. earlier Milik's *Ten Years of Discovery in the Wilderness of Judaea*, London 1959, p. 33: the Similitudes were composed by a Jew or a Jewish Christian in the first or second century; Cross, *The Ancient Library of Qumran*, p. 150 n. 7: the complete absence of the Similitudes from the Qumran fragments of Enoch indicates that this section is 'post-Essene in date, and Christian in its received form'; R. N. Longenecker, *The Christology of Early Jewish Christianity*, London 1970, pp. 82–5: 'possibly by a Jewish Christian with roots of some type in Jewish Essenism' (p. 85). The discussion is entering upon a new phase with the publication of Milik's edition of the Qumran Aramaic fragments; see M. Black, 'The "Parables" of Enoch (1 En 37–71) and the "Son of Man"', *ExpT* 78, 1976–7, pp. 5–8; also T. F. Glasson, 'The Son of Man Imagery: Enoch xiv and Daniel vii', *NTS* 23, 1976–7, pp. 82–90. The monograph of J. Theisohn, *Der auserwählte Richter: Untersuchungen zum traditionsgeschichtlichen Ort der Menschensohngestalt der Bilderreden des Äthiopischen Henoch* (Studien zur Umwelt des Neuen Testaments 12), Göttingen 1975, reached me too late for adequate discussion here.

55 Jeremias, *Theology* I, p. 269 n. 5.

56 R. Leivestad, 'Der apokalyptische Menschensohn ein theologisches Phantom', *Annual of the Swedish Theological Institute* (Jerusalem) VI, 1968, pp. 49–105; more briefly in 'Exit the Apocalyptic Son of Man', *NTS* 18, 1971–2, pp. 243–67.

57 See further below, pp. 22–3.

58 G. Vermes, *Jesus the Jew*, London 1973, p. 175.

59 N. Perrin, *Rediscovering the Teaching of Jesus*, London 1967, pp. 164–72; see his earlier statements in 'The Son of Man in Ancient Judaism and Primitive Christianity', *Biblical Research* 11, 1966, pp. 17–28; 'New Beginnings in Christology: A Review Article', *JR* 46, 1966, pp. 491–6.

60 Perrin, *Rediscovering*, pp. 166f.

61 *Ibid*., p. 167.

62 *Ibid*., p. 166 n.

63 *Ibid*., p. 260.

64 M. Black, 'The Eschatology of the Similitudes of Enoch', *JTS* N.S. 3, 1952, pp. 1–10.

65 The address to the prophet Ezekiel as Son of man (Ezek. 2.1) was for the seer the link between the two scenes.

66 Perrin, *Rediscovering*, pp. 172f.

67 *Ibid*., p. 170.

68 In a trenchant review of Perrin's book, W. G. Kümmel expresses the view that his 'contesting of the existence of a Jewish apocalyptic Son of Man figure is ... completely untenable', *JR* 49, 1969, p. 64.

69 F. Hahn, *Christologische Hoheitstitel* (FRLANT 83), Göttingen 1963, p. 22 n. 1 and p. 19 n. 3 (both omitted in ET). Albright and Mann think this absence proves nothing about the date of composition which, in view of some resemblances to the Hymns of Thanksgiving, they assign to approximately the same period, 175–140 B.C.: W. F. Albright and C. S. Mann, 'Qumran and the Essenes: Geography, Chronology, and Identification of the Sect' in *The Scrolls and Christianity*, ed. M. Black, London 1969, pp. 11–25 (pp. 25, 108 n. 9).

70 Metzger, 'Pseudepigrapha', HDB, p. 821 (following S. Mathews in the first edition (1909), p. 40).
71 Vielhauer, *Aufsätze*, p. 132; cf. H. H. Rowley, *The Relevance of Apocalyptic*, London [3]1963, p. 60 n.
72 E. Schweizer, 'The Son of Man Again', *NTS* 9, 1962–3, pp. 256–61.
73 *Ibid.*, p. 259.
74 *Ibid.*, pp. 259f.
75 Fuller, *Foundations*, pp. 37f.
76 *Ibid.*, p. 57 n. 47.
77 S. Mowinckel, *He That Cometh*, Oxford 1956, pp. 440–4; for some of the literature on 1 En. 70f. see my article, 'Son of Man-*Forschung* since "The Teaching of Jesus"' *in New Testament Essays*, ed. A. J. B. Higgins, Manchester 1959, pp. 119–35 (p. 134 n. 58).
78 Charles, *The Book of Enoch Translated*, p. 141.
79 But three of the Ethiopic manuscripts, U, V, and W, explicitly apply the title Son of man to Enoch at 70.1, in that they say that it was the name of the Son of man (i.e. Enoch) that was raised aloft to the Lord of Spirits, and not, as in the usual text, his (Enoch's) name that was raised aloft 'to that Son of man and to the Lord of Spirits'; see F. Martin, *Le Livre d'Hénoch traduit sur le texte éthiopien*, Paris 1906, pp. lxxxiii, 158; Black, 'Eschatology of the Similitudes', p. 4 n. 2; Higgins, 'The Priestly Messiah', pp. 212f. The significance of the variant is debatable.
80 Fuller, *Foundations*, pp. 40f.
81 Black, 'Eschatology of the Similitudes'. For the Manson Memorial Lecture see Black, 'The Son of Man Problem'; cf. *Peake's Commentary on the Bible* ed. M. Black and H. H. Rowley, London and Edinburgh 1962, p. 697, section 608d.
82 Black, 'The Son of Man Problem', pp. 311f.
83 Fuller, *Foundations*, p. 38, takes the opposite view, that the demonstratives, as renderings of the Greek definite article, show that a title *is* intended: '*the* Son of man'; cf. Mowinckel, *He That Cometh*, pp. 362ff., who thought it likely that both the Greek and the original Semitic texts had the corresponding demonstratives.
84 He is the anointed one, 48.10; 52.4.
85 Sjöberg, *Der Menschensohn im äthiopischen Henochbuch.* p. 158.
86 Colpe, '*ὁ υἱὸς τοῦ ἀνθρώπου*' p. 427.
87 Barrett, *Jesus and the Gospel Tradition*, p. 92.
88 *Ibid.*, p. 94.
89 *Ibid.*, p. 95; cf. Barrett, *The New Testament Background: Selected Documents*, London 1956, p. 255.
90 R. Otto, *Reichgottes und Menschensohn*, Munich 1934; ET *The Kingdom of God and the Son of Man*, London [2]1943.
91 M. Black, *An Aramaic Approach to the Gospels and Acts*, Oxford [3]1967, pp. 310–28.
92 *Ibid.*, p. 327.
93 *Ibid.*, p. 328.
94 I retain Vermes' form of the phrase without capitals in the following discussion.
95 See immediately below.
96 G. Vermes, *Jesus the Jew*, London 1973, chapter 7, I: 'The son of man in Jewish Writings', pp. 162–77.

97 Black, *Aramaic Approach*, pp. 328–30.
98 Vermes, *Jesus the Jew*, p. 189; the reference is to Black's article, 'The "Son of Man" in the Teaching of Jesus', *ExpT* 60, 1948–9, pp. 32–6, a page-long extract from which forms the major part of his critique.
99 J. Jeremias, 'Die älteste Schicht der Menschensohn-Logien', *ZNW* 58, 1967, pp. 159–72 (p. 165 and n. 9); *Theology* I, p. 261 n. 1.
100 Cf. Colpe, '*ὁ υἱὸς τοῦ ἀνθρώπου*', pp. 403f.: for 'I' *bar nasha* is not found, but only *hahu gabra*, 'that man', although a speaker could in the former include himself; R. Le Déaut, 'Le substrat araméen des évangiles: scolies en marge de l'*Aramaic Approach* de Matthew Black', *Biblica* (Rome) 49, 1968, pp. 397–9. Colpe's article in *TDNT* VIII escapes Vermes' attentions, except for honourable mention in *Jesus the Jew*, p. 261 n. 91. See also A. Gelston, 'A Sidelight on the "Son of Man" ', *SJT* 22, 1969, pp. 189–96 (p. 189 n. 2): there is also 'the wider generic sense of "man" ("I as a particular man" or "I *qua* man"), so that the phrase is more than a mere circumlocution for "I"'
101 Vermes, *Jesus the Jew*, p. 189.
102 In Black, *Aramaic Approach*, p. 327.
103 Vermes, *Jesus the Jew*, pp. 169–77.
104 *Ibid.*, p. 177.
105 See above, n. 56.
106 Leivestad, 'Exit the Apocalyptic Son of Man', p. 244: 'A Jewish Son of man title was completely unknown to Jesus and the primitive church.'
107 Leivestad, 'Der apokalyptische Menschensohn', p. 50: 'Der apokalyptische Menschensohn ist eine Erfindung der modernen Theologie'; p. 101: 'Der apokalyptische Menschensohn ist eine theologische Erfindung der letzten hundert Jahre.' Compare the late Dr Paul Winter's statement, quoted by Vermes, *Jesus the Jew*, p. 186, that if Perrin's hypothesis about the Son of man sayings is correct, 'the place of origin of the myth is not to be sought in Iran, or in Judea or even in Ugarit, but in the German universities'!
108 This is because the Greek phrase would presuppose Hebrew *ben ha-adam*, but the definite article is not used before 'son of man' in biblical or post-biblical Hebrew; the sole known exception is a second copyist's addition of it over the word for 'man' in 1QS 11.20: *The Dead Sea Scrolls of St. Mark's Monastery*, II.2: *Plates and Transcriptions of the Manual of Discipline*, ed. M. Burrows, New Haven 1951; Vermes, *Jesus the Jew*, p. 162 and p. 256 n. 8; Colpe, p. 402, following Vermes, thinks this may be an Aramaism.
109 Leivestad, 'Exit the Apocalyptic Son of Man', p. 265.
110 *Ibid.*
111 Vermes, *Jesus the Jew*, p. 177.
112 Leivestad, 'Exit the Apocalyptic Son of Man', p. 267. Rightly he does not favour Ezekiel as the inspiration of Jesus' usage; see 'Der apokalyptische Menschensohn', p. 102.
113 Ezekiel may be said to have regarded 'son of man' (= 'man') as descriptive of his prophetic office, and therefore as, in that sense, a self-designation; cf. G. W. Buchanan, *To the Hebrews: Translation, Comment and Conclusions*, New York 1972, p. 42 n. 55. But in Ezekiel in this usage *ben adam* is confined to divine address to the prophet, while Jesus is never addressed as 'son of man' by God or man.
114 For the question of languages in first-century Palestine and the place of

spoken Hebrew, see J. A. Fitzmyer, 'The Languages of Palestine in the First Century A.D.', *Catholic Biblical Quarterly* 32, 1970, pp. 501–31; also his 'Methodology in the Study of the Aramaic Substratum of Jesus' Sayings in the New Testament' in *Jésus aux origines de la christologie*, ed. J. Dupont, Louvain 1975, pp. 73–102; J. Barr, 'Which Language did Jesus Speak? – Some Remarks of a Semitist', *BJRL* 53, 1970–1, pp. 9–29; J. A. Emerton, 'The Problem of Vernacular Hebrew in the First Century A.D. and the Language of Jesus', *JTS* N.S. 24, 1973, pp. 1–23; P. Lapide, 'Insights from Qumran into the Languages of Jesus', *Revue de Qumran* 8.4 (December 1975), pp. 483–501.

115 Vermes, *Jesus the Jew*, pp. 177–86.

116 *Ibid.*, p. 182.

117 Vermes lists next Mark 10.45; 14.21; 14.41 and their parallels; for the view that the first two are developments from possibly authentic 'I' words, see *JSM*, pp. 49, 51. It is correct that Jesus' own predictions, which are the ultimate source of all the passion logia, probably referred only to his approaching death, with no mention of vindication.

118 Vermes, *Jesus the Jew*, pp. 180–2, with the notes.

119 Cf. Jeremias, *Theology* I, p. 262 and n. 1.

120 Cf. *JSM*, p. 30.

121 Vermes, *Jesus the Jew*, pp. 186, 182.

122 See below, chapter III, sections 5 and 6.

123 Vermes, *Jesus the Jew*, p. 183.

124 *Ibid.*, chapter 6, 'Jesus the Messiah', pp. 129–56.

125 *Ibid.*, p. 186.

126 O. Cullmann, *Jesus and the Revolutionaries*, New York 1970; M. Hengel, *Was Jesus a Revolutionist?*, Philadelphia 1971.

127 Vermes, *Jesus the Jew*, p. 211.

128 See, for example, N. Perrin, *The Kingdom of God in the Teaching of Jesus*, London 1963, pp. 112–29, especially pp. 124–7.

129 Yet my emphasis upon the functional and non-personal nature of Jesus' references to the Son of man renders inappropriate such a use of *bar nasha* in future sayings.

130 At least there is no problem, as there is with the Ethiopic version of the Similitudes, about the first-century date of the gospel sayings even in their Greek form.

131 Vermes, *Jesus the Jew*, p. 184.

132 See my remarks in 'Is the Son of Man Problem Insoluble?' in *Neotestamentica et Semitica: Studies in Honour of Matthew Black*, ed. E. E. Ellis and M. Wilcox, Edinburgh 1969, pp. 70–87 (pp. 85–7). On the fragment, see A. S. van der Woude, 'Melchisedek als himmlische Erlösergestalt in den neugefundenen eschatologischen Midraschim aus Qumran Höhle XI', *Oudtestamentische Studiën* XIV, ed. P. A. H. de Boer, 1965, pp. 354–73; A. S. van der Woude and M. de Jonge, '11Q Melchizedek and the New Testament', *NTS* 12, 1965–6, pp. 301–26; D. Flusser, 'Melchizedek and the Son of Man', *Christian News from Israel* 17, 1966, pp. 23–9; J. A. Emerton, 'Melchizedek and the Gods', *JTS* N.S. 17, 1966, pp. 399–401; J. A. Fitzmyer, 'Further Light on Melchizedek from Qumran Cave 11', *JBL* 86, 1967, pp. 25–41; F. L. Horton, *The Melchizedek Tradition: A Critical*

Examination of the Sources to the Fifth Century A.D. and in the Epistle to the Hebrews, Cambridge 1976, especially pp. 64–82.

133 Unless, of course, this absence is due either to the sect's ignorance of them if they existed, or to their non-existence at the time. On the probability of an original Aramaic 1 Enoch as the direct *Vorlage* of the Ethiopic version see E. Ullendorff, *Ethiopia and the Bible*, London 1968, pp. 61f.; cf. A. M. Denis, *Introduction aux Pseudépigraphes Grecs d'Ancien Testament*, Leiden 1970, p. 26; M. Black (ed.), *Apocalypsis Henochi Graece* in *Pseudepigrapha Veteris Testamenti Graece* III, ed. A. M. Denis and M. De Jonge, Leiden 1970, pp. 6f.

134 (1) However, the interpretation of van der Woude, de Jonge, and Fitzmyer, that 11QMelch represents Melchizedek as a heavenly or angelic being, has been challenged by J. Carmignac in an important article, 'Le Document de Qumran sur Melkisédeq', *Revue de Qumran* 7.3 (December 1970), pp. 343–78. He examines four hypotheses (pp. 363–9). (i) Melchizedek is the figure of past biblical history (Gen. 14.18–20). This he rejects, because this *pesher*, in common with the rest, concerns, not the time of Abraham, but the history of the Qumran community. (ii) The interpretation of van der Woude and others adopted here he also rejects. He says that the author, following Qumran usage, employs *el* when referring to God, and *elim* when referring to celestial beings, but that in quoting scripture he follows the biblical text, and consequently both *elohim* and *el* in the first line of the quotation from Ps. 82.1 refer to God, and Melchizedek cannot be meant. (iii) The sect expected someone who would be, as it were, a second Melchizedek, a 'king of righteousness' indeed (cf. Heb. 7.2) in slaying the wicked and delivering the righteous - a military leader rather than a priest. (iv) Alternatively, this expected leader would actually bear the appropriate name Melchizedek, 'king of righteousness'. Carmignac decides in favour of either (iii) or (iv).

(2) This exegesis of Carmignac has been convincingly refuted by M. Delcor in 'Melchizedek from Genesis to the Qumran Texts and the Epistle to the Hebrews', *Journal for the Study of Judaism* 2, 1971, pp. 115–35. He affirms the correctness of the interpretation of van der Woude, and sees in Melchizedek in this Qumran document a celestial being, an eschatological judge and saviour (whom he identifies with Michael, also a celestial being in the thought of the sect (pp. 124f., 133f.)).

(3) Among the many lacunae in 11QMelch there is one in line 13 between 'and Melchizedek will avenge with the vengeance of the judgments of God' and 'from the hand of Belial and from the hand of all [the spirits of] his [lot]'. F. Du Toit Laubscher, 'God's Angel of Truth and Melchizedek: A Note on 11QMelch 13b', *Journal for the Study of Judaism* 3, 1972, pp. 46–51, has proposed a conjecture for this lacuna which, if correct, is of great importance for this question of Melchizedek.

In general the contents of 11QMelch are closely related to the final conflict between the powers of light and darkness described in the War Scroll (1QM). Laubscher shows that this is true also of another text, 4QCatena A fragments 12–13. In particular he calls attention to col.1.7, '. . . his angel of truth will help all the children of light from the hand of Belial . . .' This he uses to restore the lacuna in 11QMelch 13, so that the second part of the passage may now be read as follows: 'and he [i.e. Melchizedek, the subject at the beginning of the sentence] will help all the children of light from the hand of Belial and from the hand of all the spirits of his lot'. The evidence presented by Laubscher makes this restoration of the lacuna extremely probable, and indeed virtually certain. Both Melchizedek in this text, and God's angel of truth in the corresponding context in 4QCatena A f12–13, are thus said to help the children of light from the power of Belial. This parallelism, Laubscher claims, confirms van der Woude's view that Melchizedek is a heavenly being, because in an identical context Melchizedek stands in the place of 'his angel of truth' in 4QCatena A f12–13, and so is implicitly called an angel.

There can remain no doubt as to how the figure of Melchizedek should be understood. Whether the hypothesis of possible influence from a Son of man concept is acceptable or not depends largely on one's attitude to the Son of man problem as a whole.

For the interpretation of Melchizedek in 11QMelch as a hypostasis of God rather than as an angel, see J. T. Milik, '*Milki-sedeq* et *Milki-resa* dans les anciens écrits juifs et chrétiens', *Journal of Jewish Studies* 23, 1972, pp. 95–144 (pp. 96–109).

Chapter II

1 See, for example, R. Marlow, 'The *Son of Man* in Recent Journal Literature', *Catholic Biblical Quarterly* 28, 1966, pp. 20–30: a summary of research based on the work of Cullmann and Mowinckel, down to 1955, followed by a bibliography of articles from 1953 to 1965, and brief outlines of most of them; G. Haufe, 'Das Menschensohn-Problem in der gegenwärtigen wissenschaftlichen Diskussion', *EvT* 26, 1966, pp. 130–41: covers the period 1954-64; I. H. Marshall, 'The Synoptic Son of Man Sayings', *NTS* 12, 1965–6, pp. 327–51; Marshall, 'The Son of Man in Contemporary Debate', *EQ* 42, 1970, pp. 67–87; J. N. Birdsall, 'Who is this Son of Man?' EQ 42, 1970, pp. 7–17: a review article surveying books by Tödt, Higgins, Fuller, Morna Hooker and Borsch; J. Reumann, *Jesus in the Church's Gospels*, London 1970, pp. 267–79; O. Michel, 'Der Menschensohn', *Theologische Zeitschrift* 27, 1971, pp. 81–104; H. Boers, 'Where Christology is Real', *Interpretation* 26, 1972, pp. 302–15.

2 L. Goppelt, 'Zum Problem des Menschensohns: das Verhältnis von Leidens- und Parusieankündigung' in *Mensch und Menschensohn*, ed. H. Sierig, Hamburg 1963, pp. 20–32.

3 C. F. D. Moule, *The New Testament Gospels*, London 1965, pp. 46–9; *The Phenomenon of the New Testament*, pp. 34–6; review of Tödt, *The Son of Man in the Synoptic Tradition*, in *Theology* 69, April 1966, pp. 172–4.

4 R. Maddox, 'The Function of the Son of Man According to the Synoptic Gospels', *NTS* 15, 1968–9, pp. 45–74; see further below, p. 46.

5 I. H. Marshall, 'The Synoptic Son of Man Sayings in Recent Discussion', *NTS* 12, 1965–6, pp. 327–51.

6 Barrett, *Jesus and the Gospel Tradition*, London 1967.

7 F. F. Bruce, *This is That*, Exeter 1968, pp. 26–30, 97–9; see also W. G. Kümmel, *The Theology of the New Testament*, London 1974, pp. 76–90; G. N. Stanton, *Jesus of Nazareth in New Testament Preaching*, London 1974, pp. 156–67; G. E. Ladd, *A Theology of the New Testament*, Guildford and London 1975, pp. 145–58.

8 Marshall, 'Synoptic Son of Man Sayings', p. 350.
9 Barrett, *Jesus and the Gospel Tradition*, p. 41.
10 *Ibid*., pp. 77ff.
11 E. Schweizer, 'Der Menschensohn', *ZNW* 50, 1959, pp. 185–209; 'The Son of Man', *JBL* 79, 1960, pp. 119–29; 'The Son of Man Again', *NTS* 9, 1962–3, pp. 256–61; *Lordship and Discipleship*, London 1960; *Erniedrigung und Erhöhung bei Jesus und seinen Nachfolgern*, Zürich [2]1962; *Das Evangelium nach Markus*, Göttingen 1967, pp. 94–6 (ET: *Good News according to Mark*, London 1971, pp. 166–71); *Jesus*, London 1971, pp. 20f.
12 Jub. 4.23; 10.17; Wisd. of Sol. 2–5; 1 En. 71; cf. *JSM*, pp. 23f., 206f.
13 M. Black, 'The "Son of Man" in the Old Biblical Literature', *ExpT* 60, 1948–9, pp. 11–15; 'The "Son of Man" in the Teaching of Jesus', *ExpT* 60, 1948–9, pp. 32–6; 'The Eschatology of the Similitudes of Enoch', *JTS* N.S.3, 1952, pp. 1–10; 'Servant of the Lord and Son of Man', *SJT* 6, 1953, pp. 1–11; *Peake's Commentary on the Bible*, 1962, p. 697, section 608d; *A Companion to the Bible*, ed. H. H. Rowley, London [2]1963, pp. 82f.; 'From Schweitzer to Bultmann: The Modern Quest of the Historical Jesus', *McCormick Quarterly* 20, 1966–7, pp. 271–83; 'The "Son of Man" Passion Sayings in the Gospel Tradition', *ZNW* 60, 1969, pp. 1–8.
14 M. Black, 'The Son of Man Problem in Recent Research and Debate', *BJRL* 45, 1962–3, pp. 305–18.
15 Schweizer, 'The Son of Man', *JBL* 79, 1960, p. 123.
16 E. Lohmeyer, *Kyrios Jesus: Eine Untersuchung zu Phil. 2, 5–11*, Heidelberg 1928.
17 See *JSM*, p. 151 n. 1.
18 Schweizer, 'Der Menschensohn', pp. 203–5.
19 Black, 'The Son of Man Problem', p. 316, adds Hebrews, the passages being 1.3; 2.9f.; 8.1; 10.12; 12.2, but Jesus' resurrection comes in 13.20.
20 Hahn, *Titles of Jesus in Christology*, pp. 23, 46 n. 57, complains that 1 En. 70f. is problematical and, besides, has an apocalyptic framework, while the Son of man title is lacking in Wisd. of Sol. 2–5. Hahn is also right in saying that Acts 7.56 and the Johannine Son of man passages are of no help in Schweizer's attempt to demonstrate that the concept of exaltation belongs to the original core of Jesus' own words about the Son of man. Moreover, so far from holding that the idea of Jesus' resurrection is secondary to that of exaltation and ousted it, we find Hahn, p. 131, asserting the direct opposite about, for example, Phil. 2.9, that 'the significance of the resurrection for the earliest tradition is beyond question and cannot be reduced'; cf. Teeple, 'Origin of the Son of Man Christology', pp. 228–31.
21 Black, 'The Son of Man Problem', p. 317.
22 Cf. Tödt, *The Son of Man in the Synoptic Tradition*, pp. 214f.
23 Black, 'The Son of Man Problem', p. 316.
24 G. Lindeskog, 'Das Rätsel des Menschensohnes', *Studia Theologica* 22, 1968, pp. 149–75.
25 *Ibid*., p. 167 and n. 65. Lindeskog, p. 168, accepts Tödt's demonstration that the Markan passion and resurrection predictions are dependent upon the passion kerygma and its use of proof-texts.
26 *Ibid*., p. 173 n. 83; the reference is to Vielhauer, 'Jesus und der Menschensohn', *ZTK* 60, 1963, p. 172 (= Vielhauer, *Aufsätze*, p. 135).

27 Jüngel, 'Jesus und der Menschensohn'.
28 *JSM*, p. 194.
29 R. H. Fuller, *The Mission and Achievement of Jesus*, London 1954, pp. 107f.
30 Fuller, *Foundations*, p. 122.
31 Fuller, *The Mission and Achievement of Jesus*, p. 103.
32 Fuller, *Foundations*, p. 123.
33 *Ibid.*, p. 130.
34 Higgins, 'Is the Son of Man Problem Insoluble?' *Neotestamentica et Semitica*, ed. Ellis and Wilcox, pp. 72f.; see also my review of Fuller, *Foundations* in *JBL* 85, 1966, pp. 360–2.
35 R. E. C. Formesyn, 'Was there a Pronominal Connection for the "bar nasha" Selfdesignation?', *Novum Testamentum* 8, 1966, pp. 1-35.
36 *Ibid.*, p. 12.
37 *Ibid.*, p. 25.
38 *Ibid.*, p. 26. According to Formesyn, p. 34 n. 3, we have to assume that some of the earthly sayings do not go back to Jesus, but originated in the church, e.g. Mark 2.10, and thus that the 'I' in them is the 'I' of the risen Lord, that is, of the Jesus of faith. This presumably is also to be regarded as applicable to the passion and resurrection predictions, Mark 8.31, etc.
39 *Ibid.*, p. 32.
40 Cf. Hahn, *Titles of Jesus in Christology*, p. 46 n. 49, referring to J. Y. Campbell's earlier suggestion in 'The Origin and Meaning of the Term Son of Man', *JTS* 48, 1947, pp. 145–55.
41 See the review article by I. H. Marshall, 'Professor Ferdinand Hahn's "Christologische Hoheitstitel"', *ExpT* 78, 1966–7, pp. 212–15. Unfortunately, in the English translation, *The Titles of Jesus in Christology*, 1969, the footnotes have been drastically curtailed, the subject index is reduced to only three pages, the index of references contains only about half the biblical passages in the German edition and none of those to other ancient literature, and the index of authors is not included at all. Moreover, the translation itself leaves much to be desired.
42 Hahn, *Titles of Jesus in Christology*, p. 27.
43 *Ibid.*, p. 28.
44 *Ibid.*, p. 31. Haufe, 'Das Menschensohn-Problem', strongly supports the position of Tödt, Hahn and others, with special emphasis on the pivotal importance of Luke 12.8f.
45 E. Käsemann, 'Das Problem des historischen Jesus', *ZTK* 51, 1954, pp. 125–53; *Essays on New Testament Themes*, London 1964, pp. 15–47.
46 Käsemann, *Essays*, pp. 38, 43.
47 *Ibid.*, p. 43; see further Käsemann, 'Sentences of Holy Law in the New Testament' in his *New Testament Questions of Today*, London 1969, pp. 66–81.
48 Käsemann, *Essays*, pp. 43f.
49 Teeple, 'Origin of the Son of Man Christology'.
50 *Ibid.*, p. 218.
51 *Ibid.*, p. 222.
52 *Ibid.*, p. 223.
53 *Ibid.*, p. 226.

54 *Ibid.*, p. 246.
55 E. Lohmeyer, *Galiläa und Jerusalem*, Göttingen 1936.
56 Perrin, *Rediscovering*, pp. 173ff.
57 Cf. Perrin, 'Recent Trends in Research in the Christology of the New Testament' in *Transitions in Biblical Scholarship*, ed. J. C. Rylaarsdam, Chicago 1968, p. 221: 'I am of the considered opinion that every single Son of man saying is a product of the theologizing of the early Church.'
58 Perrin, 'Mark XIV. 62: The End Product of a Christian Pesher Tradition', *NTS* 12, 1965–6, pp. 150–5.
59 Barnabas Lindars, *New Testament Apologetic*, London 1961.
60 Lindars, *New Testament Apologetic*, pp. 48f.
61 Perrin, *Rediscovering*, p. 198, cf. pp. 191, 203.
62 *Ibid.*, p. 191.
63 *Ibid.*, pp. 189–91.
64 The extent of the influence of Dan. 7.13 on Jesus' thought is disputed, but it seems likely that the primary influence was that of a Son of man concept.
65 The influence of Perrin (and of Käsemann) is evident in R. A. Edwards' article, 'The Eschatological Correlative as a *Gattung* in the New Testament', *ZNW* 60, 1969, pp. 9–20, in which he concludes that the Son of man christology probably originated in the *pesher* tradition of the early church. On Edwards' subsequent book, *The Sign of Jonah in the Theology of the Evangelists and Q*, London 1971, see below, chapter IV, section 3 (i).
66 See above, pp. 14 and 22–3.
67 Leivestad, 'Der apokalyptische Menschensohn', pp. 50f. J. C. O'Neill, 'The Silence of Jesus', *NTS* 15, 1968–9, pp. 153–67, maintains that Jesus' messianic consciousness was not expressed by the use of any of the messianic titles. He distinguishes between authentic sayings in which 'Son of man' is a self-designation devoid of messianic meaning, and unauthentic sayings in which it has become a title, and cites as an example Luke 12.8, a genuine saying in which the Aramaic term 'Son of man' refers, as a self-designation, to the speaker's humility, while par. Mark 8.38, with its titular use, is unauthentic. It is of some interest that Anthony Purver, a Quaker schoolmaster, in his *A New and Literal Translation of all the Books of the Old and New Testaments, with Notes Critical and Explanatory*, London 1764, always renders *ὁ υἱὸς τοῦ ἀνθρώπου* in the New Testament by 'The Man'; see H. A. Guy, 'An Eighteenth Century N.E.B.', *ExpT* 81, 1969–70, pp. 148–50.
68 Leivestad, 'Der apokalyptische Menschensohn', pp. 56–9.
69 Leivestad quotes as a later example the words of James to the scribes and Pharisees reported by Hegesippus (*c.* A.D. 180), 'Why do you ask me about Jesus the Son of man?' (Eusebius, *H. E.* ii. 23. 13). But 'Jesus' is not part of the text in all the manuscripts; see *Eusebius: Kirchengeschichte*, ed. E. Schwartz, kleine Ausgabe, Leipzig [4]1932, p. 69.
70 A very late example of this occurs in the fourteenth-century Arabic apocryphal Gospel of John: *Iohannis Evangelium Apocryphum Arabice*, ed. I. Galbiati [text with Latin translation], Milan 1957, 22.2. The Arabic is based upon a seventh-century Syriac work, according to the editor of this sumptuous volume; cf. A. de Santos Otero, *Los Evangelios Apocrifos*, Madrid [2]1963, pp. 23f.

71 That is, there is no explicit identification of Jesus with the Son of man by the church in the third person, because Jesus did not explicitly state the identity himself. Colpe, '*ὁ υἱὸς τοῦ ἀνθρώπου*', p. 439, explains that such explicit identifications as 'I am the Son of man', 'I as Son of man', 'the Son of man, I am he' are not to be expected 'in the Palestinian mode of thought as yet uninfluenced by this principle [of identity]'.

72 Leivestad, 'Der apokalyptische Menschensohn', pp. 71f.

73 *Ibid.*, p. 81.

74 Tödt, p. 57.

75 Leivestad, 'Der apokalyptische Menschensohn', pp. 96–8.

76 *Ibid.*, p. 99.

77 *Ibid.*, p. 100.

78 Except in Mark 2.10 parr.; Luke 7.34, par. Matt. 11.19; Luke 9.58, par. Matt. 8.20 in a non-messianic sense, 'a (certain) man' or 'someone (you know who)' – but admittedly perhaps more frequently than the gospel records might suggest.

79 Of special interest is a discussion by L. Gaston, *No Stone on Another: Studies in the Significance of the Fall of Jerusalem in the Synoptic Gospels*, Leiden 1970, pp. 370–409. He, too, eliminates an apocalyptic Son of man figure from the picture; but in its place he revives the collective or corporate interpretation of the Son of man based on Dan. 7 and associated especially with the name of T. W. Manson: *The Teaching of Jesus*, London [2]1935; 'The Son of Man in Daniel, Enoch and the Gospels', *BJRL* 32, 1949–50, pp. 171–93, reprinted in his *Studies in the Gospels and Epistles*, ed. M. Black, Manchester 1962, pp. 123–45; *The Servant-Messiah*, London 1953, pp. 72–4 (cf. Cadoux, *The Historic Mission of Jesus*, London 1941, especially pp. 90–103, and *The Life of Jesus*, West Drayton 1948, pp. 123f.) – but with a difference. Gaston rightly recognizes as the essential weakness of Manson's presentation its dependence on Mark as providing a reliable outline of Jesus' ministry and, resting on this, the idea of the development of the meaning of 'the Son of man' from the community of his followers to Jesus alone: 'the very fact that Manson must posit a development is a confession that he can find no unified concept underlying the Son of Man sayings' (*No Stone on Another*, p. 394). Gaston locates the development not in the thought of Jesus, but in that of the church. To Jesus 'the Son of man' meant the community he founded; to that community, the church as it came to be, it meant Jesus himself. This does not mean that Gaston succeeds in vindicating the collective interpretation of the Son of man in Jesus' teaching. One consequence of his approach is his drastic solution of the problem of 'the days' and 'the day' in Luke 17.22-30 (a passage discussed in detail in chapter III, below), namely, excision of verses 22 and 30 as Lukan creations, and of the references to the Son of man in verses 24 and 26 as Lukan additions to Proto-Luke, which is said to have referred to the coming not of the Son of man, but of the kingdom of God (*No Stone on Another*, pp. 348–51).

80 Cf. Schweizer, *Das Evangelium nach Markus*, pp. 95f. (ET: *Good News according to Mark*, pp. 168–70).

81 *JSM*, pp. 15f.

82 Leivestad, 'Der apokalyptische Menschensohn', pp. 102f. A somewhat

similar suggestion is made by J. B. Cortés and Florence M. Gatti, 'The Son of Man or The Son of Adam', *Biblica* 49, 1968, pp. 457–502. This is that Jesus spoke of himself as the Son of Adam, using a Hebrew expression *ben ha-adam* (literally, 'the Son of the Man (Adam)'), from which was derived the 'more ambiguous' Aramaic *bar nasha* (p. 486). 'The entire NT would offer clearer unity, and its theology would appear more unified if, in the Gospels, "Son of Man" were always translated by its equivalent "the Son of Adam", or "second Adam" ', because Paul's doctrine of the second or last Adam is a correct interpretation of Jesus' own thought (p. 490). This suggestion serves as the basis for the understanding of Jesus' self-designation as the expression of his solidarity with men in his redemptive ministry and passion. 'Jesus simply added *ben* to the expression *ha-adam* so often encountered in Genesis as designating Adam' (p. 482). Unfortunately for this theory, while the plural *bene ha-adam* often occurs in the Old Testament, the singular *ben ha-adam* never does; see above, chapter I, n. 108. The thesis of the authors is therefore founded on the derivation of the Aramaic *bar nasha* from a purely hypothetical Hebrew prototype. Their further suggestion (pp. 465f.) that the Greek ὁ υἱὸς τοῦ ἀνθρώπου in the gospels may have been derived from Jesus' own use of the expression with the literal meaning 'the Son of Man', can hardly be taken seriously.

83 Perrin's *Rediscovering the Teaching of Jesus* appeared only a short time before Borsch's *SMMH*, and is mentioned there only three times.

84 *SMMH*, pp. 314–401.

85 *Ibid*., p. 314.

86 *Ibid*., p. 315 and n. 2.

87 *Ibid*., pp. 319f.

88 *Ibid*., p. 320.

89 *Ibid*., pp. 400f.

90 *Ibid*., pp. 333f.

91 *Ibid*., p. 400, cf. p. 333 n. 2.

92 *Ibid*., p. 230.

93 See my discussion in *Neotestamentica et Semitica*, pp. 73–9. Reumann, *Jesus in the Church's Gospels*, p. 435, succinctly remarks that Dr Hooker's 'observations tell us more about Markan redaction than the historical Jesus'.

94 R. Maddox, 'The Function of the Son of Man According to the Synoptic Gospels', *NTS* 15, 1968–9, pp. 45–74.

95 *Ibid*., p. 57 n. 1.

96 *Ibid*., p. 68.

97 Matt. 24.27, par. Luke 17.24; Matt. 24.37, par. Luke 17.26; Luke 17.30; 18.8b; 21.36; 22.69; Matt. 10.23; 24.30a.

98 Colpe, pp. 439–41.

99 Cf. *JSM*, p. 23: 'Even if we do not attach too much importance to Dan. 7 as the background of the thought of Jesus, I do not see how the ideas of the kingdom of God and the Son of man could have been kept completely isolated in his teaching.'

100 Käsemann, Vielhauer, Conzelmann, Teeple, Perrin, *et al.*

101 E. Bammel, 'Erwägungen zur Eschatologie Jesu', *Studia Evangelica* III, ed. F. L. Cross, Berlin 1964, pp. 3–32.

102 Colpe, 'ὁ υἱος τοῦ ἀνθρώπου', p. 441: 'The apocalyptic Son of Man is a

symbol of Jesus' assurance of perfecting ... a dynamic and functional equating of Jesus and the coming Son of Man with the future perfecting of Jesus in view'; cf. *JSM*, especially pp. 202f.

103 Colpe, '*ὁ υἱὸς τοῦ ἀνθρώπου*', pp. 439f. P. Hoffmann, *Studien zur Theologie der Logienquelle*, Münster 1972, p. 88, sees as the main difficulty in Colpe's hypothesis the reconstruction of the fourth Son of man tradition he finds embedded in the synoptic gospels, and asks whether the reduction of apocalyptic ideas in the relevant sayings is really a feature of the supposed Jewish tradition, and not rather a characteristic of the oldest Jesus tradition.

104 Jeremias, 'Die älteste Schicht'; *Theology* I, pp. 262–4.

105 Counting the synoptic parallels once only.

106 The sole Johannine example, John 1.51, is also in Jeremias' lists.

107 Jeremias, *Theology* I, p. 263, excludes from his earlier list in 'Die älteste Schicht', p. 172 (cf. p. 170), Matt. 8.20, par. Luke 9.58, as having originally an indefinite sense, *Theology* I, p. 262 (contrast 'Die älteste Schicht', p. 171).

108 Barnabas Lindars, 'Re-enter the Apocalyptic Son of Man', *NTS* 22, 1975–6, pp. 52–72.

109 Vermes, *Jesus the Jew*, p. 179.

110 *Ibid*., p. 186.

111 Lindars, 'Re-enter the Apocalyptic Son of Man', p. 59.

112 *Ibid*., p. 64.

113 *Ibid*., p. 67.

114 *Ibid*., pp. 68f.

115 *Ibid*., p. 71.

116 Vermes, *Jesus the Jew*, p. 186.

117 Lindars, 'Re-enter the Apocalyptic Son of Man', p. 72.

118 *Ibid*., p. 71.

119 See Lindars' reference on p. 52 of 'Re-enter the Apocalyptic Son of Man' to Leivestad's article entitled 'Exit the Apocalyptic Son of Man', *NTS* 18, 1971–2, pp. 243–67.

120 Abel and Joshua are cited by Lindars as further possible examples on p. 377 of his 'The Apocalyptic Myth and the Death of Christ', *BJRL* 57, 1974–5, pp. 366–87, in which the suggestions offered in the article discussed in this excursus are used to good effect.

Chapter III

1 *JSM*, p. 185.

2 *Ibid*., pp. 82–91. A. Harnack, *The Sayings of Jesus*, London 1908, pp. 106–8, argued for the secondary character of Luke 17.24, 26f. compared with Matt. 24.27, 37–9. But there is no reason to depart from the view (cf. *JSM*, p. 83) that it is a matter not of Lukan modification of the Q text as exhibited in Matthew, but of Matthaean modification of the Q text basically as exhibited in Luke. See a valuable discussion in C. H. Talbert and E. V. McKnight, 'Can the Griesbach Hypothesis be Falsified?', *JBL* 91, 1972, pp. 364–7, where McKnight shows that in Luke 17.26f. the evangelist did not use Matt. 24.37–9 as a source, but that Luke's basically Q text has been adapted by Matthew. The decisive criteria for the secondary nature of Matthew here are given as: (1) Luke preserves the Semitic poetic structure,

while Matthew breaks it; (2) the term παρουσία is confined to Matthew among the gospels, and there is no plausible explanation of Luke's omission of it had he used Matthew; (3) the differences of Matt. 24. 37–9 from the Lukan parallel are due to Matthew's purpose of appealing throughout chapters 24 and 25 to Christians, despite its delay, to be watchful and prepared for the sudden advent of the Son of man.

3 Jüngel, 'Jesus und der Menschensohn', pp. 240f., 244.

4 *Ibid*., p. 239.

5 R. Morgenthaler, *Statistik des neutestamentlichen Wortschatzes*, Zürich and Frankfurt am Main 1958, pp. 104, 181.

6 Omitted by 𝔓[75] B D a b d e i sa.

7 Jüngel, 'Jesus und der Menschensohn', p. 253.

8 *Ibid*., p. 255, following Tödt, *The Son of Man in the Synoptic Tradition*, p. 51 (German text, p. 47).

9 Colpe, 'ὁ υἱὸς τοῦ ἀνθρώπου', p. 450.

10 *Ibid*., p. 434 n. 255.

11 Cf. *JSM*, p. 88.

12 See also Colpe, 'ὁ υἱὸς τοῦ ἀνθρώπου', p. 458 n. 396.

13 Fuller, *Foundations*, p. 175 n. 8.

14 Hahn, *Titles of Jesus in Christology*, p. 49 n. 105.

15 Leivestad, 'Der apokalyptische Menschensohn', pp. 86–8.

16 Borsch, *SMMH*, p. 356 n. 2, thinks that in Luke 17.22ff. the evangelist uses the plural and singular forms with much the same meaning; cf. W. G. Kümmel, *Promise and Fulfilment*, London 1957, pp. 37f., who more unambiguously equates them and attributes them to Jesus. Maddox, 'The Function of the Son of Man', p. 51, rightly distinguishes them, but without committing himself to acceptance of 'the days of the Son of man' as representing Jesus' language, rather than as the evangelist's understanding of the phrase to denote Jesus' earthly days.

17 Perrin, *Rediscovering*, pp. 195–7.

18 T. W. Manson, *The Sayings of Jesus*, London 1949, p. 142; see *JSM*, p. 87.

19 See the next two paragraphs, and *JSM*, pp. 86–9.

20 Cf. R. Schnackenburg, 'Der eschatologische Abschnitt Lk 17, 20–37' in *Mélanges Bibliques en hommage au R. P. Béda Rigaux*, ed. A. Descamps and A. de Halleux, Gembloux 1970, p. 221; for the general frequency of ἡμέρα in the Lukan writings see Morgenthaler, *Statistik*, p. 104: Luke 83, Acts 94, as compared with Matthew 45, Mark 27, John 31, Paul (including the Pastorals) 50.

21 So Schnackenburg, 'Eschatologische Abschnitt', p. 221; but Jeremias, *The Parables of Jesus*, London 1963, p. 129 n. 75, regards it as 'a stylistic peculiarity of the Lucan source'.

22 Schnackenburg, 'Eschatologische Abschnitt', pp. 219–22, judges verse 22 to be probably 'lukanische Redaktion', apart from the words ἐλεύσονται ἡμέραι which, he suggests, were followed immediately in the source by verse 23.

23 Cf. *JSM*, p. 89 n. 2.

24 See n. 6 above; Leaney, *St Luke*, pp. 69f.; B. M. Metzger, *A Textual Commentary on the Greek New Testament*, London and New York 1971, p. 167.

25 A. Merx, *Die Evangelien des Markus und Lukas: Die vier kanonischen Evangelien nach ihrem ältesten bekannten Texte* II.2, Berlin 1905, p. 348, explains the shorter text as the result of intentional 'correction' by the omission of 'in his day'; cf. M. J. Lagrange, *Critique Textuelle du Nouveau Testament* II: *La Critique Rationelle*, Paris 1935, p. 52, in whose view the words were omitted because of their absence from par. Matt. 24.27; another possible reason for correction may have been the wish to remove an apparent inconsistency with 'one of the days' in verse 22, cf. Lagrange, *Evangile selon Saint Luc*, Paris ^{3}1927, p. 463.

26 *JSM*, pp. 86ff.

27 Merx, *Die vier Evangelien*, pp. 347f.

28 *Ibid.*, p. 347: 'Hier ist die Parusie Jesu in den Text gebracht, wo Syrsin [*sic*] nur den Tag des Weltgerichts bezeichnet.'

29 The centre of our present exegesis of the whole passage suggests that the teaching of Jesus, which forms its basis, was directed towards the day of the Son of man, the day of his entry into the heavenly court of judgment.

30 There is an analogy at 1 Cor. 1.8, ἐν τῇ ἡμέρᾳ τοῦ κυρίου ἡμῶν Ἰησοῦ, where ἡμέρᾳ is replaced by παρουσίᾳ in D G it.

31 Cf. E. Klostermann, *Das Lukasevangelium*, Tübingen ^{2}1929, p. 175.

32 Cf. R. Bultmann, *The History of the Synoptic Tradition*, Oxford ^{2}1968, p. 117; Tödt, *The Son of Man in the Synoptic Tradition*, p. 51.

33 Manson, *Sayings of Jesus*, p. 143.

34 On verse 25 see below, n. 43.

35 Manson, *Sayings of Jesus*, p. 144.

36 Cf. *ibid.*, p. 145.

37 Cf. C. K. Barrett, *The First Epistle to the Corinthians*, London ^{2}1971, p. 88.

38 A more exact correspondence to 1 Cor. 3.13 would, of course, have been οὕτως ἡ ἡμέρα τοῦ υἱοῦ τοῦ ἀνθρώπου ἀποκαλύπτεται.

39 Cf. 1 En. 69.26, 'Because the name of that Son of man had been revealed to them'; 69.29, 'For that Son of man has appeared, and has seated himself on the throne of his glory'; Mowinckel, *He That Cometh*, pp. 388–93, on the 'epiphany' of the Son of man, and p. 303 on the self-revelation of the Messiah in the Targums, who is revealed as such by the accomplishment of his saving messianic work.

40 Luke 17.30 is reminiscent of the apocalyptic idea of the pre-existence and concealment of the Son of man in heaven until his revelation to the world; cf. Hoffmann, *Studien*, pp. 93, 97. R. G. Hamerton-Kelly, *Pre-existence, Wisdom, and the Son of Man*, London 1973, pp. 45f., classifies other sayings, including Luke 17.24, 26, with this one in this respect, but without justification.

41 This use of 'days' belongs to the Q source, for cf. par. Matt. 24.37, and also the Matthaean addition (38a), 'in the days before the flood', with the same meaning as 'the days of Noah'; similarly, ἄχρι ἧς ἡμέρας (Luke 17.27, par. Matt. 24.38) is from Q.

42 Lightning is much more conspicuous at night. 'The day of the Son of man' is not necessarily restricted to the daytime, but is a general indication of time; cf. Schnackenburg, 'Eschatologische Abschnitt', p. 225, with reference to Luke 17.34.

43 Cf. 2 Baruch 53.9, 'Now that lightning shone exceedingly, so as to illumi

nate the whole earth.' On Luke 17.25 see *JSM*, pp. 78f., and for another view Borsch, *SMMH*, p. 347 n. 3. The verse is an abbreviated form of the Markan passion predictions, in particular of Luke 9.22, par. Mark 8.31, and is the redactional work of the evangelist. The clue to the purpose of this insertion into the Q pericope is the reference to the rejection of the Son of man by 'this generation' (τῆς γενεᾶς ταύτης), which by that act would prove that it was no better than the men of the days of Noah and of Lot, and deserved a similar fate. The interpolation has the effect of underlining the fundamental identity of the theme of Luke 17.24, 26–30 with that of Luke 11.29–32, which depicts 'this generation' as unworthy, because of its rejection of Jesus' message, of any sign except the sign of Jonah, and as deserving the adverse testimony of the Queen of the South and of the Ninevites in the judgment.

44 The addition of οὐκ ἔγνωσαν ἕως ('they did not know until') in Matt. 24.39 to the text of Q serves to link the passage with the evangelist's stress, in the pericope 24.36–42 as a whole, on the lack of knowledge of the day and the hour of Jesus' coming as the Son of man (with verse 30; no one knows, neither the angels nor the Son, verse 36), or as the Lord ('you do not know', verse 42); cf. McKnight in Talbert and McKnight, 'The Griesbach Hypothesis', p. 367.

45 SB III, p. 619; cf. however, 2 Esdras 13.52, '. . . no one on earth can see my Son [= the Messiah] or those who are with him, except in the time of his day' (RSV, following the Syriac; cf. SB II, p. 237; IV, p. 859).

46 Mowinckel, *He That Cometh*, p. 392.

47 See J. N. D. Kelly, *The Epistles of Peter and of Jude*, London 1969, pp. 332–4.

48 Jeremias, *Parables*, p. 49: 'Here, too, events, although of extreme antiquity, which overwhelmed men unprepared, are used by Jesus as a warning of terrors to come.' Jeremias (cf. C. H. Dodd, *The Parables of the Kingdom*, London 1936, pp. 168f.) regards the parable of the burglar as also drawn from an actual (but recent) happening; cf. also the parable of the steward awaiting his master's return, Luke 12. 42–6, par. Matt. 24.45–51.

49 Manson, *Sayings of Jesus*, p. 77.

50 It is certainly arguable that it is Matthew who represents the Q-text in not including the Lot pericope, and that Luke's twin comparisons with the days of Noah and the days of Lot reflect the influence of the use of the Flood and the destruction of Sodom in paraenetic tradition as stock examples of the visitation of divine punishment, cf. Ecclus. 16.7f.; Wisd. of Sol. 10.4, 6 f.; Jub. 20.5; Test. Naphtali 3. 4f.; Jude 5–7; 2 Pet. 2.4–8; Josephus, *Bellum Judaicum* V. 566 (xiii.6): ἂν . . . ἢ κατακλυσθῆναι τὴν πόλιν ἢ τοὺς τῆς Σοδομηνῆς μεταλαβεῖν κεραυνούς. However, the case for Luke as more accurately following Q by the inclusion of the Lot pericope remains a strong one; and the traditional use of the Flood and the destruction of Sodom as dire warnings does not reduce the probability that Jesus also appealed to them. For the first view see D. Lührmann, 'Noah und Lot (Lk 17.26–29) – ein Nachtrag', *ZNW* 63, 1972, pp. 130–2 (p. 130).

51 T. F. Glasson, 'The Second Advent – 25 Years Later', *ExpT* 82, 1970–1, pp. 307–9.

52 Cf. Matt. 25.31, 'When the Son of man comes in his glory, and all the angels with him...'

53 Gaston, *No Stone on Another*, pp. 448f., goes beyond Käsemann's opinion that early Christian prophets kept alive the parousia hope (E. Käsemann, *New Testament Questions of Today*, London 1969, p. 79), and maintains that they created it. 'The doctrine of the parousia is in the New Testament a creation of the New Testament prophets, expressed in language derived from Old Testament theophanies and based on sayings of Jesus concerning the Son of Man' – and, we may add, especially sayings concerning the Son of man's day, as in Luke 17.

54 On Mark 8.38 in this sense see already *JSM*, p. 59: 'The parousia or descent of the Son of man from heaven may [however] not be present in Mark 8.38. The Son of man may be described as taking up his place in the presence of God, and the angels are his entourage'; but this was not pressed, *ibid*., p. 60.

55 Jeremias, *Theology* I, p. 274. For the 'assumption' by God as a synonym for exaltation, see ἀνάλημψις in Luke 9.51 (Vulgate *assumptio*) and ἀναλάμβανειν in Mark 16.19; Acts 1.2, 11, 22; 1 Tim. 3.16 (Vulgate *assumere* in all cases).

56 Or even, according to some critics, the absence of a Son of man concept of any kind.

57 On the problems of the interpretation of 71.14, 'Thou art the Son of man', see *JSM*, pp. 200f.; Fuller, *Foundations*, pp. 40f.

58 Since, however, the thrones are also in par. Luke 22. 28–30, this feature must have belonged to the common tradition behind both versions; cf. also Rev. 3.21.

59 Jeremias, *Theology* I, pp. 273f.

60 δοξάζεσθαι in John is synonymous with ὑψοῦσθαι, and elucidation of its meaning is not dependent upon Luke 24.26.

61 Luke 24.26, 51; cf. Acts 1.9–11.

62 This view is not adversely affected by clear evidence of editorial and redactional work on the source: the change of audience in verse 22a; the rest of this verse, because of the Lukan 'days of the Son of man' (again in verse 26); the Markan-type passion prediction in verse 25; the present arrangement of verses 28–30. Cf. Mark 8.38, parousia of the Son of man (see above, n. 54), followed by 9.1, the kingdom of God.

63 The parallelism becomes much closer if this sentence is thus given an eschatological interpretation. Jeremias, *Theology* I, p. 101, explains that the difference of tense (ἐστιν, ἔσται) arose when the sayings in Aramaic, which has not these tense distinctions, were translated into Greek.

64 ἐν ἡμέρᾳ κρίσεως occurs in Matt. 10.15 (par. Luke 10.12, ἐν τῇ ἡμέρᾳ ἐκείνῃ); Matt. 11.22 (par. Luke 10.14, ἐν τῇ κρίσει); Matt. 11.24; 12.36 (Matt. 7.22, ἐν ἐκείνῃ τῇ ἡμέρᾳ).

65 See especially Luke 13.1–5. How far this aspect of Jesus' proclamation was influenced by contemporary events is a disputed question. But standing in the prophetic tradition, he cannot have been unaffected by events nor have failed to foresee the inevitability of the Jewish disaster a few decades later; cf. e.g. G. B. Caird, *The Gospel of St Luke*, Harmondsworth 1963, pp. 198f.

66 *JSM*, chapter 7.

67 Colpe, 'ὁ υἱὸς τοῦ ἀνθρώπου', p. 435.

68 *SMMH*, p. 364 n. 1.
69 *Ibid.*, p. 363.
70 Mark 8.38 parr.; 13.26 parr.; 14.62, par. Matt. 26.64; Luke 12.40, par. Matt. 24.44; Matt. 10.23; 16.28; 25.31.
71 Leivestad, 'Der apokalyptische Menschensohn', p. 89: 'Es ist vielleicht der rätselhafteste Spruch in der ganzen Überlieferung.'
72 Jeremias, *Parables*, p. 155 n. 13; on πλήν and ὁ υἱὸς τοῦ ἀνθρώπου respectively, see F. Rehkopf, *Die lukanische Sonderquelle*, Tübingen 1959, pp. 96 and 97.
73 *SMMH*, p. 364 n. 1.
74 *Ibid.*
75 *Ibid.*, p. 319 and n. 2.
76 Jüngel, 'Jesus und der Menschensohn', p. 239.
77 Bultmann, *Tradition*, p. 119.
78 F. W. Beare, *The Earliest Records of Jesus*, Oxford 1964, p. 217.
79 Cf. Black, *Aramaic Approach*, p. 134.
80 Cf. *JSM*, p. 94.
81 Colpe, 'ὁ υἱὸς τοῦ ἀνθρώπου', pp. 436f.
82 Cf. J. Jeremias, *Jesus' Promise to the Nations*, London 1958, pp. 34f.
83 H. Schürmann, 'Zur Traditions- und Redaktionsgeschichte von Mt 10, 23', *Biblische Zeitschrift*, N.F.3, 1959, pp. 82–8.
84 This involves assigning Matt. 10.23 also to Q (cf. Tödt, *The Son of Man in the Synoptic Tradition*, p. 48), an attribution regarded by Fuller, *Foundations*, p. 176 n. 22, as 'speculative'. Schürmann points out that W. Haupt proposed a similar solution in 1913.
85 Yet Mark 13.10 is given in an expanded form at Matt. 24.14.
86 F. Hahn, *Mission in the New Testament*, London 1965, p. 54 n. 5.
87 Perrin, *Rediscovering*, pp. 201f.
88 D. R. A. Hare, *The Theme of Jewish Persecution of Christians in the Gospel according to St Matthew*, London 1967, pp. 110–12.
89 *SMMH*, pp. 391–4.
90 *Ibid.*, p. 391 n. 4.
91 F. H. Borsch, 'Mark XIV.62 and 1 Enoch LXII.5', *NTS* 14, 1967–8, pp. 565–7.
92 *Ibid.*, p. 567 n. 3.
93 Cf. *JSM*, pp. 107f., 117.
94 Perrin, *Rediscovering*, pp. 173ff., and 'End Product', pp. 150–5; see my discussion in *Neotestamentica et Semitica*, pp. 79–85.
95 Except in Matt. 25.31; παρουσία occurs twenty times in the epistles.
96 In an article ('The Origin of the Son of Man Concept as applied to Jesus') in *JBL* 91, 1972, pp. 482–90, W. O. Walker asks why precisely Ps. 110.1 was interpreted with the use of Dan. 7.13 so as to refer to Jesus' exaltation as Son of man in Mark 14.62a and Acts 7.56. Perrin's explanation of the Son of man christology as originating in a *pesher* type of early Christian scriptural exegesis is accepted, but it fails to account for the combination of these two particular texts. The explanation offered is that the link between them is to be found in Ps. 8, the key passage being Mark 12.36. Here the quotation from Ps. 110 (LXX 109).1 has not the Septuagint reading ὑποπόδιον τῶν ποδῶν, but ὑποκάτω τῶν ποδῶν from Ps. 8.6 (LXX 7).

Further, υἱὸς ἀνθρώπου in Ps. 8.4 (LXX 5) led to the connection with Dan. 7.13. 'Psalm 8 forms the most probable link between the primitive Christian use of Ps. 110.1 to interpret the resurrection of Jesus as his exaltation to the right hand of God as "Lord" and the subsequent use of Dan. 7.13 to interpret further that exaltation as the exaltation of Jesus as "*Son of Man*"' (Walker, 'Origin', pp. 488f., his italics. Cf. O. J. F. Seitz's suggestion that Ps. 80.17 is 'the catalytic agent' in the fusion of Ps. 110.1 and Dan. 7.13, in 'The Future Coming of the Son of Man: Three Midrashic Formulations in the Gospel of Mark', *Studia Evangelica* VI, TU 112, ed. E. A. Livingstone, Berlin 1973, pp. 478–94 (pp. 481–8). Walker goes on to claim that the dissimilarities between the corresponding Hebrew in the two psalms passages, and between the Hebrew and Aramaic for 'son of man' in Ps. 8.4(5) and Dan. 7.13 respectively, exclude their association and consequently the production of a Son of man christology in a Semitic milieu. The christology must rather have arisen, not in the Aramaic-speaking Palestinian church, but among Greek-speaking Hellenistic Jewish Christians. This suggestion fails on two grounds. Firstly, traditio-historical criticism shows that the Son of man christology belongs to the earliest strata of the tradition; secondly, its creation virtually on the basis of Greek verbal similarities is highly improbable. Far more significant to the early Christians were correspondences of basic ideas in two or more passages of scripture.

97 Colpe, 'ὁ υἱὸς τοῦ ἀνθρώπου', pp. 435f.; cf. Jeremias, *Theology* 1, p. 273; Leivestad, 'Der apokalyptische Menschensohn', pp. 92f.; Vincent Taylor, *The Passion Narrative of St Luke*, ed. O. E. Evans, London 1972, pp. 82f., but allowing for the possibility of modification of Mark.

98 Examples of this Aramaic periphrasis for 'God' in G. Dalman, *The Words of Jesus*, Edinburgh 1902, pp. 200–2, and A. Schlatter, *Der Evangelist Matthäus*, Stuttgart [3]1948, p. 760. Dalman, *Words*, p. 200, cites as a parallel to Luke's 'the power of God' the description of Simon Magus in Acts 8.10 as ἡ δυναμις τοῦ θεοῦ ἡ καλουμένη μεγάλη, a Lukan substitute for 'the great Power'.

99 Lindars, *New Testament Apologetic*, p. 49 and n. 3, thinks the second part of Mark 14.62 was omitted by Luke to remove the inconsistency with the first part, and finds a parallel in Luke 9.27, which lacks the words 'come in power' of Mark 9.1. But it may be noted that Luke 22.69 resembles 1 En. 62.5 in speaking of the Son of man only as sitting, and not also as coming.

> And they shall be terrified,
> And they shall be downcast of countenance,
> And pain shall seize them,
> When they see that Son of man
> Sitting on the throne of his glory.

This is in agreement with the absence of a parousia idea in Jewish apocalyptic.

100 See especially there section 3 (ii).

Chapter IV

1 Hoffmann, *Studien*, pp. 155f., points out that in the Q context the saying concerns the church's missionary situation, and the preceding verses indicate

the danger in which those who confess Jesus, both the preachers and their hearers, find themselves. Regarding the saying as in all probability not from Jesus, but a community formulation, Hoffmann describes it as a clear example of advanced christological thought, and as a conscious definition of the relationship of Jesus and the Son of man. This reasoning is not altogether convincing; and the context of the saying in Q may be due to the community's application of an authentic utterance of Jesus to its missionary situation.

2 Fuller, *Foundations*, p. 123.

3 Leivestad, 'Der apokalyptische Menschensohn', pp. 82f.

4 G. Voss, *Die Christologie der lukanischen Schriften in Grundzügen*, Paris 1965, p. 40.

5 Bultmann, *Tradition*, pp. 112, 151f.; Jeremias, *Theology* I, p. 29.

6 Tödt, *The Son of Man in the Synoptic Tradition*, p. 55.

7 Hahn, *Titles of Jesus in Christology*, pp. 28–34.

8 W. Pannenberg, *Jesus – God and Man*, London ²1970, pp. 58f.

9 Cf. *ibid*., p. 59.

10 *Ibid*., p. 59 n. 22.

11 *JSM*, pp. 57–60, 197, 202f.

12 See above, p. 33.

13 Pannenberg, *Jesus – God and Man*, p. 59 n. 22.

14 *Ibid*., p. 69.

15 Käsemann, *Essays on New Testament Themes*, p. 43; *New Testament Questions of Today*, p. 77: 'Prophecy proclaims blessing and curse on those members of the community who confess and those who deny by establishing within it the eschatological *jus talionis*.' Gaston, *No Stone on Another*, p. 404, notes that for the Christian prophets who, he agrees, formulated this saying and its later modified version in Mark 8.38, Jesus and the Son of man were identical, and no distinction between them was intended.

16 So Hahn, *Titles of Jesus in Christology*, pp. 29f.; Pannenberg, *Jesus – God and Man*, pp. 59f. n. 22; E. Lövestam, *Spiritus Blasphemia: eine Studie zu Mk 3, 28f par Mt 12, 31f, Lk 12, 10,* Lund 1968, p. 66 n. 43.

17 𝔓⁴⁵ 245 e sys bo(pt).

18 *καὶ ὁμολογήσω τὸ ὄνομα αὐτοῦ ἐνώπιον τοῦ πατρός μου καὶ ἐνώπιον τῶν ἀγγέλων αὐτοῦ.*

19 Cf. Lindeskog, 'Das Rätsel des Menschensohnes', p. 153.

20 Hahn, *Titles of Jesus in Christology*, pp. 30f., 49 n. 98 (excluding *τοῦ θεοῦ* as a later addition); cf. Jüngel, 'Jesus und der Menschensohn', p. 260.

21 Cf. Borsch, *SMMH*, p. 363 n. 4, who points out that 'the judge in any Semitic situation . . . was always judge, defence counsellor and prosecuting attorney rolled into one'. There is therefore no contradiction in the portrayal of the Son of man as both judge and advocate. One may add that there is also a certain fluidity in the ideas of the counsel and the witness.

22 F. H. Borsch, *The Christian and Gnostic Son of Man*, London 1970 (cited as *CGSM*), pp. 16–19; cf. Haufe, 'Das Menschensohn-Problem', p. 136.

23 Perrin, *Rediscovering*, pp. 188–91; cf. his *What is Redaction Criticism*? London 1970, pp. 46–8. Perrin's argument is refuted by Hamerton-Kelly, *Pre-existence*, pp. 93f. But although the latter regards Luke 12.8 as

'probably authentic', this is on the ground that it coheres with all the Q sayings concerning the Son of man on earth (p. 95), whereas, in all probability, no authentic saying of Jesus speaks of the Son of man as a messianic figure on earth.

24 Lindeskog, 'Das Rätsel des Menschensohnes', p. 160.

25 Cf. Perrin, *Rediscovering*, pp. 187f.

26 See Jeremias, *Theology* I, p. 7 n. 2: 'to be ashamed of' (ἐπαισχύνεσθαι, Mark 8.38, par. Luke 9.26) and 'to deny' (ἀρνεῖσθαι, Luke 12.9, par. Matt. 10.33) represent Aramaic variants, *ḥaphar* and *kephar* respectively, dating from the oral tradition.

27 Lindeskog agrees with Perrin in presupposing a single *Urwort*, but differs in looking for it not in an older non-Son of man form of Luke 12.8, but behind Mark 8.38, the verb 'to be ashamed of' being viewed provisionally as more 'authentic' than 'to deny' in Q. On the other hand, Perrin (*Rediscovering*, p. 186) treats Mark 8.38 as a revision of Luke 12.8f. par.

28 See also, e.g. Conzelmann, *Theology*, p. 132: Luke 12.8 is secondary to Matt. 10.32; D. R. Catchpole, *The Trial of Jesus*, Leiden 1971, p. 138: Matt. 10.32 is the earlier, Luke 12.8 the later redactional form; cf. W. Bousset, *Kyrios Christos*, ET New York 1970, p. 38.

29 Colpe, 'ὁ υἱὸς τοῦ ἀνθρώπου', pp. 442, 447.

30 *Ibid.*, p. 442 n. 297.

31 Jeremias, 'Die älteste Schicht', p. 170.

32 Perrin, *Rediscovering*, p. 189, refers to Rev. 3.5b, 'I will confess'.

33 Borsch, *CGSM*, p. 16.

34 Jeremias, *Theology* I, pp. 275f.

35 R. Bultmann, *Theology of the New Testament* I, London 1956, pp. 30–32.

36 W. Marxsen, *The Beginnings of Christology*, ET Philadelphia 1969, pp. 30-3, focusses upon Luke 12.8f. and Mark 8.38 as evidence of a stage in the tradition in which the Son of man title had not yet been unequivocally applied to Jesus by the community, as in the later versions in Matt. 10.32f., in which the title is replaced by 'I', and in Matt. 16.27, where it is virtually just a name of Jesus. On these texts see further my article '"Menschensohn" oder "ich" in Q: Lk 12, 8–9/Mt 10, 32–33' in *Jesus und der Menschensohn: für Anton Vögtle*, ed R. Pesch and R. Schnackenburg with O. Kaiser, Freiburg im Breisgau 1975, pp. 117–23, and in the same volume W. G. Kümmel, 'Das Verhalten Jesus gegenüber . . . ', pp. 210–24. C. K. Barrett examines Mark 8.38 and parallels in connection with their relevance to the understanding of Rom. 1.16 in his *New Testament Essays*, London 1972, pp. 119–27, 135–8.

37 Both these plurals are renderings of the Aramaic *bar nasha* in a generic or collective sense ('man' = 'men'); cf. J. Wellhausen, *Das evangelium Marci*, Berlin [2]1909, pp. 26f.; E. Klostermann, *Das Markusevangelium*, Tübingen [5]1971, p. 38.

38 Cf. Black, *Aramaic Approach*, pp. 194f.

39 Cf. e.g. E. E. Ellis, *The Gospel of Luke*, London 1966, p. 165.

40 Cf. V. Taylor, 'The Original Order of Q' in *New Testament Essays*, ed. A. J. B. Higgins, Manchester 1959, pp. 246–69.

41 Cf. J. M. Creed, *The Gospel according to St Luke*, London 1930, p. 172: 'The verse preceding does not prepare us for the view that speech against the Son of Man is venial.'

42 The standard patristic interpretation of the Q version, irrespective of its different contexts in Matthew and Luke, is that blasphemy (or speaking) against the Son of man is a sin committed by the heathen, and is forgivable (in baptism), whereas such speech directed against the Holy Spirit, being a post-baptismal sin, is unforgivable; cf. C. K. Barrett, *The Holy Spirit and the Gospel Tradition*, London 1947, p. 106. Another interpretation is that Jews who reject Jesus the Son of man have a second chance after Pentecost, but subsequent rejection means blasphemy against the Spirit operating in the disciples, and is unforgivable; cf. Ellis, *Luke*, p. 175.

43 Lagrange, *Évangile selon Saint Luc*, pp. 355f.; cf. W. Grundmann, *Das Evangelium nach Lukas*, Berlin 1961, p. 255. P. Bonnard, *L'Évangile selon Saint Matthieu*, Neuchâtel 1963, p. 182, stresses, without benefit of a parallel to Luke 12.9 in this context, the christological significance of speaking against the Holy Spirit: the Pharisees are guilty not of blasphemy against the Spirit in general, but as operative in Jesus' healing of demoniacs.

44 Lövestam, *Spiritus Blasphemia*, pp. 46–8.

45 E. Bammel, review of *Spiritus Blasphemia* in *JTS* N.S. 22, 1971, pp. 192–4.

46 *Ibid*., p. 194.

47 Tödt, *The Son of Man in the Synoptic Tradition*, p. 118.

48 *Ibid*., p. 119 n. 1; cf. Borsch, *CGSM*, p. 9, who says the Q version fits the Markan context of accusations against Jesus, where Mark's own version does not.

49 Lövestam, *Spiritus Blasphemia*, p. 68 n. 46. In support of this preference for Mark, Lövestam (p. 47 n. 96) maintains that logion 44 of the Gospel of Thomas makes explicit the sin of blasphemy against the Father already implied in the sins and blasphemies in Mark 3.28. Logion 44 reads: 'He who blasphemes against the Father will be forgiven, and he who blasphemes against the Son will be forgiven, but he who blasphemes against the Holy Spirit will not be forgiven, either on earth or in heaven' (Metzger's translation in K. Aland, *Synopsis Quattuor Evangeliorum*, Stuttgart ^{4}1967, p. 522). It is, however, much more likely that it is the Q version that is the basis of the one in Thomas; here 'the Son of man' is abbreviated to 'the Son' and a reference to blasphemy against the Father is prefixed to the logion, in the interests of Trinitarian doctrine. W. Schrage, *Das Verhältnis des Thomas-evangeliums zur synoptischen Tradition und zu den koptischen Evangelienübersetzungen*, Berlin 1964, p. 100, rightly says that this expansion does not sound gnostic, and points out that the same expansion occurs in the Tuscan Gospel Harmony, the text of which reads: 'chiunque dirà parola contra 'l Padre, gli sarà perdonato' (*Diatessaron Toscano* 63, in *Il Diatessaron in Volgare Italiano: Testi Inediti Secoli XIII–XIV*, ed. V. Todesco, A. Vaccari and M. Vattasso, Città del Vaticano 1938, p. 244). The conclusion in Thomas 44 is an alteration (perhaps gnostic in intention) in spatial terms of Matt. 12.32, 'either in this age or the age to come'.

50 Edwards, *The Sign of Jonah*, pp. 67f.

51 Tödt, *The Son of Man in the Synoptic Tradition*, p. 119.

52 Jeremias, 'Die älteste Schicht', p. 165; *Theology* I, p. 261.

53 R. Schippers, 'The Son of Man in Matt. xii.32 = Lk. xii.10, compared with Mk. iii.28', *Studia Evangelica* IV, ed. F. L. Cross, Berlin 1968, pp. 231–5. For Colpe's somewhat similar approach but different conclusions see below, Excursus 1, pp. 116–17.

54 Schippers' reconstruction is: *kol (man) diygaddeph barnasha yishtebeq leh* (my simplified transliteration).
55 Rendered by Q (Matt. 12.32; Luke 12.10) as 'speak a word against'.
56 Schippers, 'The Son of Man in Matt. xii. 32', p. 235.
57 See below, Excursus 1, pp. 116–17.
58 A possible objection, the inconsistency between Mark 3.28, if authentic, and Matt. 5.22 (again, if authentic), is pointed out by Borsch, *CGSM*, p. 11.
59 See below, pp. 109–11.
60 On all these texts, cf. *JSM*, pp. 133–40.
61 Colpe, '*ὁ υἱὸς τοῦ ἀνθρώπου*', pp. 449f.
62 This rendering takes *τί* in the exclamatory sense, cf. Black, *Aramaic Approach*, p. 123; *εἰ* represents the Semitic form of affirmative asseveration equivalent to a negation.
63 Perrin, *Rediscovering*, p. 193.
64 *Ibid.*: 'The sign of Jonah saying itself is certainly authentic.'
65 *Ibid.*, p. 194. Cf. Hoffmann, *Studien*, p. 181: Luke 11.30 is a Q addition to Jesus' word in verse 29 and a reinterpretation of the sign of Jonah as the Son of man coming in judgment. R. H. Hiers, *The Historical Jesus and the Kingdom of God*, Gainesville, Florida 1973, pp. 57–9, rejects both the Matthaean and the Lukan explanations on the ground that they do not fit the context, and finds the genuine sequel in 'something greater than Jonah *is here*' (my italics) – John the Baptist as the coming Elijah, possibly designated by Jesus as 'the sign of Jonah' or even 'the sign of John' (cf. J. H. Michael, '"The Sign of John"', *JTS* 21, 1920, pp. 146–59).
66 Jeremias, 'Die älteste Schicht', p. 168.
67 Matt. 16.4, in its use of Mark 8.12, adds 'except the sign of Jonah' from Q, and replaces (with omission of *αμην λέγω ὑμῖν*) Mark's wording, including the Semitic *εἰ δοθήσεται*, with the exact Greek wording of Q: *καὶ σημεῖον οὐ δοθήσεται αὐτῇ εἰ μὴ τὸ σημεῖον Ἰωνᾶ*.
68 *JSM*, pp. 134f.; cf. Bultmann, *Tradition*, p. 118: 'the interpretation of the sign of Jonah in terms of the death and resurrection of Jesus is a quite secondary formulation of the Church'; Hoffmann, *Studien*, p. 181 n. 92: 'Mt 12,40 entstammt sicher der Redaktion des Evangelisten.'
69 Moreover, if Luke were supposed to have used Matthew in the composition of his own gospel, why would he have replaced this with his own indeterminate and enigmatic version? E. V. McKnight remarks: 'The inclusion of 12:40 by Matthew makes complete nonsense of the condemnation of "this generation" as evil and adulterous and the declaration that no sign will be given. The insertion of vs. 40 in Matthew 12 clearly destroys the purpose of the entire pericope as Luke presents it and demonstrates the priority of the form preserved by Luke' (Talbert and McKnight, 'The Griesbach Hypothesis', p. 361).
70 K. Stendahl, *The School of St Matthew*, Lund [2]1968, pp. 132f.; cf. also his commentary on Matthew in *Peake's Commentary on the Bible*, 1962, p. 785, section 684t.
71 There is no textual evidence for its omission.
72 Perhaps the simplest explanation is that Matt. 12.40 is both a later deutero-Matthaean interpretation of the sign of Jonah, and the earliest interpretation of the Q saying at Luke 11.30 showing *how* Jonah was *a* sign to the

Ninevites, and replacing it. If Stendahl is correct, this substitution had not been made in the text of Matthew known to Justin. McKnight, 'The Griesbach Hypothesis', p. 362, suggests that 'Matt. 12:40 is an expansion of Luke 11.30 designed to form a prediction-echo pattern with Matt. 27:63 to set forth the resurrection of Jesus as the σημεῖον to substantiate Jesus' unique claim to authority.' This he supports by pointing out that Matthew has no other resurrection-prediction attributed to Jesus and heard by the Jewish authorities (scribes and Pharisees), to which the chief priests and Pharisees of 27.63 could refer; and that the use of μετὰ τρεῖς ἡμέρας there instead of Matthew's customary formula τῇ τρίτῃ ἡμέρᾳ (16.21; 17.23; 20.19) is intended to correspond to 'three days and three nights' in 12.40. I do not find this very convincing.

73 Edwards, *The Sign of Jonah*, pp. 5f.; cf. his earlier article, 'The Eschatological Correlative', *ZNW* 60, 1969, pp. 9–20, and see Perrin's remarks in 'Son of Man', *Biblical Research* 13, 1968, pp. 9f. Perrin's name for the eschatological correlatives is 'comparison sayings', from their comparison of the past or the present ('as') with the future ('so'); see Perrin, *Rediscovering*, p. 191.

74 Edwards, *The Sign of Jonah*, p. 20.

75 *Ibid.*, pp. 49ff.

76 On this, otherwise known as the 'comparative clause', see J. H. Moulton, *A Grammar of New Testament Greek* III: *Syntax* (by N. Turner), Edinburgh 1963, pp. 319f. Since, however, the comparative clause is a feature of Hebrew (E. Kautzsch (ed.), *Gesenius' Hebrew Grammar*, ET by A. E. Cowley, Oxford ^{2}1910, p. 499) and Aramaic (H. Odeberg, *The Aramaic Portions of Bereshit Rabba* II: *Short Grammar of Galilaean Aramaic*, Lund and Leipzig 1939, p. 146) as well as of Greek, the eschatological correlative could have been created in a Semitic milieu, a consideration of some relevance to the argument that follows.

77 Following Edwards, *The Sign of Jonah*, pp. 49f., but with modification of his enumeration. The four Q sayings are those in the left-hand column; nos. 3 and 4 represent Q more faithfully in essentials than does Matthew. The only other eschatological correlative in the synoptics is Matt. 13.40f., where the Son of man occurs not in the apodosis, as in the rest, but in the following explanatory expansion.

78 Käsemann, 'Sentences of Holy Law in the New Testament' and 'The Beginnings of Christian Theology' in *New Testament Questions of Today*, pp. 66–81, 82–107. Käsemann (pp. 77, 102, 104) actually refers to the parr. Matt. 10.32f. and Mark 8.38, not to Luke 12.8 itself.

79 The other saying, Luke 12.39f., par. Matt. 24.43f., contains 'Son of man' in an addition to an already existing parable.

80 Perrin, *Rediscovering*, pp. 185f.; 'Son of Man', pp. 8f.

81 This NEB rendering approximates to the chiastic form of the Greek: εἴ τις τὸν ναὸν τοῦ θεοῦ φθείρει, φθερεῖ τοῦτον ὁ θεός. Other similar sayings are Matt. 6.14f.; Mark 4.24; 1 Cor. 14.38. On 1 Cor. 16.22, 'If a man does not love the Lord, let him be anathema (accursed)', Käsemann, 'Sentences', p. 70, notes that, in distinction from passages where the same verb occurs in both parts, 'talion is now expressed no longer by the correspondence of the verb but directly through the curse'; cf. Gal. 1.9; Matt. 5.19; Rev. 22.18f. Chiasmus, referred to above, is not a constant formal feature of sayings of this category.

82 Edwards, *The Sign of Jonah*, p. 53.
83 *Ibid.*, p. 54.
84 Of the former, Edwards, *ibid.*, p. 55, claims that 'Tödt is wrong in asserting the authenticity of those sayings.'
85 Perrin, 'Son of Man', p. 9.
86 Edwards, *The Sign of Jonah*, p. 75; cf. above, n. 62.
87 *Ibid.*, p. 80.
88 *Ibid.*, p. 83.
89 Another but less forcible objection to the priority of Mark's version is advanced by Perrin, *Rediscovering*, pp. 192f., that Mark, who emphasizes Jesus' mighty deeds as the authentication of his messiahship, would have omitted any other sign pointing in that direction.
90 Edwards, *The Sign of Jonah*, pp. 83–7.
91 *Ibid.*, p. 84.
92 *Ibid.*, p. 86.
93 *Ibid.*, p. 106; cf. p. 86: 'Both σημεῖον and Ἰωνᾶ come from the tradition which Q has received and combined – σημεῖον from the saying about refusing a sign and Ἰωνᾶ from the double saying. The correlation of Jonah and Son of Man was expressed as *the Sign* of Jonah and the Son of Man' (Edwards' italics).
94 *Ibid.*, p. 86. In fact, the present investigation will establish that there is nothing fortuitous about it at all.
95 *Ibid.*, p. 87.
96 Perrin, *Rediscovering*, pp. 173ff.
97 *Ibid.*, p. 183.
98 Edwards, *The Sign of Jonah*, p. 54.
99 *Ibid.*, p. 87.
100 Perrin, 'Son of Man', p. 5.
101 Perrin, 'Mark XIV.62: The End Product of a Christian Pesher Tradition?', *NTS* 12, 1965–6, pp. 150–5.
102 Perrin, 'Son of Man', pp. 9–11.
103 *Ibid.*, p. 10.
104 Perrin, *Rediscovering*, p. 193. 'The sign of Jonah saying itself is certainly authentic: exhibiting an Aramaic idiom, it must be early; it stands at the beginning of a stream of tradition the history of which we can trace; it coheres with teaching attested elsewhere (Luke 17.20, 21).'
105 Edwards, *The Sign of Jonah*, p. 86.
106 Perrin, *Rediscovering*, pp. 194f.
107 Colpe, 'ὁ υἱὸς τοῦ ἀνθρώπου', p. 449 n. 349.
108 The eschatological construction is used three times by Paul in comparing Christ and Adam: Rom. 5.19; 1 Cor. 15.22, 49. The correlative (but not the *eschatological* correlative) construction occurs six times in the Fourth Gospel. Only in John 3.14 is the Son of man the subject of the apodosis: 'As (καθώς) Moses lifted up the serpent in the wilderness, so (οὕτως) must the Son of man be lifted up.' In the remaining instances (except 15.4) Jesus is called or speaks as the Son: 5.21; 5.26; 12.50; 14.31. To these should be added examples with καθώς . . . καί: 15.9, 'As the Father has loved me, so have I loved you'; 17.18, 'As thou didst send me into the world, so I have sent them into the world'; 20.21, 'As the Father has sent

me, even so I send you'; also 1 John 2.18; 4.17 (2.6, καθώς ... οὕτως). The examples in the Fourth Gospel are probably not later non-future derivatives from the eschatological correlative in Q, but may represent independent development of a form drawn not from the Q usage but from a Johannine tradition of Jesus' words. On the correlative construction or comparative clause as Semitic, as well as Greek, see above, n. 76.

109 In Matt. 13.40f., where the correlative form is broken by the Son of man not being mentioned in the apodosis but in the next sentence, Edwards, *The Sign of Jonah*, p. 51, suggests that the evangelist has borrowed the form from Q and adapted it to parabolic use.

110 That it is τοῖς Νινευείταις in Luke 11.30, but ἄνδρες Νινευεῖται in Luke 11.32 = Matt. 12.41, could be an indication of independence, but is more probably without significance, and the longer form is merely intended to balance βασίλισσα νότου.

111 It may be noted that γενεά occurs in every verse of Luke 11. 29–32.

112 N. Turner, *Grammatical Insights into the New Testament*, Edinburgh 1965, p. 60, takes the genitive in 'the sign of Jonah' as epexegetical, and the meaning as 'the sign *which is* Jonah' (Turner's italics). Jesus thus promised to his generation Jonah himself as a sign. Jesus is both Jonah and 'more than Jonah' – 'the prophet to the Gentiles, but without the lack of sympathy which curtailed Jonah's usefulness'. One may disagree with Turner's opinion that grammar alone points to the correct solution in this instance.

113 Jeremias, ''Ἰωνᾶς', *TDNT* III, 1966, pp. 406–10, p. 409, points out that this is excluded by the future tense ἔσται, and that to describe the preaching of repentance as a σημεῖον is 'highly unusual' ('ganz ungewöhnlich'), since a sign consists not in what men do, but in God's intervention in affairs. Hamerton-Kelly, *Pre-existence*, p. 34, sees the Son of man in Luke 11.30 as Jesus on earth, the preacher of repentance, who is superior to Jonah 'because in his preaching men encounter the summons of the eschatological judge. On their response to the Son of Man now depends their status in the judgement. The future judgement takes place in the present, in the preaching of Jesus.' This exegesis conflicts with the understanding that it is men's response to the message of *Jesus* now that will determine their status before the *Son of man* in the judgment.

114 Matthew remodels so as to produce another eschatological correlative, 24. 38f.

115 The first of the series of eschatological correlatives, Luke 17.24 (par. Matt. 24.27), is not followed by an explanation, because it serves as an introduction to the teaching on the suddenness of the day of the Son of man illustrated by the historical examples of Noah and Lot.

116 For ἐγερθήσεται and ἀναστήσονται in this sense and κατακρίνειν meaning 'provide the standard for condemnation', see Jeremias, *Theology* I, p. 135 n. 2 (after Wellhausen); on ἀναστῆναι (ἐγείρεσθαι) μετά as a Semitism, to which ἐν τῇ κρίσει is added for the sake of clarity, see Black, *Aramaic Approach*, p. 134.

117 Cf. ἡ γενεὰ αὕτη in Luke 11.30, 31, 32 with implied pejorative meaning (explicit in verse 29, γενεὰ πονηρά ἐστιν) parallel to 'the (evil) days' of Noah and of Lot.

118 To admit Luke 11.30 into the category of dominical sayings is to go against

recent critical opinion; besides R. A. Edwards and Perrin, cf. Colpe, 'ὁ υἱὸς τοῦ ἀνθρώπου', p. 449: Luke 11.30 is an expansion (introducing the Son of man) of Jesus' enigmatic *mashal*-type saying into a complete analogy. Hahn, *Titles of Jesus in Christology*, p. 33, is uncertain of its authenticity. On the other hand, even Perrin, *Rediscovering*, p. 193, although preferring to see in Luke 11.30 an early addition by the community, admits the possibility that it may come from Jesus. Fuller, *Foundations*, p. 123, accepts the saying as probably authentic, following Tödt, *The Son of Man in the Synoptic Tradition*, p. 224, cf. p. 211.

119 The exception is Luke 21.36b.

120 *JSM*, pp. 140f.

121 Edwards, *The Sign of Jonah*, p. 51.

122 Note Matthew's substitution of φυλακῇ for ὥρᾳ and the addition of ἐγρηγόρησεν ἂν καί in the parable.

123 Perrin, *Rediscovering*, pp. 185f.

124 Käsemann, *New Testament Questions of Today*, p. 92.

125 Edwards, *The Sign of Jonah*, p. 53.

126 *Titles of Jesus in Christology*, pp. 29f.

127 See above, n. 76.

128 Käsemann, *New Testament Questions of Today*, pp. 76f., citing Rom. 10.11 (Isa. 28. 16), 13 (Joel 2.32), and Gal. 3.12 (Lev. 18.5).

129 SB I, pp. 636–8, on Matt. 12.32.

130 Cf. the similar use of καί in the correlatives in John 15.9; 17.18; 20.21.

131 Their *Sitz im Leben* is 'the situation in which primitive Christian prophecy "judges" the messianic people of God, as once the old prophets "judged" Israel', Käsemann, *New Testament Questions of Today*, p. 79; see *ibid*., p. 76, on 1 Cor. 3.17 and Rev. 22.18f.

132 M. E. Boring, 'How May We Identify Oracles of Christian Prophets in the Synoptic Tradition? Mark 3:28–29 as a Test Case', *JBL* 91, 1972, pp. 501–21. Boring lends convincing support to Käsemann's hypothesis. Käsemann, *New Testament Questions of Today*, pp. 102f., concerns himself with Matt. 12.32: the Son of man is Jesus in his earthly life, and misunderstanding of this could be forgiven; but opposition to the primitive mission is in fact resistance to the prophetic Spirit, and is therefore unforgivable.

133 Bultmann, *Tradition*, pp. 127f.

134 Boring, 'Oracles of Christian Prophets', p. 501 n. 2.

135 J. Moffatt, *The First Epistle of Paul to the Corinthians*, London 1938, p. 80.

136 F. Neugebauer, 'Geistsprüche und Jesuslogien', *ZNW* 53, 1962, pp. 218–28; cf. F. F. Bruce, *Tradition Old and New*, Exeter 1970, pp. 64f., for support.

137 Neugebauer, 'Geistsprüche und Jesuslogien', p. 226.

138 Cf. Rom. 11.25ff.; 1 Cor. 14.6; 15.23ff., 51ff. G. Friedrich, 'προφήτης': D. Prophets and Prophecies in the New Testament, *TDNT* VI, 1968, pp. 828–56, p. 850, stresses Paul's rating of prophecy above other spiritual gifts, 1 Cor. 14.1. On prophets in Acts, see E. E. Ellis, 'The Role of the Christian Prophets in Acts', in *Apostolic History and the Gospel: Biblical and Historical Essays presented to F. F. Bruce on his 60th Birthday*, ed. W. W. Gasque and R. P. Martin, Exeter 1970, pp. 55–67, especially pp. 64f., on the overlapping of the functions of prophet and apostle.

139 See F. W. Beare, 'Sayings of the Risen Jesus in the Synoptic Tradition', in *Christian History and Interpretation: Studies presented to John Knox*, ed. W. R. Farmer, C. F. D. Moule, and R. R. Niebuhr, London 1967, pp. 161–81. In a discussion of prophets in the early church, Gaston assumes 'that their activities included the transmission of sayings of Jesus, *the head of their prophetic school*' (*No Stone on Another*, p. 446, my italics), but also the uttering of pronouncements of their own, some of which came to be transmitted in the tradition as his (ibid., p. 448). As a particularly relevant example of the creative role of prophets in the developing tradition the prophetic origin of 'the parousia of the Son of man' in Matt. 24 may perhaps be cited (if 'the day of the Son of man' in Luke 17 comes from Jesus, and is not a mere equivalent of 'the parousia' in Matthew); see above, chapter III, n. 53.

140 J. Jeremias, *The Prayers of Jesus*, London 1967, pp. 34f.

141 Boring, 'Oracles of Christian Prophets', p. 516.

142 K. Berger, 'Zu den sogenannten Sätzen Heiligen Rechts', *NTS* 17, 1970–1, pp. 10–40; see also D. Hill, 'On the Evidence for the Creative Role of Christian Prophets', *NTS* 20, 1973–4, pp. 262–74, especially pp. 270–3.

143 Berger, 'Sogenannte Sätze', pp. 20f.

144 E.g. Mark 10.15.

145 K. Berger, *Die Amen-Worte Jesu. Eine Untersuchung zum Problem der Legitimation in apokalyptischer Rede*, BZNW 39, Berlin 1970. V. Hasler, *Amen: Redaktionsgeschichtliche Untersuchung zur Einführungsformel der Herrenworte 'Wahrlich ich sage euch'*, Zürich 1969, assigns the origin of the amen-formula to charismatic prophets in the worship of the Hellenistic communities; critiques by Berger, *Die Amen-Worte Jesu*, pp. 153–63, and Jeremias, *Theology* I, p. 36 n. 2.

146 See earlier *JSM*, pp. 89f., 138–41.

147 In Mark 2.10; Luke 7.34, par. Matt. 11.19; Luke 9.58, par. Matt. 8.20 Jesus uses *bar nasha* in the sense of 'a (certain) man', 'someone (you know who)', in reference to himself; the early church came to regard these as Son of man sayings in the 'messianic' sense.

148 Borsch states that the result of his analyses of texts is 'that the various tools of source, form and redactional criticism tend to point, sometimes rather conclusively, to the priority of the Son of Man designation in traditions where there are probable parallels without the Son of Man' (*CGSM*, p. 27).

149 See further *JSM*, pp. 119–21; Borsch, *CGSM*, p. 23.

150 *CGSM*, pp. 20f.; *SMMH*, pp. 372ff.

151 *SMMH*, pp. 378f.

152 Jeremias, 'Die älteste Schicht', p. 168.

153 'Or his tradition', says Borsch, *CGSM*, p. 20.

154 *Ibid.*, pp. 21f.

155 See the full discussion in *JSM*, pp. 36–50; cf. Jeremias, 'Die älteste Schicht', p. 166.

156 *CGSM*, p. 27.

157 Rev. 3.21 resembles Luke's as well as Matthew's form of the traditional saying: compare ὁ νικῶν with 'you who have continued with me in my trials' (Luke 22.28), and δώσω αὐτῷ καθίσαι with καὶ καθήσεσθε (Luke 22.30).

158 Colpe, 'ὁ υἱὸς τοῦ ἀνθρώπου', p. 443.
159 *Ibid.*, pp. 452f.
160 See above, pp. 99, 104–5.
161 Colpe, 'ὁ υἱὸς τοῦ ἀνθρώπου', p. 437 and n. 282.
162 K. H. Rengstorf, 'σημεῖον', *TDNT* VII, 1971, p. 237 and n. 264.
163 Nor, indeed, can it bear this meaning in any case, against J. Schniewind, *Das Evangelium nach Matthäus*, Göttingen 1956, pp. 244f., and Bonnard, *L'Évangile selon Saint Matthieu*, p. 352.
164 T. F. Glasson, 'The Ensign of the Son of Man (Matt. XXIV.30)', *JTS* N.S. 15, 1964, pp. 299f.; this suggestion is accepted by Jeremias, 'Die älteste Schicht', p. 167; *Theology* I, p. 264 n. 2, and by Colpe, p. 437 n. 283.
165 See my article, 'The Sign of the Son of Man (Matt. xxiv. 30)', *NTS* 9, 1962–3, pp. 380–2; *JSM*, pp. 108–14.
166 Cf. Jeremias, *Theology* I, pp. 257ff.
167 Jeremias, 'Die älteste Schicht', p. 162.
168 Jeremias, *Parables*, pp. 81–5.
169 R. M. Grant and D. N. Freedman, *The Secret Sayings of Jesus according to the Gospel of Thomas*, London 1960, p. 156.
170 Jeremias, 'Die älteste Schicht', p. 160. I give Metzger's translation of Thomas in Aland, *Synopsis*, pp. 520 and 529.
171 Thomas 103 appears to include a mere remnant of an interpretation of the parable such as that in 21b.
172 Grant and Freedman, *Secret Sayings*, p. 172; R. McL. Wilson, *Studies in the Gospel of Thomas*, London 1960, p. 59; B. Gärtner, *The Theology of the Gospel of Thomas*, London 1961, pp. 60f. R. Kasser, *L'Évangile selon Thomas*, Neuchâtel 1961, p. 104, comments: 'Jésus, n'ayant pas de "repos" terrestre, jouira du repos céleste: de même son disciple'; cf. Schrage, *Thomas-Evangelium und Tradition*, p. 169: the Son of man is only the prototype of 'the sons of man' (logion 106) who likewise are homeless and without rest in this world.
173 Jeremias, 'Die älteste Schicht', p. 161.
174 *Ibid.*, p. 163.
175 Hamerton-Kelly, *Pre-existence*, p. 100.
176 *Ibid.*, p. 41.
177 *Ibid.*, pp. 37f.
178 *Ibid.*, p. 101.
179 Tödt, *The Son of Man in the Synoptic Tradition*, p. 302, against E. Sjöberg, *Der verborgene Menschensohn in den Evangelien*, Lund 1955.

Chapter V

1 Cf. John 5.27: '... and has given him authority to execute judgment, because he is the Son of man'; *JSM*, pp. 165–8.
2 Opinion is divided, but the case for genuineness is not strong.
3 Mark 2.10 parr.; Luke 7.34, par. Matt. 11.19; Luke 9.58, par. Matt. 8.20 were given a christological Son of man content they did not originally possess.
4 These present the Matthaean interpretation of the Q sayings recorded also in Luke 17 in a generally more reliable form.
5 The only other undoubted apocalyptic touch is the verb ἀποκαλύπτεται with

the Son of man as subject in Luke 17.30 (cf. 1 En. 69.26, 29). Although ἀστραπή (in the plural) is employed in apocalyptic (Rev. 4.5; 8.5; 11.19; 16.18), its use in Luke 17.24 is perhaps more directly akin to Jesus' word at Luke 10.18, 'I saw Satan fall like lightning from heaven' (cf. Rev. 12.8f.). The day of the Son of man resembles lightning both in its suddenness and in its pervasive effects; nothing can escape its glare, all are affected, just as the flood and the fire and brimstone (Luke 17.27, 29) brought destruction upon all (πάντας).

6 The most significant feature of the kernel sayings is the degree of distinctiveness of the Son of man concept both from Jewish thought and from early Christian faith. Among more recent discussions of criteria utilized by traditio-historical criticism to determine the authenticity of sayings of Jesus, may be mentioned the following: Teeple, 'Origin of the Son of Man Christology', *JBL* 84, 1965, pp. 213–50; R. H. Fuller, *A Critical Introduction to the New Testament*, London 1966, pp. 94–8; Perrin, *Rediscovering*, pp. 39–47, and *What is Redaction Criticism*? p. 71; Bruce, *Tradition Old and New*, pp. 47–57; D. G. A. Calvert, 'An Examination of the Criteria for Distinguishing the Authentic Words of Jesus', *NTS* 18, 1971–2, pp. 209–19; R. S. Barbour, *Traditio-Historical Criticism of the Gospels*, London 1972, contains much acute critical comment on the use and misuse of the criteria.

7 The difficulty is not resolved by the theory, based largely on Luke 12.8f. and Mark 8.38, that by the Son of man Jesus meant a transcendent figure other than himself, who would validate his ministry in the approaching judgment (Bultmann, Tödt, Fuller and others, with varying emphases). This idea seems never to have occurred to the early church; cf. Seitz, 'The Future Coming of the Son of Man', *Studia Evangelica* VI, 1973, p. 493: 'the saying [Mark 8.38] presents no reliable evidence for the assertion that Jesus looked forward to the coming of another whom he referred to in the imagery of Dan. 7.13 as the Son of man. Certainly neither Mark nor any of the other evangelists believed that he did so.'

8 Cf. H. R. Balz, *Methodische Probleme der neutestamentlichen Christologie*, Neukirchen 1967, p. 120.

9 1 En. 48.4–7; 51.2; 62.13f.; Mowinckel, *He That Cometh*, pp. 401–3.

SELECT BIBLIOGRAPHY

Aland, K. (ed.), *Synopsis Quattuor Evangeliorum*, Stuttgart ^{4}1967.

Albright, W. F. and Mann, C. S., 'Qumran and the Essenes: Geography, Chronology, and Identification of the Sect' in *The Scrolls and Christianity*, ed. M. Black, London 1969, pp. 11-25.

Andel, C. P. van, *De Structuur van de Henoch-Traditie en het Nieuwe Testament*, Utrecht 1955.

Balz, H. R., *Methodische Probleme der neutestamentlichen Christologie* (Wissenschaftliche Monographien zum Alten und Neuen Testament 25), Neukirchen 1967.

Bammel, E., 'Erwägungen zur Eschatologie Jesu', *Studia Evangelica* III, TU 88, ed. F. L. Cross, Berlin 1964, pp. 3-32.

Barbour, R. S., *Traditio-Historical Criticism of the Gospels*, London 1972.

Barr, J., 'Messiah', HDB, p. 651.

'Which Language did Jesus speak? – Some Remarks of a Semitist', *BJRL* 53, 1970-71, pp. 9-29.

Barrett, C. K., *The Holy Spirit and the Gospel Tradition*, London 1947.

The New Testament Background: Selected Documents, London 1956.

Jesus and the Gospel Tradition, London 1967.

The First Epistle to the Corinthians, London ^{2}1971.

'I am not Ashamed of the Gospel', *New Testament Essays*, London 1972, pp. 116-43.

Beare, F. W., *The Earliest Records of Jesus*, Oxford 1964.

'Sayings of the Risen Jesus in the Synoptic Tradition' in *Christian History and Interpretation: Studies presented to John Knox*, ed. W. R. Farmer, C. F. D. Moule, and R. R. Niebuhr, London 1967, pp. 161-81.

Berger, K., *Die Amen-Worte Jesu. Eine Untersuchung zum Problem der Legitimation in apokalyptischer Rede* (BZNW 39), Berlin 1970.

'Zu den sogenannten Sätzen Heiligen Rechts', *NTS* 17, 1970-1, pp. 10-40.

Birdsall, J. N., 'Who is this Son of Man?', *EQ* 42, 1970, pp. 7-17.

Black, M., 'The "Son of Man" in the Old Biblical Literature', *ExpT* 60, 1948-9, pp. 11-15.

'The "Son of Man" in the Teaching of Jesus', *ExpT* 60, 1948-9, pp. 32-6.

'The Eschatology of the Similitudes of Enoch', *JTS* N.S. 3, 1952, pp. 1-10.

'Servant of the Lord and Son of Man', *SJT* 6, 1953, pp. 1–11.
'The Son of Man Problem in Recent Research and Debate', *BJRL* 45, 1962–3, pp. 305–18.
'From Schweitzer to Bultmann: The Modern Quest of the Historical Jesus', *McCormick Quarterly* (Chicago) 20, 1966–7, pp. 271–83.
An Aramaic Approach to the Gospels and Acts, Oxford ³1967.
'The "Son of Man" Passion Sayings in the Gospel Tradition', *ZNW* 60, 1969, pp. 1–8.
(ed.), *Apocalypsis Henochi Graece* in *Pseudepigrapha Veteris Testamenti Graece* III, ed. A. M. Denis and M. de Jonge, Leiden 1970.
'The "Parables" of Enoch (1 En 37–71) and the "Son of Man" ', *ExpT* 78, 1976–7, pp. 5–8.
Boers, H., 'Where Christology is Real', *Interpretation* (Richmond, Virginia) 26, 1972, pp. 302–15.
Bonnard, P., *L'Évangile selon Saint Matthieu* (Commentaire du Nouveau Testament 1), Neuchâtel 1963.
Boring, M. E., 'How May We Identify Oracles of Christian Prophets in the Synoptic Tradition? Mark 3:28–29 as a Test Case', *JBL* 91, 1972, pp. 501–21.
Borsch, F. H., *The Son of Man in Myth and History*, London 1967.
'Mark XIV.62 and 1 Enoch LXII.5', *NTS* 14, 1967–8, pp. 565–7.
The Christian and Gnostic Son of Man (SBT second series 14), London 1970.
Bousset, W., *Kyrios Christos* (1913, ²1921), ET by J. E. Steely, New York 1970.
Bruce, F. F., *This is That*, Exeter 1968.
Tradition Old and New, Exeter 1970.
Buchanan, G. W., *To the Hebrews: Translation, Comment and Conclusions* (Anchor Bible 36), New York 1972.
Bultmann, R., *Theology of the New Testament* I, ET by K. Grobel, London 1956.
The History of the Synoptic Tradition, ET by J. Marsh, Oxford ²1968.
Burrows, M. (ed.), *The Dead Sea Scrolls of St. Mark's Monastery* II.2: *Plates and Transcription of the Manual of Discipline*, New Haven 1951.
More Light on the Dead Sea Scrolls, New York 1958.
Cadoux, C. J., *The Historic Mission of Jesus*, London 1941.
The Life of Jesus (Penguin Books), West Drayton 1948.
Caird, G. B., *The Gospel of St Luke* (Pelican Commentaries), Harmondsworth 1963.
Calvert, D. G. A., 'An Examination of the Criteria for Distinguishing the Authentic Words of Jesus', *NTS* 18, 1971–2, pp. 209–19.
Campbell, J. Y., 'The Origin and Meaning of the Term Son of Man', *JTS* 48, 1947, pp. 145–55.
Carmignac, J., 'Le Document de Qumran sur Melkisédeq', *Revue de Qumran* (Paris) 7.3 (December 1970), pp. 343–78.
Catchpole, D. R., *The Trial of Jesus* (Studia Post-Biblica XVIII), Leiden 1971.
Charles, R. H., *The Book of Enoch or 1 Enoch Translated from the Editor's Ethiopic Text*, Oxford 1912.

Colpe, C., 'Der Spruch von der Lästerung des Geistes', in *Der Ruf Jesu und die Antwort der Gemeinde: Exegetische Untersuchungen Joachim Jeremias zum 70. Geburtstag gewidmet von seinen Schülern*, ed. E. Lohse, C. Burchard and B. Schaller, Göttingen 1970, pp. 63-79.
'ὁ υἱὸς τοῦ ἀνθρώπου', *TDNT* VIII, 1972, pp. 400-77.
Conzelmann, H., 'Gegenwart und Zukunft in der synoptischen Tradition', *ZTK* 54, 1957, pp. 277-96.
'Jesus Christus', *RGG*[3] III, Tübingen 1959, cols. 619-53; ET *Jesus*, by J. R. Lord, ed. J. Reumann, Philadelphia 1973.
An Outline of the Theology of the New Testament, ET by J. Bowden, London 1969.
Cortés, J. B. and Gatti, Florence M., 'The Son of Man or The Son of Adam', *Biblica* (Rome) 49, 1968, pp. 457-502.
Creed, J. M., *The Gospel according to St Luke*, London 1930.
Cross, F. M., *The Ancient Library of Qumran and Modern Biblical Studies*, New York 1958.
Cullmann, O., *Jesus and the Revolutionaries*, ET by G. Putnam, New York 1970.
Dalman, G., *The Words of Jesus*, ET by D. M. Kay, Edinburgh 1902.
Delcor, M., 'Melchizedek from Genesis to the Qumran Texts and the Epistle to the Hebrews', *Journal for the Study of Judaism* (Leiden) 2, 1971, pp. 115-35.
Denis, A. M., *Introduction aux Pseudépigraphes Grecs d'Ancien Testament* (Studia in Veteris Testamenti Pseudepigrapha I, ed. A. M. Denis and M. de Jonge), Leiden 1970.
Dodd, C. H., *The Parables of the Kingdom*, London 1936.
Edwards, R. A., 'The Eschatological Correlative as a *Gattung* in the New Testament', *ZNW* 60, 1969, pp. 9-20.
The Sign of Jonah in the Theology of the Evangelists and Q (SBT second series 18), London 1971.
Review of F. H. Borsch, *The Son of Man in Myth and History*, 1967 and *The Christian and Gnostic Son of Man*, 1970, in *JBL* 90, 1971, pp. 235-7.
Ellis, E. E., *The Gospel of Luke* (New Century Bible), London 1966.
'The Role of the Christian Prophets in Acts' in *Apostolic History and the Gospel: Biblical and Historical Essays presented to F. F. Bruce on his 60th Birthday*, ed. W. W. Gasque and R. P. Martin, Exeter 1970, pp. 55-67.
Emerton, J. A., 'The Origin of the Son of Man Imagery', *JTS* N.S. 9, 1958, pp. 225-42.
'Melchizedek and the Gods', *JTS* N.S. 17, 1966, pp. 399-401.
'The Problem of Vernacular Hebrew in the First Century A.D. and the Language of Jesus', *JTS* N.S. 24, 1973, pp. 1-23.
Fitzmyer, J. A., S. J., 'Further Light on Melchizedek from Qumran Cave 11', *JBL* 86, 1967, pp. 25-41, reprinted in his *Essays on the Semitic Background of the New Testament*, London 1971, pp. 245-67.
'The Languages of Palestine in the First Century A.D.', *Catholic Biblical Quarterly* (Washington D.C.) 32, 1970, pp. 501-31.
'Methodology in the Study of the Aramaic Substratum of Jesus' Sayings

in the New Testament' in *Jésus aux origines de la christologie*, ed. J. Dupont (Bibliotheca Ephemeridum Theologicarum Lovaniensium XL), Louvain 1975, pp. 73-102.

Flusser, D., 'Melchizedek and the Son of Man', *Christian News from Israel* (Jerusalem) 17, 1966, pp. 23-9.

Formesyn, R. E. C., 'Was there a Pronominal Connection for the "bar nasha" Selfdesignation?', *Novum Testamentum* (Leiden) 8, 1966, pp. 1-35.

Freedman, D. N., see under Grant.

Friedrich, G., 'προφήτης': D. Prophets and Prophecies in the New Testament, *TDNT* VI, 1968, pp. 828-56.

Fuller, R. H., *The Mission and Achievement of Jesus* (SBT 12), London 1954.

The Foundations of New Testament Christology, London 1965.

A Critical Introduction to the New Testament, London 1966.

Gärtner, B., *The Theology of the Gospel of Thomas*, ET by E. J. Sharpe, London 1961.

Galbiati, I. (ed.), *Iohannis Evangelium Apocryphum Arabice*, Milan 1957.

Gaston, L., *No Stone on Another: Studies in the Significance of the Fall of Jerusalem in the Synoptic Gospels* (Supplements to *Novum Testamentum* XXIII), Leiden 1970.

Gatti, Florence M., see under Cortés.

Gelston, A., 'A Sidelight on the "Son of Man"', *SJT* 22, 1969, pp. 189-96.

Glasson, T. F., *The Second Advent: The Origin of the New Testament Doctrine*, London 1945.

'The Ensign of the Son of Man (Matt. XXIV. 30)', *JTS* N.S. 15, 1964, pp. 299f.

'The Second Advent - 25 Years Later', *ExpT* 82, 1970-1, pp. 307-9.

'The Son of Man Imagery: Enoch xiv and Daniel vii', *NTS* 23, 1976-7, pp. 82-90.

Goppelt, L., 'Zum Problem des Menschensohns: das Verhältnis von Leidens- und Parusieankündigung' in *Mensch und Menschensohn* (Festschrift für Bischof Professor D. Karl Witte), ed. H. Sierig, Hamburg 1963, pp. 20-32.

Grant, R. M. and Freedman, D. N., *The Secret Sayings of Jesus according to the Gospel of Thomas*, London 1960.

Grundmann, W., *Das Evangelium nach Lukas* (Theologischer Handkommentar zum Neuen Testament 3), Berlin 1961.

Guy, H. A., 'An Eighteenth Century N.E.B.', *ExpT* 81, 1969-70, pp. 148-50.

Hahn, F., *Christologische Hoheitstitel* (FRLANT 83), Göttingen 1963 (^{2}1964, ^{3}1966); ET *The Titles of Jesus in Christology*, by H. Knight and G. Ogg, London 1969.

Mission in the New Testament, ET by F. Clarke (SBT 47), London 1965.

Hamerton-Kelly, R. G., *Pre-existence, Wisdom, and the Son of Man* (SNTSMS 21), London 1973.

Hare, D. R. A., *The Theme of Jewish Persecution of Christians in the Gospel according to St. Matthew* (SNTSMS 6), London 1967.

Harnack, A., *The Sayings of Jesus*, ET by J. R. Wilkinson, London 1908.

Harvey, A. E., review of F. H. Borsch, *The Son of Man in Myth and History*, 1967, and *The Christian and Gnostic Son of Man*, 1970, in *JTS* N.S. 22, 1971, pp. 203–6.
Hasler, V., *Amen: Redaktionsgeschichtliche Untersuchung zur Einführungsformel der Herrenworte 'Wahrlich ich sage euch'*, Zürich 1969.
Haufe, G., 'Das Menschensohn-Problem in der gegenwärtigen wissenschaftlichen Diskussion', *EvT* 26, 1966, pp. 130–41.
Hengel, M., *Was Jesus a Revolutionist?*, ET by W. Klassen, Philadelphia 1971.
Hiers, R. H., *The Historical Jesus and the Kingdom of God* (University of Florida Humanities Monograph 38), Gainesville 1973.
Higgins, A. J. B., 'Son of Man-*Forschung* since "The Teaching of Jesus"' in *New Testament Essays: Studies in Memory of T. W. Manson*, ed. A. J. B. Higgins, Manchester 1959, pp. 119–35.
'The Sign of the Son of Man (Matt. xxiv.30)', *NTS* 9, 1962–3, pp. 380–2.
'The Old Testament and Some Aspects of New Testament Christology' in *Promise and Fulfilment: Essays Presented to Professor S. H. Hooke*, ed. F. F. Bruce, Edinburgh 1963, pp. 128–41.
Jesus and the Son of Man, London 1964.
Menschensohn-Studien (Franz Delitzsch-Vorlesungen 1961), Stuttgart 1965.
Review of R. H. Fuller, *The Foundations of New Testament Christology*, 1965 in *JBL* 85, 1966, pp. 360–2.
'The Priestly Messiah', *NTS* 13, 1966–7, pp. 211–39.
'The Son of Man Concept and the Historical Jesus', *Studia Evangelica* V, TU 103, ed. F. L. Cross, Berlin 1968, pp. 14–20.
'Is the Son of Man Problem Insoluble?' in *Neotestamentica et Semitica: Studies in Honour of Matthew Black*, ed. E. E. Ellis and M. Wilcox, Edinburgh 1969, pp. 70–87.
'"Menschensohn" oder "ich" in Q: Lk 12,8–9/Mt 10,32–33?' in *Jesus und der Menschensohn: für Anton Vögtle*, ed. R. Pesch and R. Schnackenburg with O. Kaiser, Freiburg im Breisgau 1975, pp. 117–23.
Hill, D., 'On the Evidence for the Creative Rôle of Christian Prophets', *NTS* 20, 1973–4, pp. 262–74.
Hindley, J. C., 'Towards a Date for the Similitudes. An Historical Approach', *NTS* 14, 1967–8, pp. 551–65.
Hoffmann, P., *Studien zur Theologie der Logienquelle* (Neutestamentliche Abhandlungen N.F. 8), Münster 1972.
Hooker, Morna D., *The Son of Man in Mark*, London 1967.
Horton, F. L., *The Melchizedek Tradition: A Critical Examination of the Sources to the Fifth Century A.D. and in the Epistle to the Hebrews* (SNTSMS 30), Cambridge 1976.
Jeremias, J., *Jesus' Promise to the Nations*, ET by S. H. Hooke (*SBT* 24), London 1958.
The Parables of Jesus, ET by S. H. Hooke, London 1963.
'Ἰωνᾶς', *TDNT* III, 1966, pp. 406–10.
'Die älteste Schicht der Menschensohn-Logien', *ZNW* 58, 1967, pp. 159–72.

The Prayers of Jesus (SBT second series 6), London 1967.
New Testament Theology I, ET by J. Bowden, London 1971.

Jonge, M. de, see under Denis, and under Woude, van de.

Jüngel, E., 'Jesus und der Menschensohn', *Paulus und Jesus* (Hermeneutische Untersuchungen zur Theologie 2), Tübingen ^{4}1972, pp. 215-62.

Käsemann, E., 'Das Problem des historischen Jesus', *ZTK* 51, 1954, pp. 125-53.
Essays on New Testament Themes, ET by W. J. Montague (SBT 41), London 1964.
'Sentences of Holy Law in the New Testament' (ET of 'Sätze Heiligen Rechtes im Neuen Testament', *NTS* 1, 1954-5, pp. 248-60), *New Testament Questions of Today*, ET by W. J. Montague, London 1969, pp. 66-81; 'The Beginnings of Christian Theology', *ibid.*, pp. 82-107.

Kasser, R., *L'Évangile selon Thomas*, Neuchâtel 1961.

Kautzsch, E. (ed.), *Gesenius' Hebrew Grammar*, ET (revised) by A. E. Cowley, Oxford ^{2}1910.

Kelly, J. N. D., *The Epistles of Peter and of Jude*, London 1969.

Klostermann, E., *Das Lukasevangelium* (Handbuch zum Neuen Testament 5), Tübingen ^{2}1929.
Das Markusevangelium (Handbuch zum Neuen Testament 3), Tübingen ^{5}1971.

Kümmel, W. G., *Promise and Fulfilment*, ET by Dorothea M. Barton (SBT 23), London 1957.
The Theology of the New Testament, ET by J. E. Steely, London 1974.
'Das Verhalten Jesus gegenüber . . .' in *Jesus und der Menschensohn: für Anton Vögtle*, ed. R. Pesch and R. Schnackenburg with O. Kaiser, Freiburg im Breisgau 1975, pp. 210-24.

Ladd, G. E., *A Theology of the New Testament*, Guildford and London 1975.

Lagrange, M. J., *Évangile selon Saint Luc*, Paris ^{3}1927.
Critique Textuelle du Nouveau Testament II: *La Critique Rationelle*, Paris 1935.

Lapide, P., 'Insights from Qumran into the Languages of Jesus', *Revue de Qumran* (Paris) 8.4 (December 1975), pp. 483-501.

Laubscher, F. du Toit, 'God's Angel of Truth and Melchizedek: A Note on 11QMelch 13b', *Journal for the Study of Judaism* (Leiden) 3, 1972, pp. 46-51.

Leaney, A. R. C., *The Gospel according to St Luke*, London 1958.
The Rule of Qumran and its Meaning, London 1966.

Le Déaut, R., 'Le substrat araméen des évangiles: scolies en marge de l'*Aramaic Approach* de Matthew Black', *Biblica* (Rome) 49, 1968, pp. 397-9.

Leivestad, R., 'Der apokalyptische Menschensohn ein theologisches Phantom', *Annual of the Swedish Theological Institute* (Jerusalem) VI, 1968, pp. 49-105.
'Exit the Apocalyptic Son of Man', *NTS* 18, 1971-2, pp. 243-67.

Lindars, Barnabas, S.S.F., *New Testament Apologetic*, London 1961.
'The Apocalyptic Myth and the Death of Christ', *BJRL* 57, 1974-5, pp. 366-87.

'Re-enter the Apocalyptic Son of Man', *NTS* 22, 1975–6, pp. 52–72.
Lindeskog, G., 'Das Rätsel des Menschensohnes', *Studia Theologica* (Lund) 22, 1968, pp. 149–75.
Lövestam, E., *Spiritus Blasphemia: eine Studie zu Mk 3, 28f par Mt 12, 31f, Lk 12, 10* (Scripta Minora Regiae Societatis Humaniorum Literarum Lundensis, 1966–7, no. 1), Lund 1968.
Lohmeyer, E., *Kyrios Jesus: Eine Untersuchung zu Phil. 2, 5–11* (Sitzungsberichte der Heidelberger Akademie der Wissenschaften, Phil.-Hist. Klasse, Jahr. 1927–8, 4. Abh.), Heidelberg 1928, ²1961.
Galiläa und Jerusalem (FRLANT 34), Göttingen 1936.
Longenecker, R. N., *The Christology of Early Jewish Christianity* (SBT second series 17), London 1970.
Lührmann, D., 'Noah und Lot (Lk 17.26–29) – ein Nachtrag', *ZNW* 63, 1972, pp. 130–2.
McKnight, E. V., see under Talbert.
Maddox, R., 'The Function of the Son of Man according to the Synoptic Gospels', *NTS* 15, 1968–9, pp. 45–74.
Mann, C. S., see under Albright.
Manson, T. W., *The Teaching of Jesus*, London ²1935.
The Sayings of Jesus, London 1949.
'The Son of Man in Daniel, Enoch and the Gospels', *BJRL* 32, 1949–50, pp. 171–93.
The Servant-Messiah, London 1953.
Studies in the Gospels and Epistles, ed. M. Black, Manchester 1962.
Marlow, R., S. J., 'The *Son of Man* in Recent Journal Literature', *Catholic Biblical Quarterly* (Washington D.C.) 28, 1966, pp. 20–30.
Marshall, I. H., 'The Synoptic Son of Man Sayings in Recent Discussion', *NTS* 12, 1965–6, pp. 327–51.
'Professor Ferdinand Hahn's "Christologische Hoheitstitel"', *ExpT* 78, 1966–7, pp. 212–15.
'The Son of Man in Contemporary Debate', *EQ* 42, 1970, pp. 67–87.
Martin, F., *Le Livre d'Hénoch traduit sur le texte éthiopien*, Paris 1906.
Marxsen, W., *The Beginnings of Christology*, ET by P. J. Achtemeir, Philadelphia 1969.
Merx, A., *Die Evangelien des Markus und Lukas: Die vier kanonischen Evangelien nach ihrem ältesten bekannten Texte* II.2, Berlin 1905.
Metzger, B. M., 'Pseudepigrapha', HDB, p. 821.
Evangelium Thomae Copticum, ET, in Aland, *Synopsis*, pp. 517–30.
A Textual Commentary on the Greek New Testament, United Bible Societies, London and New York 1971.
Michael, J. H., '"The Sign of John"', *JTS* 21, 1920, pp. 146–59.
Michel, O., 'Der Menschensohn', *Theologische Zeitschrift* (Basel) 27, 1971, pp. 81–104.
Milik, J. T., *Ten Years of Discovery in the Wilderness of Judaea*, ET by J. Strugnell (SBT 26), London 1959.
'Problèmes de la littérature Hénochique à la lumière des fragments araméens de Qumrân', *Harvard Theological Review* (Cambridge, Mass.) 64, 1971, pp. 333–78.

'*Milki-sedeq* et *Milki-resa* dans les anciens écrits juifs et chrétiens', *Journal of Jewish Studies* (London) 23, 1972, pp. 95-144.
The Books of Enoch: Aramaic Fragments of Qumrân Cave 4, edited by J. T. Milik with the collaboration of Matthew Black, Oxford 1976.
Moffatt, J., *The First Epistle of Paul to the Corinthians*, London 1938.
Morgenthaler, R., *Statistik des neutestamentlichen Wortschatzes*, Zürich and Frankfurt am Main 1958.
Moule, C. F. D., *The New Testament Gospels*, BBC Publications, London 1965.
Review of H. E. Tödt, *The Son of Man in the Synoptic Tradition*, ET 1965, in *Theology* (London) 69, no. 550, April 1966, pp. 172-4.
The Phenomenon of the New Testament (SBT second series 1), London 1967.
Moulton, J. H., see under Turner.
Mowinckel, S., *He That Cometh*, ET by G. W. Anderson, Oxford 1956.
Neugebauer, F., 'Geistsprüche und Jesuslogien', *ZNW* 53, 1962, pp. 218-28.
Nineham, D. E., *The Gospel of St Mark* (Pelican Commentaries), Harmondsworth 1963.
Odeberg, H., *The Aramaic Portions of Bereshit Rabba* II: *Short Grammar of Galilaean Aramaic*, Lund and Leipzig 1939.
O'Neill, J. C., 'The Silence of Jesus', *NTS* 15, 1968-9, pp. 153-67.
Otto, R., *Reichgottes und Menschensohn*, Munich 1934; ET *The Kingdom of God and the Son of Man*, by F. V. Filson and B. Lee-Woolf, London ²1943.
Pannenberg, W., *Jesus - God and Man*, ET by L. Wilkins and Duane A. Priebe, London ²1970.
Peake's Commentary on the Bible, ed. M. Black and H. H. Rowley, London and Edinburgh 1962.
Perrin, N., *The Kingdom of God in the Teaching of Jesus*, London 1963.
'Mark XIV.62: The End Product of a Christian Pesher Tradition?', *NTS* 12, 1965-6, pp. 150-5.
'The Son of Man in Ancient Judaism and Primitive Christianity: a Suggestion', *Biblical Research* (Chicago) 11, 1966, pp. 17-28.
'New Beginnings in Christology: A Review Article' [of Fuller, *Foundations*], *JR* 46, 1966, pp. 491-6.
Rediscovering the Teaching of Jesus, London 1967.
'The Son of Man in the Synoptic Tradition', *Biblical Research* (Chicago) 13, 1968, pp. 3-25.
'Recent Trends in Research in the Christology of the New Testament' in *Transitions in Biblical Scholarship*, ed. J. C. Rylaarsdam, Chicago 1968, pp. 217-33.
What is Redaction Criticism?, London 1970.
The New Testament: An Introduction - Proclamation and Parenesis, Myth and History, New York 1974.
Rehkopf, F., *Die lukanische Sonderquelle*, Tübingen 1959.
Rengstorf, K. H., 'σημεῖον', *TDNT* VII, 1971, pp. 200-61.
Reumann, J., *Jesus in the Church's Gospels*, London 1970.
Rowley, H. H., *The Relevance of Apocalyptic*, London ³1963.
(ed.), *A Companion to the Bible*, Edinburgh ²1963.
Santos Otero, A. de, *Los Evangelios Apocrifos*, Madrid ²1963.

Schippers, R., 'The Son of Man in Matt. xii.32 = Lk. xii.10, compared with Mk. iii.28', *Studia Evangelica* IV, TU 102, ed. F. L. Cross, Berlin 1968, pp. 231-5.
Schlatter, A., *Der Evangelist Matthäus*, Stuttgart ^{3}1948.
Schnackenburg, R., 'Der eschatologische Abschnitt Lk 17, 20-37' in *Mélanges Bibliques en hommage au R. P. Béda Rigaux*, ed. A. Descamps and A. de Halleux, Gembloux 1970, pp. 213-34.
Schniewind, J., *Das Evangelium nach Matthäus* (Das Neue Testament Deutsch 2), Göttingen 1956.
Schrage, W., *Das Verhältnis des Thomas-evangeliums zur synoptischen Tradition und zu den koptischen Evangelienübersetzungen* (BZNW 29), Berlin 1964.
Schürmann, H., 'Zur Traditions- und Redaktionsgeschichte von Mt 10, 23', *Biblische Zeitschrift* (Paderborn) N.F. 3, 1959, pp. 82-8, reprinted in *Traditionsgeschichtliche Untersuchungen zu den synoptischen Evangelien*, Düsseldorf 1968, pp. 150-6.
Schwartz, E. (ed.), *Eusebius: Kirchengeschichte*, kleine Ausgabe, Leipzig ^{4}1932.
Schweizer, E., *Lordship and Discipleship* (SBT 28), London 1960, ET of the first edition (1955) of the next item.
Erniedrigung und Erhöhung bei Jesus und seinen Nachfolgern, Zürich ^{2}1962.
'Der Menschensohn', *ZNW* 50, 1959, pp. 185-209, reprinted in his *Neotestamentica*, Zürich 1963, pp. 56-84.
'The Son of Man', *JBL* 79, 1960, pp. 119-29.
'The Son of Man Again', *NTS* 9, 1962-3, pp. 256-61, reprinted in his *Neotestamentica*, Zürich 1963, pp. 85-92.
Das Evangelium nach Markus (Das Neue Testament Deutsch 1), Göttingen 1967; ET *The Good News according to Mark*, by D. H. Madvig, London 1971.
Jesus, ET by D. E. Green, London 1971.
Seitz, O. J. F., 'The Future Coming of the Son of Man: Three Midrashic Formulations in the Gospel of Mark', *Studia Evangelica* VI, TU 112, ed. E. A. Livingstone, Berlin 1973, pp. 478-94.
Sjöberg, E., *Der Menschensohn im äthiopischen Henochbuch*, Lund 1946.
Der verborgene Menschensohn in den Evangelien, Lund 1955.
Stanton, G. N., *Jesus of Nazareth in New Testament Preaching* (SNTSMS 27), London 1974.
Stendahl, K., *The School of St Matthew*, Lund ^{2}1968.
Talbert, C. H. and McKnight, E. V., 'Can the Griesbach Hypothesis be Falsified?' *JBL* 91, 1972, pp. 338-68.
Taylor, V., 'The Original Order of Q' in *New Testament Essays: Studies in Memory of T. W. Manson*, ed. A. J. B. Higgins, Manchester 1959, pp. 246-69, reprinted in the posthumous collection of Taylor's shorter writings, *New Testament Essays*, London 1970, pp. 95-118.
The Passion Narrative of St Luke, ed. O. E. Evans (SNTSMS 19), London 1972.
Teeple, H. M., 'The Origin of the Son of Man Christology', *JBL* 84, 1965, pp. 213-50.

Todesco, V., Vaccari, A., S. J., and Vattasso, M. (edd.), *Il Diatessaron in Volgare Italiano: testi inediti secoli XIII–XIV* (Studi e Testi 81), Città del Vaticano 1938.
Tödt, H. E., *Der Menschensohn in der synoptischen Überlieferung*, Gütersloh 1959; *ET The Son of Man in the Synoptic Tradition* from the second edition 1963, by Dorothea M. Barton, London 1965.
Turner, N., *A Grammar of New Testament Greek* by J. H. Moulton, III: *Syntax*, Edinburgh 1963.
Grammatical Insights into the New Testament, Edinburgh 1965.
Ullendorff, E., *Ethiopia and the Bible*, London 1968.
Vermes, G., 'The Use of *bar nash/bar nasha* in Jewish Aramaic', in M. Black, *An Aramaic Approach to the Gospels and Acts*, Oxford ³1967, pp. 310–28.
Jesus the Jew, London 1973.
Vielhauer, P., 'Gottesreich und Menschensohn in der Verkündigung Jesu' in *Festschrift für Günther Dehn*, ed. W. Schneemelcher, Neukirchen 1957, pp. 51–79, reprinted in *Aufsätze zum Neuen Testament* (Theol. Bücherei 31), Munich 1965, pp. 55–91.
'Jesus und der Menschensohn: zur Diskussion mit Heinz Eduard Tödt und Eduard Schweizer', *ZTK* 60, 1963, pp. 133–77, reprinted in *Aufsätze*, pp. 92–140.
Voss, G., *Die Christologie der lukanischen Schriften in Grundzügen*, Paris 1965.
Walker, W. O., 'The Origin of the Son of Man Concept as Applied to Jesus', *JBL* 91, 1972, pp. 482–90.
Wellhausen, J., *Das Evangelium Marci*, Berlin ²1909.
Wilson, R. McL., *Studies in the Gospel of Thomas*, London 1960.
Woude, A. S. van der, 'Melchisedek als himmlische Erlösergestalt in den neugefundenen eschatologischen Midraschim aus Qumran Höhle XI', *Oudtestamentische Studiën* (Leiden) XIV, ed. P. A. H. de Boer, 1965, pp. 354–73.
Woude, A. S. van der and Jonge, M. de, '11Q Melchizedek and the New Testament', *NTS* 12, 1965–6, pp. 301–26.

INDEX OF AUTHORS

Albright, W. F., 130
Andel, C. P. van, 129

Balz, H. R., 158
Bammel, E., 87, 140, 150
Barbour, R. S., 158
Barr, J., 13, 129, 133
Barrett, C. K., 3, 19, 29, 30, 127, 131, 135, 136, 143, 149, 150
Beare, F. W., 74, 146, 156
Bentzen, A., 4
Berger, K., 111, 156
Birdsall, J. N., 135
Black, M., 13, 15, 18, 20, 21, 30, 31, 129–32, 136, 146, 149, 151, 154
Boers, H., 135
Bonnard, P., 150, 157
Boring, M. E., 109, 110, 155, 156
Borsch, F. H., 3–7, 12, 43–5, 73, 74, 77, 78, 84, 113–16, 123, 128, 129, 135, 140, 142, 144, 146, 148–51, 156
Bousset, W., 149
Bowker, J. W., 127
Bruce, F. F., 29, 135, 155, 158
Buchanan, G. W., 132
Bultmann, R., 34–6, 73, 74, 80, 81, 84, 109, 143, 146, 148, 149, 151, 155, 158
Burrows, M., 129

Cadoux, C. J., 139
Caird, G. B., 145
Calvert, D. G. A., 158
Campbell, J. Y., 137
Carmignac, J., 134
Catchpole, D. R., 149
Charles, R. H., 9, 18, 128, 131
Colpe, C., 3, 7–12, 15, 19, 25, 40, 46–8, 57, 72–5, 78, 79, 83, 84, 89–91, 95, 100, 116–18, 128, 129, 131, 132, 139–42, 145–7, 149–51, 153, 155, 157
Conzelmann, H., 3, 128, 140, 149
Cortés, J. B., 140
Creed, J. M., 149
Cross, F. M., 129, 130
Cullmann, O., 133, 135

Dalman, G., 147
Delcor, M., 134
Denis, A. M., 134
Dodd, C. H., 144

Edwards, R. A., 87, 88, 92–100, 123, 138, 150, 152–5
Ellis, E. E., 149, 150, 155
Emerton, J. A., 128, 133
Engnell, I., 4

Fitzmyer, J. A., 133, 134
Flusser, D., 28, 133
Formesyn, R. E. C., 35, 137
Freedman, D. N., 157
Friedrich, G., 155
Fuller, R. H., 3, 17, 34, 57, 80, 98, 127, 129, 131, 135, 137, 142, 145, 146, 148, 155, 158

Gärtner, B., 157
Galbiati, I., 138
Gaston, L., 139, 145, 148, 156
Gatti, Florence M., 140
Gelston, A., 132
Glasson, T. F., 68, 118, 119, 129, 130, 144, 157
Goppelt, L., 29, 135
Grant, R. M., 157
Grundmann, W., 150
Guy, H. A., 138

Hahn, F., 3, 16, 35, 36, 57, 76, 80, 82, 108, 127, 130, 136, 137, 142, 146, 148, 155

Hamerton-Kelly, R. G., 121, 122, 143, 148, 154, 157
Hare, D. R. A., 77, 146
Harnack, A., 141
Harvey, A. E., 163
Hasler, V., 156
Haufe, G., 135, 137, 148
Haupt, W., 146
Hengel, M., 133
Hiers, R. H., 151
Higgins, A. J. B., 129, 131, 135, 137
Hilgenfeld, A., 129
Hill, D., 156
Hindley, J. C., 13, 129
Hoffmann, P., 141, 143, 147, 148, 151
Hofmann, J. C. K. von, 129
Hooker, Morna D., 45, 135, 140
Horton, F. L., 133

Jeremias, J., 1, 21, 25, 48, 70, 73–5, 83, 84, 89, 91, 110, 112–14, 116, 119, 121, 123, 127, 129, 130, 132, 133, 141, 142, 144–7, 149–51, 154, 156, 157
Jonge, M. de, 133, 134
Jüngel, E., 3, 33, 56, 57, 61, 74, 127, 137, 142, 146, 148

Käsemann, E., 11, 36, 94, 95, 107, 108, 109, 111, 123, 137, 138, 140, 145, 148, 152, 155
Kasser, R., 157
Kautzsch, E., 152
Kelly, J. N. D., 144
Klostermann, E., 143, 149
Kümmel, W. G., 130, 135, 142, 149

Ladd, G. E., 135
Lagrange, M. J., 86, 143, 150
Lapide, P., 133
Laubscher, F. du Toit, 134, 135
Leaney, A. R. C., 128, 142
Le Déaut, R., 132
Leivestad, R., 14, 22, 23, 40–4, 53, 57, 58, 73, 80, 128, 130, 132, 138, 139, 141, 142, 146–8
Lietzmann, H., 20
Lindars, B., 39, 40, 49–53, 78, 127, 138, 141, 147
Lindeskog, G., 32, 33, 83, 136, 148, 149
Lövestam, E., 86, 87, 90, 148, 150
Lohmeyer, E., 30, 39, 136, 138
Longenecker, R. N., 130
Lührmann, D., 144

McKnight, E. V., 141, 144, 151, 152
Maddox, R., 29, 46, 135, 140, 142
Mann, C. S., 130
Manson, T. W., 12, 59, 63, 67, 139, 142–4
Marlow, R., 135
Marshall, I. H., 29, 135–7
Martin, F., 131
Marxsen, W., 149
Mathews, S., 130
Merx, A., 61, 143
Metzger, B. M., 16, 130, 142, 150, 157
Meyer, A., 20
Michael, J. H., 151
Michel, O., 135
Milik, J. T., 14, 130, 135
Moffatt, J., 109, 110, 155
Morgenthaler, R., 142
Moule, C. F. D., 13, 29, 129, 135
Moulton, J. H., 152
Mowinckel, S., 18, 66, 131, 135, 143, 144, 158

Neugebauer, F., 109, 155
Nineham, D. E., 3, 127

Odeberg, H., 152
O'Neill, J. C., 138
Otto, R., 20, 131

Pannenberg, W., 80, 81, 148
Perrin, N., 15, 16, 39, 40, 44, 58, 76–8, 83, 91, 92, 94, 95, 97–9, 107, 121, 123, 128, 130, 132, 133, 138, 140, 142, 146, 148, 149, 151–3, 155, 158
Philippi, F., 129
Purver, A., 138

Rehkopf, F., 146
Rengstorf, K. H., 118, 157
Reumann, J., 135, 140
Rowley, H. H., 131

Santos Otero, A. de, 138
Schippers, R., 88, 89, 116, 117, 150, 151
Schlatter, A., 147
Schnackenburg, R., 142, 143
Schniewind, J., 157
Schrage, W., 150, 157
Schürmann, H., 75, 76, 146
Schweizer, E., 16, 17, 30, 31, 43, 128, 131, 136, 139
Seitz, O. J. F., 147, 158

Sjöberg, E., 128, 131, 157
Stanton, G. N., 135
Stendahl, K., 91, 92, 151, 152

Talbert, C. H., 141, 144, 151
Taylor, V., 147, 149
Teeple, H. M., 3, 37–9, 128, 136, 137, 140, 158
Theisohn, J., 130
Todesco, V., 150
Tödt, H. E., 3, 35, 42, 73, 80, 81, 87, 91, 92, 98, 121, 122, 127, 128, 135–7, 139, 142, 143, 146, 148, 150, 153, 155, 157, 158
Torrey, C. C., 59
Turner, N., 152, 154

Ullendorff, E., 134

Vaccari, A., 150
Vattasso, M., 150
Vermes, G., 1, 15, 20–7, 49, 51, 53, 127, 128, 130–3, 141
Vielhauer, P., 3, 16, 33, 38, 81, 92, 128, 131, 136, 140
Volkmar, G., 129
Voss, G., 80, 148

Walker, W. O., 146, 147
Weisse, H., 129
Wellhausen, J., 149, 154
Wilson, R. McL., 157
Woude, A. S. van der, 133, 134

INDEX OF REFERENCES

Old Testament
Genesis
14 49
14. 18–20 134
19. 26 63
Leviticus
18. 5 155
Psalms
8. 4 147
8. 6 146
16 4
18 4
21 4
22 4
69 4
80. 17 147
82. 1 28, 134
89 4
110. 1 15, 39, 40, 70, 77, 79, 97, 98, 125, 146, 147
116 4
118 4
Isaiah
11. 12 118
18. 3 118
27. 13 118
28. 16 155
Ezekiel
1 15, 39
2. 1 130
Daniel
7 12, 13, 15, 16, 30, 39, 46, 47, 121, 130, 139, 140
7. 13 8, 10, 11, 14, 15, 16, 21, 22, 23, 25–7, 30, 39, 40, 49, 53, 70, 77, 79, 97, 98, 125, 138, 146, 147, 158
7. 13f. 8
7. 21 8
7. 27 8
Joel
2. 32 155
Amos
5. 18 67
Jonah
2. 1 92
Zechariah
12. 10 77
12. 10ff. 39, 97
14. 5 68

Apocrypha
2 Esdras
13 8, 9, 12, 14–17, 21, 22, 41, 46, 121
13. 3 9
13. 52 144
Wisdom
2–5 136
10. 4, 6f. 144
Ecclesiasticus
16. 7f. 144

New Testament
Note. For Matthew, Mark and Luke see also table of contents, pp. v–vi.
Matthew
5. 1f. 113
5. 11 24, 77, 115
5. 12 63
5. 19 152
5. 21f. 125
5. 22. 151
6. 14f. 152
7. 22 145
8. 10 74
8. 20 2, 12, 25, 29, 46, 50, 120, 139, 141, 156f.
9. 13 32

10. 5f. 75, 76
10. 15 67, 145
10. 19f. 76
10. 23 11, 42, 48, 69, 72, 78, 124, 140, 146
10. 32 30, 94
10. 32f. 33, 97, 115, 149, 152
10. 33 149
11. 19 2, 12, 25, 29, 32, 50, 139, 156, 157
11. 21–3 67
11. 21–4 102
11. 22 145
11. 23–4 67
11. 24 145
12. 3–6 101
12. 22–32 86
12. 27f. 85
12. 28 86
12. 30 85
12. 31 87, 89
12. 31f. 86, 109, 117, 148
12. 32 25, 29, 115, 116, 150, 151, 155
12. 36 145
12. 38 96
12. 39 118
12. 39f. 115
12. 40 24, 33, 151, 152
12. 41 96, 154
12. 41f. 101
13. 37 48, 119
13. 40 107, 154
13. 40f. 107, 152
13. 41 42, 119, 124
13. 37–43 119
15. 24 32, 75, 76
16. 4 151
16. 13 24, 41, 42, 114, 115
16. 20 115
16. 21 152
16. 27 33, 42, 78, 114, 124, 149
16. 28 48, 59, 76, 77, 78, 115, 124, 146
17. 9 102
17. 22 48
17. 23 152
19. 28 42, 69, 78, 124
20. 19 152
23. 34 77
24 156
24. 3 60, 67, 68, 78, 118, 119
24. 14 146
24. 26f. 125
24. 27 10, 33, 36, 56, 64, 65, 68, 78, 93, 107, 124, 140, 141, 143, 154
24. 30 11, 59, 77, 78, 97, 118, 124, 129, 140, 157
24. 30f. 42, 118
24. 31 118
24. 36–42 144
24. 37 10, 42, 48, 56, 65, 68, 78, 93, 107, 124, 140, 143
24. 37–9 33, 36, 64, 65, 125, 141, 142
24. 38 143
24. 38f. 94, 100, 154
24. 39 42, 48, 60, 68, 78, 107, 125, 144
24. 43 67
24. 43f. 94, 107, 120, 152
24. 44 29, 42, 78, 124, 146
24. 45–51 144
25. 31 42, 48, 69, 78, 124, 145, 146
26. 2 48
26. 21 120
26. 24 120, 121
26. 32 120
26. 45 121
26. 46 121
26. 64 10, 59, 146
27. 63 152

Mark
1. 15 38, 53, 126
2. 5 24
2. 10 2, 12, 24, 25, 29, 32, 46, 137, 139, 156, 157
2. 17 32
2. 20 60
2. 27f. 24
2. 28 29
3. 28 48, 150, 151
3. 28f. 25, 83, 115, 148, 155
4. 24 152
8. 12 115, 125, 151
8. 27 24, 41, 42, 114, 115
8. 31 2, 24, 29, 115, 137, 144
8. 38 12, 23, 29, 32–4, 36, 37, 39, 69, 78, 80,

Mark-contd.
95, 97, 114, 124, 125, 138, 145, 146, 148, 149, 152, 158
9. 1 48, 75–7, 114, 115, 145
9. 9 24, 120
9. 12 24
9. 12f. 2
9. 31 2, 24, 29
9. 41 111
10. 15 111, 156
10. 29f. 111
10. 33f. 2, 24, 29
10. 38 24
10. 45 29, 32, 115, 133
11. 23 111
12. 36 146
13. 4 60
13. 9 76
13. 10 76, 146
13. 11 76
13. 15f. 63
13. 26 11, 12, 26, 39, 48, 59, 69, 77, 78, 97, 98, 124, 125, 146
13. 30 75, 76
14. 18 120, 121
14. 21 29, 120, 121, 133
14. 28 120
14. 41 121, 133
14. 42 121
14. 62 10, 12, 26, 29, 39, 40, 46, 48, 50, 59, 68–70, 97–9, 124, 126, 138, 146, 147, 153
14. 72 87
16. 19 145
Luke
5. 17 60
5. 32 32
5. 35 60
6. 20 113
6. 22 24, 77, 115
6. 23 63
6. 26 63
7. 9 74
7. 34 2, 12, 25, 32, 50, 139, 156, 157
7. 48 24
8. 22 60
9. 18 24, 41
9. 22 144
9. 26 32, 33, 78, 149
9. 27 147
9. 51 145
9. 58 2, 12, 25, 50, 120, 139, 141, 156, 157
10. 12 67, 145
10. 13–15 67, 102
10. 14 145
10. 18 56, 158
11. 16 96
11. 19f. 85
11. 20 86
11. 23 85, 86
11. 29 118, 151
11. 29f. 80, 115, 118, 123, 125
11. 29–32 101, 103, 105, 106, 112, 124, 144, 154
11. 30 24, 33, 39, 123, 151, 152, 154, 155
11. 30–32 102
11. 31f. 101–5, 126
11. 32 96, 154
11. 49 77
12. 2ff. 87
12. 8 23, 29, 30, 34, 40, 75, 94, 95, 108, 126, 138, 148, 149, 152
12. 8f. 16, 29, 32–4, 36, 37, 39, 50, 80, 113–5, 123–5, 137, 149, 158
12. 9 40, 81, 149, 150
12. 10 25, 48, 80, 83, 115, 148, 150, 151
12. 11f. 75, 76, 87
12. 22 67
12. 35–8 67
12. 39 67
12. 39f. 94, 107, 120, 152
12. 40 29, 38, 78, 107, 124, 146
12. 42–6 144
12. 49f. 102
12. 50 24
13. 1–5 145
13. 2–5 63, 102
13. 3, 5 106, 126
13. 32f. 24
15. 4–10 63
15. 16 60
16. 21 60
17 145, 156, 157
17. 20f. 59, 153
17. 20–30 70

17. 20–37 142
17. 21 70, 71
17. 22 48, 145
17. 22ff. 142
17. 22–30 139
17. 22–31 56
17. 22–37 68
17. 23 70
17. 23–37 62
17. 24 10, 33, 36, 38, 39, 47, 48, 79, 80, 93, 97, 105, 106, 112, 123, 124, 140, 141, 143, 144, 154, 158
17. 25 2, 144, 145
17. 26 10, 33, 43, 47, 48, 79, 80, 93, 101, 106, 107, 112, 123, 140, 143, 145
17. 26f. 10, 36, 39, 97, 103, 123, 126, 141
17. 26–9 144
17. 26–30 38, 106, 112, 124, 144
17. 27 143, 158
17. 28f. 36
17. 28a, 30 94, 103, 106, 107 112, 123
17. 28b, 29 103
17. 28–30 10, 57, 101, 123, 125, 126, 145
17. 29 63, 158
17. 30 10, 33, 47, 48, 79, 80, 108, 140, 143, 158
17. 31 56, 63
17. 32 63
17. 34 143
18. 8b 10, 29, 48, 78, 124, 140
19. 10 25, 32
19. 43 60
20. 1 60
21. 6 60
21. 27 78
21. 34–6 10
21. 36 10, 11, 42, 48, 72, 73, 75, 124, 140, 155
22. 15 60
22. 21 120
22. 22 120, 121
22. 27 115
22. 28 156
22. 28–30 145
22. 30 156
22. 48 29
22. 69 10, 70, 78, 79, 140, 147
23. 29 60
23. 35 14
23. 42 115
24. 7 2, 24
24. 26 145
24. 51 145

John
1. 51 141
3. 13 70
3. 14 31, 32, 70, 153
5. 21 153
5. 26 153
5. 27 157
6. 62 70
7. 33 121
8. 28 31, 70
12. 23 70
12. 32 31
12. 34 31, 70
12. 50 153
13. 21 121
13. 31f. 70
14. 2 121
14. 31 153
15. 4 153
15. 9 153, 155
17. 18 153, 155
19. 11 121
19. 37 39, 97
20. 21 153, 155

Acts
1. 2, 11, 22 145
1. 9–11 145
2. 32 31
2. 32f. 32
2. 33 31
3. 17ff. 87
5. 30 31
5. 30f. 32
5. 31 31
7. 56 31, 39, 97, 136, 146
8. 10 147
8. 30 73

Romans
1. 16 149
1. 17 63
1. 18 63
5. 19 153
8. 18 63
10. 11 155
10. 13 155
11. 25ff. 155

1 Corinthians
1. 8 66, 143
1. 24, 30 104
3. 13 63, 143
3. 17 94, 155
5. 5 66
7. 10–13 109
7. 25f. 109
14. 1 155
14. 6 155
14. 38 152
15. 3f. 32
15. 4 32
15. 22 153
15. 23ff., 51ff. 155
15. 49 153
16. 22 97, 152
2 Corinthians
1. 14 66
Galatians
1. 9 152
3. 12 155
Philippians
2. 5–11 136
2. 6–11 30
2. 9 31, 32, 136
1 Thessalonians
4. 16 68
5. 2 66
2 Thessalonians
2. 2 66
2. 3, 6 63
2. 8 63
1 Timothy
3. 16 145
Hebrews
1. 3 136
2. 9f. 136
7. 2 134
8. 1 136
10. 12 136
12. 2 136
13. 20 136
1 Peter
1. 5 63
5. 1 63
2 Peter
2. 4–8 66, 144
1 John
2. 6 154
2. 18 154
4. 17 154
Jude
5–7 144

Revelation
1. 7 39, 97
3. 5 149
3. 5b 82
3. 21 145, 156
4. 4 70, 115
4. 5 158
8. 5 158
11. 19 158
12. 1 119
12. 3 119
12. 8f. 158
15. 1 119
16. 18 158
22. 18f. 152, 155

Qumran
CD 12. 23f.; 14. 19; 19. 10f.; 20. 1 129
1QH 3. 7–10 128
1QM 134
1QS 4. 20–3 128
1QS 11. 20 132
1QSa 2. 12, 20; 2. 14 129
4QCatena A, f12–13 134, 135
4QPatr 3 129
11QMelch 28, 49, 133, 134
11QMelch 13 134
Cave 1, f30 129

Other Sources

A. Jewish
1 Enoch
14 130
14. 8f. 15
26. 29 158
37–69 18
37–71 8, 12–21, 46, 49, 121
45. 3 66, 69, 71, 115
46. 1 8
46. 2 22, 128
46. 3 22
46. 4 17
47. 1–4 14
48. 2 17
48. 4–7 158
48. 10 131
49. 3 104
51. 2 158

52. 4	131
55. 4	66, 69, 115
56. 5–7	13, 14
60	15
61. 5	66
61. 8	69, 115
62. 1–3	66
62. 2, 3, 5	69, 115
62. 5	66, 69, 77, 78, 146, 147
62. 9	17
62. 11	14
62. 13f.	158
62. 14	17
63. 11	17
69. 26	143, 158
69. 26f.	17
69. 27	71, 115
69. 27, 29	66, 69, 78, 115
69. 29	143, 158
70f.	15, 17–20, 69, 128, 131, 136
70. 1	9, 17, 19, 69, 131
70. 1f.	18
70. 3	18
71	136
71. 1	18
71. 14	9, 14, 17, 19, 22, 41, 49, 145
71. 17	19
108. 12	70, 115
2 Enoch	19

Psalms of Solomon	
17	16
Jubilees	
4. 23	136
10. 17	136
20. 5	144
Testaments of the XII Patriarchs	
T. Naphtali	
3. 4f.	144
2 Baruch	
53. 9	143
Josephus, *Bellum Judaicum*	
V.566 (xiii.6)	144

B. Christian

Gospel of Thomas	
21	120, 157
44	150
57	119
86	120
103	120, 157
106	157
Tuscan Diatessaron	
63	150
Didache	
11. 7	110
Justin Martyr, *Trypho*	
107	91
Eusebius, *H. E.* ii.	
23. 13	138